Writing Academic English

FOURTH EDITION

Alice Oshima
Ann Hogue

PEARSON
Longman

Writing Academic English, Fourth Edition

Pearson Education, 10 Bank Street, White Plains, NY 10606

Editorial Director: Laura Le Dréan
Development editor: Molly Sackler
Vice president, director of design and production: Rhea Banker
Associate managing editor: Jane Townsend
Production editor: Lynn Contrucci
Production supervisor: Christine Edmonds
Marketing director: Oliva Fernandez
Senior manufacturing buyer: Nancy Flaggman
Photo research: Rhea Banker
Cover design: Jill Lehan
Cover images: (left) Sumerian cuneiform. Bildarchiv Preussischer Kulturbesitz/Art Resource, NY.
  (right) Computer circuit board, close-up (digital composite) by Jan Franz. Collection: Stone. Getty Images.
Text composition: Integra
Text font: 11.5/13 Times Roman
Credits: See page 337.

Library of Congress Cataloging-in-Publication Data
Hogue, Ann.
   Writing academic English/Ann Hogue and Alice Oshima.—4th ed.
      p.   cm.
   Includes index.
   ISBN 0-13-152359-7 (alk. paper)
   1. English language—Rhetoric—Handbooks, manuals, etc.   2. English language—Grammar—Handbooks,
manuals, etc.   3. English language—Textbooks for foreign speakers.   4. Academic writing—Handbooks,
manuals, etc.   5. Report writing—Handbooks, manuals, etc.
   I. Oshima, Alice. II.   Title.
PE1408.H6644 2006
808'.042—dc22

                                                                                              2005017872

LONGMAN ON THE **WEB**

Longman.com offers online resources for teachers and students. Access our Companion Websites, our online catalog, and our local offices around the world.

Visit us at **longman.com**.

ISBN: 0-13-152359-7

Printed in the United States of America
   3 4 5 6 7 8 9 10—BAH—09 08 07 06

Contents

PART II   WRITING AN ESSAY 55

Chapter 4   From Paragraph to Essay 56

Chapter 5   Chronological Order: Process Essays 81

Chapter 6   Cause/Effect Essays 94

Preface

Writing Academic English, Fourth Edition, is a comprehensive rhetoric and sentence structure textbook/workbook for high-intermediate to advanced English language learners who are in college or are college bound. The book teaches writing in a straightforward manner, using a step-by-step approach. Clear, relevant models illustrate each step, and varied practices reinforce each lesson.

The first part of the book provides a quick review of paragraph writing and summarizing, followed by a chapter that introduces the essay. The second part of the book offers comprehensive chapters on process, cause/effect, comparison/contrast, and argumentative essays. Sentence structure, with special emphasis on subordinated structures, is taught in the third part of the book.

Throughout the book, models and practices feature general academic topics that are timely and relevant to students living in a rapidly changing world. In addition, readings from current, real-world publications conclude the chapters on different essay forms. Most chapters offer a variety of writing assignments, and each chapter ends with a review of the main teaching points.

Appendices explain the writing process; give punctuation rules; show charts of connecting words, transition signals, and editing symbols; and teach students basic research and documentation skills. Self-editing and peer-editing worksheets and model scoring rubrics are also provided. References to the appendices appear within the chapters where students are likely to benefit most from using this material.

What's New in the Fourth Edition

Instructors familiar with the third edition will find these changes:

- Part I, Writing a Paragraph, has been condensed from seven to three chapters in order to move students more quickly to writing essays.
- Part II, Writing an Essay, has been expanded from two to five chapters. Each pattern of essay organization now has its own chapter.
- A new chapter on argumentative essays has been added. This chapter also serves as an introduction to using supporting materials from outside sources.
- Each essay chapter concludes with one or two short readings, selected because of their high interest and because they employ the pattern of organization taught in the chapter. Following the readings are exercises asking students to analyze rhetorical devices and patterns and/or to summarize the content. Writing assignments based on the readings are also provided.
- Instruction in basic research and documentation skills has been added in Appendix E. Examples of MLA-style in-text citations appear throughout the text.
- The sections on summarizing and paraphrasing have been expanded to include intermediate-step exercises to help students master these difficult skills.
- Both self-editing and peer-editing worksheets are provided in Appendix F, along with scoring rubrics for use by instructors.
- Finally, models have been updated, practice materials freshened, and explanations streamlined, always with the intention of making the material more accessible to students.

Order of Lesson Presentation	*Writing Academic English* is intended to be covered in one fifteen-week semester, with classes meeting five hours a week. The chapters in Part I, Writing a Paragraph, and Part II, Writing an Essay, should be taught in sequence. The sentence structure chapters in Part III should be taught alongside the chapters in Parts I and II in order to encourage students to write a variety of complex structures. Chapter 10, Types of Sentences, should be taught at the beginning of the course; subsequent sentence structure chapters may be taught in any order. Wherever possible, instructors should integrate sentence structure with rhetoric. For example, adverbial time clauses in Part III may be taught simultaneously with chronological order in Chapter 5.

For courses shorter than fifteen weeks, the text is flexible enough to allow instructors to pick and choose chapters that best suit the needs of their classes. Sentence structure is presented separately from rhetoric, so these chapters may be omitted altogether, leaving the instructor free to concentrate solely on writing. For twelve-week terms, we suggest omitting Chapters 8 and 9. For even shorter terms, instructors may elect to concentrate solely on the essay, Chapters 4 through 9.

Topic Suggestions	The topics listed for each writing assignment are only suggestions. Some chapters have more than one kind of topic. (1) Some are academic in nature but still general enough so that students from different disciplines can tackle them. (2) Topics on the Lighter Side allow students to draw on personal experience. (3) Topics for content-based writing assignments that follow the reading at the end of essay chapters relate to the readings. (4) Topics for timed writings are offered in several chapters in order to give students practice in this important skill.

Of course, we encourage instructors to keep their eyes open for topics from current news or for graphs, photographs, and charts in newspapers on which to base writing assignments.

In-Class Writing	Group brainstorming and in-class writing of first drafts are especially helpful in the early stages because the instructor is available for immediate consultation. Also, the instructor can check to make sure everyone is on the right track. Pair and group collaboration is appropriate for brainstorming and editing work; however, writing is essentially an individual task even when done in class.

Writing under Pressure	Special assignments are included to be done in class under time pressure to stimulate the experience of writing essay examinations—valuable practice for college-bound students. Instructors should adjust time limits depending on the needs of the class.

Practice Exercises	The final practice exercises of the sentence-structure chapters usually ask students to write original sentences. Because these practices prove whether the students understand the structures and can produce them correctly on their own, we encourage instructors to use them.

Editing	For most chapters, self-editing and peer-editing worksheets are printed back-to-back in Appendix F. Instructors can use one or the other, or both, as they prefer. One method of using the peer-editing worksheet is to have peer editors record their comments on the worksheet. An alternative method is to have each student read his or

her draft out loud to a small group of classmates and then to elicit oral comments and suggestions by asking the checklist questions. The student who has read then writes down the group's suggestions on his or her own paper. Instructors can also respond to student writing by using the peer-editing checklist.

Scoring Rubrics	Two sample scoring rubrics are provided at the beginning of Appendix F, one for paragraphs and one for essays. Their purpose is twofold: to show students how instructors might evaluate their writing, and to suggest a schema for instructors to do so. Instructors are invited to photocopy the rubrics. Of course, the rubrics may be modified to suit individual assignments and individual preferences.
Chapter-Opening Photographs	The photographs introducing each chapter of the book depict some of the forms of written communication used by diverse cultures throughout the evolution of civilization.

Acknowledgments

Many people have contributed to this edition of *Writing Academic English*. We especially thank Laura Le Dréan, who traveled countless miles and spent countless hours gathering valuable feedback from users of the previous edition. Thanks also to our development editor, Molly Sackler, for making sure of the accuracy of our information and the consistency of its presentation, and to our production editors, Lynn Contrucci and Jane Townsend, for their expertise in fitting all these words onto the printed page. Special thanks also to Rhea Banker, who found the beautiful photographs that appear on the opening pages of each part and each chapter.

To the many students and teachers who took the time to offer suggestions, we extend our heartfelt thanks: David Ross, Intensive English Program, Houston, Texas; Marsha Gerechter Abramovich, Tidewater Community College, Virginia Beach, Virginia; Alex Jones, Seattle, Washington; Anita Sokmen, Director, English Language Programs Extension Courses & Marketing, University of Washington, Seattle, Washington; Patty Heises, University of Washington, Seattle, Washington; Angelina Arellanes-Nuñez, University of Texas at El Paso; Dorrie Brass, Annapolis, Maryland; Barbara Smith-Palinkas, Tampa, Florida; Jacqueline Smith, Brooklyn, New York; and Diana Savas, Pasadena City College, Pasadena, California. We hope you recognize the many places where your advice has helped to improve the book.

Writing a Paragraph

1

Paragraph Structure

Petroglyphs in Canyonlands, Utah

A **paragraph** is a group of related sentences that discuss one (and usually only one) main idea. A paragraph can be as short as one sentence or as long as ten sentences. The number of sentences is unimportant; however, the paragraph should be long enough to develop the main idea clearly.

A paragraph may stand by itself. In academic writing, you often write a paragraph to answer a test question such as the following: "Define management by objective, and give one example of it from the reading you have done for this class." A paragraph may also be one part of a longer piece of writing such as an essay or a book.

We mark a paragraph by indenting the first word about a half inch (five spaces on a typewriter or computer) from the left margin.

The following model contains all the elements of a good paragraph. Read it carefully two or three times. Then answer the Writing Technique questions that follow, which will help you analyze its structure.

MODEL

Paragraph Structure

Gold

[1]Gold, a precious metal, is prized for two important characteristics. [2]First of all, gold has a lustrous[1] beauty that is resistant to corrosion.[2] [3]Therefore, it is suitable for jewelry, coins, and ornamental purposes. [4]Gold never needs to be polished and will remain beautiful forever. [5]For example, a Macedonian coin remains as untarnished[3] today as the day it was made 25 centuries ago. [6]Another important characteristic of gold is its usefulness to industry and science. [7]For many years, it has been used in hundreds of industrial applications, such as photography and dentistry. [8]The most recent use of gold is in astronauts' suits. [9]Astronauts wear gold-plated heat shields for protection when they go outside spaceships in space. [10]In conclusion, gold is treasured not only for its beauty but also for its utility.

Writing Technique Questions

1. What is the topic of the paragraph?
2. What two main points does the writer make about the topic?
3. In which two sentences does the writer say that there are two main points?
4. What examples does the writer use to support each point?

The Three Parts of a Paragraph

All paragraphs have a **topic sentence** and **supporting sentences**, and some paragraphs also have a **concluding sentence**.

The **topic sentence** states the main idea of the paragraph. It not only names the topic of the paragraph, but it also limits the topic to one specific area that can be discussed completely in the space of a single paragraph. The part of the topic sentence that announces the specific area to be discussed is called the **controlling idea**. Notice how the topic sentence of the model states both the topic and the controlling idea:

TOPIC   CONTROLLING IDEA

(Gold,) a precious metal, is prized for two important characteristics.

Supporting sentences develop the topic sentence. That is, they explain or prove the topic sentence by giving more information about it. Following are some of the supporting sentences that explain the topic sentence about gold.

First of all, gold has a lustrous beauty that is resistant to corrosion.

For example, a Macedonian coin remains as untarnished today as the day it was made 25 centuries ago.

Another important characteristic of gold is its usefulness to industry and science.

The most recent use of gold is in astronauts' suits.

---

[1]**lustrous:** glowing
[2]**corrosion:** chemical damage
[3]**untarnished:** unchanged in color

The **concluding sentence** signals the end of the paragraph and leaves the reader with important points to remember:

In conclusion, gold is treasured not only for its beauty but also for its utility.

Concluding sentences are customary for stand-alone paragraphs. However, paragraphs that are parts of a longer piece of writing usually do not need concluding sentences.

The Topic Sentence

Every good paragraph has a topic sentence, which clearly states the topic and the controlling idea of the paragraph.

A topic sentence is the most important sentence in a paragraph. It briefly indicates what the paragraph is going to discuss. For this reason, the topic sentence is a helpful guide to both the writer and the reader. The writer can see what information to include (and what information to exclude). The reader can see what the paragraph is going to be about and is therefore better prepared to understand it. For example, in the model paragraph on gold, the topic sentence alerts the reader to look for *two* characteristics.

Here are three important points to remember about a topic sentence.

1. A topic sentence is a complete sentence; that is, it contains at least one subject and one verb. The following are *not* complete sentences because they do not have verbs:

   Driving on freeways.

   How to register for college classes.

   The rise of indie films.[1]

2. A topic sentence contains both a topic and a controlling idea. It names the topic and then limits the topic to a specific area to be discussed in the space of a single paragraph.

TOPIC   CONTROLLING IDEA

(Driving on freeways) requires <u>skill and alertness</u>.

TOPIC   CONTROLLING IDEA

(Registering for college classes) can be <u>a frustrating experience for new students</u>.

TOPIC   CONTROLLING IDEA

(The rise of indie films) is due to <u>several factors</u>.

---

[1] **indie films:** independent films; films not made in or by Hollywood studios

3. A topic sentence is the most general statement in the paragraph because it gives only the main idea. It does not give any specific details. A topic sentence is like the name of a particular course on a restaurant menu. When you order food in a restaurant, you want to know more about a particular course than just "meat" or "soup" or "salad." You want to know generally what kind of salad it is. Potato salad? Mixed green salad? Fruit salad? However, you do not necessarily want to know all the ingredients. Similarly, a reader wants to know generally what to expect in a paragraph, but he or she does not want to learn all the details in the first sentence.

Following is a general statement that could serve as a topic sentence.

The Arabic origin of many English words is not always obvious.

The following sentence on the other hand, is *too specific*. It could serve as a supporting sentence but not as a topic sentence.

The slang expression *so long* (meaning "good-bye") is probably a corruption of the Arabic *salaam*.

This sentence is *too general*.

English has been influenced by other languages.

Position of Topic Sentences

The topic sentence is usually (but not always) the first sentence in a paragraph. Experienced writers sometimes put topic sentences in other locations, but the best spot is usually right at the beginning. Readers who are used to the English way of writing want to know what they will read about as soon as they begin reading.

Synonyms

Synonyms, words that have the same basic meaning, do not always have the same emotional meaning. For example, the words *stingy* and *frugal* both mean "careful with money." However, calling someone stingy is an insult, but calling someone frugal is a compliment. Similarly, a person wants to be slender but not skinny, aggressive but not pushy. Therefore, you should be careful in choosing words because many so-called synonyms are not really synonymous at all.

Sometimes a topic sentence comes at the end. In this case, the paragraph often begins with a series of examples. Other paragraphs may begin with a series of facts, and the topic sentence at the end is the conclusion from these facts.

Medical Miracles to Come

By the year 2009, a vaccine[1] against the common cold will have been developed. By the same year, the first human will have been successfully cloned.[2] By the year 2014, parents will be able to create designer children. Genetic therapy will be able to manipulate genes for abilities, intelligence, and hair, eye, and skin color. By 2020, most diseases will be able to be diagnosed and treated at home, and by 2030, cancer and heart disease will have been wiped out. <u>These are just a few examples of the medical miracles that are expected in the next few decades.</u>

PRACTICE 1

Recognizing Topic Sentences

A. Remember that a topic sentence is a complete sentence and is neither too general nor too specific.

Step 1 Read the sentences in each group, and decide which sentence is the best topic sentence. Write *best TS* (for "best topic sentence") on the line next to it.

Step 2 Decide what is wrong with the other sentences. They may be too general, or they may be too specific, or they may be incomplete sentences. Write *too general, too specific,* or *incomplete* on the lines next to them.

The first one has been done for you as an example.

Group 1

too specific	a. A lunar eclipse is an omen of a coming disaster.
too general	b. Superstitions have been around forever.
best TS	c. People hold many superstitious beliefs about the moon.
incomplete	d. Is made of green cheese.

Group 2

_____	a. The history of astronomy is interesting.
_____	b. Ice age people recorded the appearance of new moons by making scratches in animal bones.
_____	c. For example, Stonehenge in Britain, built 3500 years ago to track the movement of the sun.
_____	d. Ancient people observed and recorded lunar and solar events in different ways.

---

[1]**vaccine:** medicine that prevents a specific disease such as polio
[2]**cloned:** made an exact copy of

Group 3

_____ a. It is hard to know which foods are safe to eat nowadays.

_____ b. In some large ocean fish, there are high levels of mercury.

_____ c. Undercooked chicken and hamburger may carry _E. coli_ bacteria.

_____ d. Not to mention mad cow disease.

_____ e. Food safety is an important issue.

Group 4

_____ a. Hybrid automobiles more economical to operate than gasoline-powered cars.

_____ b. The new hybrid automobiles are very popular.

_____ c. Hybrid cars have good fuel economy because a computer under the hood decides to run the electric motor, the small gasoline engine, or the two together.

_____ d. The new hybrid automobiles are popular because of their fuel economy.

Group 5

_____ a. The North American Catawba Indians of the Southeast and the Tlingit of the Northwest both see the rainbow as a kind of bridge between heaven and earth.

_____ b. A rainbow seen from an airplane is a complete circle.

_____ c. Many cultures interpret rainbows in positive ways.

_____ d. Rainbows are beautiful.

_____ e. The belief that you can find a pot of gold at a rainbow's end.

B. Remember that the topic sentence is the most general statement in a paragraph. Read the following scrambled paragraphs and decide which sentence is the topic sentence. Write _TS_ on the line next to that sentence.

Paragraph 1

_____ a. A notes/memo function lets you make quick notes to yourself.

_____ b. Other capabilities include word processing, spreadsheets, and e-mail.

_____ c. A voice recorder that uses a built-in microphone and speaker works like a tape recorder.

_____ d. Basic tools include a calendar to keep track of your appointments, an address and phone number book, to-do lists, and a calculator.

_____ e. MP3 playback lets you listen to digital music files, and a picture viewer lets you look at digital photos.

_____ f. Most personal digital assistants (PDAs) have tools for basic tasks as well as for multimedia functions.

_____ g. A few models also include a built-in digital camera and keyboard.

Paragraph 2

_____ a. Twelve years after *Sputnik*, the United States caught up by becoming the first nation to land a man on the moon.

_____ b. The Europeans have joined the competition, vowing to land European astronauts on the moon by 2025 and on Mars by 2035.

_____ c. The number of nations competing in the "space race" has grown since the early days of space exploration.

_____ d. China joined the competition in 2003 when it launched *Shenzhou 5*.

_____ e. Initially, the former Soviet Union took the lead when it sent the first man into Earth orbit in the spaceship *Sputnik* in 1957.

_____ f. For almost 50 years, the United States and Russia were the only competitors in the contest to explore space using manned spacecraft.

Paragraph 3

_____ a. Another important change was that people had the freedom to live and work wherever they wanted.

_____ b. The earliest significant change was for farming families, who were no longer isolated.

_____ c. The final major change brought by the automobile was the building of superhighways, suburbs, huge shopping centers, and theme parks such as Disney World in Florida.

_____ d. The automobile revolutionized the way of life in the United States.

_____ e. The automobile enabled them to drive to towns and cities comfortably and conveniently.

_____ f. In fact, people could work in a busy metropolitan city and drive home to the quiet suburbs.

Paragraph 4

_____ a. In time, this melted part rises as magma.[1]

_____ b. The formation of a volcanic eruption is a dramatic series of events.

_____ c. As the plate[2] sinks, friction and Earth's heat cause part of it to melt.

_____ d. The magma produces heat, steam, and pressure.

_____ e. First of all, most volcanoes are formed where two plates collide.[3]

_____ f. Then one of the plates is forced under the other and sinks.

_____ g. When the heat, steam, and pressure from the magma finally reach the surface of Earth, a volcanic eruption occurs.

---

[1]**magma:** melted rock inside Earth
[2]**plate:** large, solid section of rock
[3]**collide:** crash into each other

The Two Parts of a Topic Sentence

As noted earlier a topic sentence has two essential parts: the **topic** and the **controlling idea**. The topic names the subject of the paragraph. The controlling idea limits or controls the topic to a specific area that you can discuss in the space of a single paragraph.

TOPIC   CONTROLLING IDEA

(Convenience foods) are <u>easy to prepare</u>.

The reader immediately knows that this paragraph will discuss how easy it is to prepare convenience foods and perhaps give some examples (canned soup, frozen dinners, and so on).

CONTROLLING IDEA   TOPIC

<u>Immigrants have contributed many delicious foods</u> to (U.S. cuisine.)

The reader of this topic sentence expects to read about various ethnic foods popular in the United States: tacos, egg rolls, sushi, baklava, pizza, and so on.

A topic sentence should not have controlling ideas that are unrelated. The three parts of the following controlling idea are too unrelated for a single paragraph. They require three separate paragraphs (and perhaps more) to explain fully.

TOO MANY IDEAS   Indie films are characterized by experimental techniques, low production costs, and provocative themes.

GOOD   Independent films are characterized by experimental techniques.

PRACTICE 2

Identifying the Parts of a Topic Sentence

Circle the topic and underline the controlling idea in each of the following sentences. The first one has been done for you as an example.

1. (Driving on freeways) <u>requires skill and alertness</u>.
2. Driving on freeways requires strong nerves.
3. Driving on freeways requires an aggressive attitude.
4. The Caribbean island of Trinidad attracts tourists because of its calypso music.
5. Spectacular beaches make Puerto Rico a tourist paradise.
6. Moving away from home can be a stressful experience for young people.
7. Many religious rules arose from the health needs of ancient times.
8. A major problem for many students is the high cost of tuition and books.
9. Participating in class discussions is a problem for several different groups of students.
10. In my opinion, television commercials for cosmetics lie to women.
11. Owning an automobile is a necessity for me.
12. It is an expensive luxury to own an automobile in a large city.
13. Taste and appearance are both important in Japanese cuisine.

Writing Topic Sentences

When you write a topic sentence, remember these three points:

1. A topic sentence must be a complete sentence, with a subject and a verb.
2. A topic sentence should be neither too general nor too specific. If it is too general, the reader cannot tell exactly what the paragraph is going to discuss. If it is too specific, the writer will not have anything to write about in the rest of the paragraph.
3. A topic sentence should not have unrelated controlling ideas.

PRACTICE 3

Writing Topic Sentences

A. Write good topic sentences for the following paragraphs. Remember to include both a topic and a controlling idea.

Paragraph 1

_____
_____.

English speakers relaxing at home, for example, may put on *kimonos*, which is a Japanese word. English speakers who live in a warm climate may take an afternoon *siesta* on an outdoor *patio* without realizing that these are Spanish words. In their gardens, they may enjoy the fragrance of *jasmine* flowers, a word that came into English from Persian. They may even relax on a *chaise* while snacking on *yogurt*, words of French and Turkish origin, respectively. At night, they may *shampoo* their hair and put on *pajamas*, words from the Hindi language of India.

Paragraph 2

_____
_____.

In European universities, students are not required to attend classes. In fact, professors in Germany generally do not know the names of the students enrolled in their courses. In the United States, however, students are required to attend all classes and may be penalized if they do not. Furthermore, in the European system, students usually take just one comprehensive examination at the end of their entire four or five years of study. In the North American system, on the other hand, students usually have numerous quizzes, tests, and homework assignments, and they almost always have to take a final examination in each course at the end of each semester.

Paragraph 3

_____

_____.

For example, the Eskimos, living in a treeless region of snow and ice, sometimes build temporary homes out of thick blocks of ice. People who live in deserts, on the other hand, use the most available materials, mud or clay, which provide good insulation from the heat. In Northern Europe, Russia, and other areas of the world where forests are plentiful, people usually construct their homes out of wood. In the islands of the South Pacific, where there is an abundant supply of bamboo and palm, people use these tough, fibrous plants to build their homes.

B. On a piece of paper, write two or three topic sentences for each of the following topics. In other words, give two or three controlling ideas for the same topic.

Example

Topic: cell phones

Topic sentences: 1. Using a cell phone while driving can be dangerous.
                  2. There are certain rules of cell phone manners that
                     everyone should know.
                  3. Cell phones have changed the way we communicate.

Topics

Movies   Your home town
Word processors   Advertising

C. With your classmates, choose three topics that interest you as a group. Write a topic sentence for each topic. Be sure to include a controlling idea.

Supporting Sentences

Supporting sentences explain or prove the topic sentence. One of the biggest problems in student writing is that student writers often fail to support their ideas adequately. They need to use specific details to be thorough and convincing.

There are several kinds of specific supporting details: examples, statistics, and quotations.

PRACTICE 4

Supporting Sentences

Step 1 Read Paragraphs A and B about red-light running. Notice the different specific supporting details that have been added to Paragraph B.

Step 2 Locate the topic sentence in Paragraph B. Circle the topic and underline the controlling idea.

Step 3 Which supporting sentences in Paragraph B contain the kinds of details listed below? Give the sentence numbers of each kind.
An example: _____
A statistic: _____
A quotation: _____

Paragraph A: Paragraph without Support

Red-Light Running

Although some people think that red-light running is a minor traffic violation that is no worse than jaywalking,[1] it can, in fact, become a deadly crime. Red-light runners cause accidents all the time. Sometimes people are seriously injured and even killed. It is especially a problem in rush hour traffic. Everyone is in a hurry to get home, so drivers run red lights everywhere. The police do not do much about it because they are too busy. The only time they pay attention is when there is an accident, and then it is too late. In conclusion, running a red light is a serious offense.

Paragraph B: Paragraph with Support

Red-Light Running

[1]Although some people think red-light running is a minor traffic violation that is no worse than jaywalking, it can, in fact, become a deadly crime. [2]Red-light runners cause hundreds of accidents, including deaths and injuries as well as millions of dollars in damages. [3]Each year more than 900 people die, and nearly 200,000 are injured in crashes that involve red-light running. [4]Motorists run red lights all the time. [5]For example, in Fairfax, Virginia, a five-month-long survey at five busy intersections revealed that a motorist ran a red light every 20 minutes. [6]Red-light runners are seldom caught. [7]According to the Insurance Institute for Highway Safety, "Communities don't have the resources to allow police to patrol intersections as often as would be needed to ticket all motorists who run red lights" ("Q&A").[2]

The next section shows you how to use examples as support. Other types of support—facts, statistics, and quotations—are explained in Chapter 3.

Examples

Examples are perhaps the easiest kind of supporting detail to use because you can often take examples from your own knowledge and experience. You don't have to search the library or the Internet for supporting material. Furthermore, examples make your writing lively and interesting, and your reader is more likely to remember your point if you support it with a memorable example.

Words and phrases that introduce examples include *for example, for instance,* and *such as.* See Transition Signals on pages 25–29 in Chapter 2 for more information.

---

[1]**jaywalking:** crossing a street where there is no marked area for it
[2]"Q&A: Red Light Running." Insurance Institute for Highway Safety June 2003. 26 Feb. 2004 <http://www.hwysafety.org/safety_facts/qanda/rlc.htm>.

MODEL

Paragraph Supported with Examples

Language and Perception

Although we all possess the same physical organs for sensing the world—eyes for seeing, ears for hearing, noses for smelling, skin for feeling, and mouths for tasting—our perception of the world depends to a great extent on the language we speak, according to a famous hypothesis[3] proposed by linguists Edward Sapir and Benjamin Lee Whorf. They hypothesized that language is like a pair of eyeglasses through which we "see" the world in a particular way. A classic example of the relationship between language and perception is the word *snow*. Eskimo languages have as many as 32 different words for snow. For instance, the Eskimos have different words for falling snow, snow on the ground, snow packed as hard as ice, slushy snow, wind-driven snow, and what we might call "cornmeal" snow. The ancient Aztec languages of Mexico, in contrast, used only one word to mean snow, cold, and ice. Thus, if the Sapir-Whorf hypothesis is correct and we can perceive only things that we have words for, the Aztecs perceived snow, cold, and ice as one and the same phenomenon.[4]

Writing Technique Questions

1. What is the main idea of this paragraph? Underline the part of the topic sentence that expresses the main idea.
2. What examples does the writer use to support this idea? Put brackets [ ] around them.
3. What words and phrases introduce the examples? Circle them.

The Concluding Sentence

A concluding sentence serves two purposes:

1. It signals the end of the paragraph.
2. It leaves the reader with the most important ideas to remember. It can do this in two ways:
   - By summarizing the main points of the paragraph
     OR
   - By repeating the topic sentence in different words

A paragraph does not always need a concluding sentence. For single paragraphs, especially long ones, a concluding sentence is helpful to the reader because it is a reminder of the important points. However, a concluding sentence is not needed for every paragraph in a multiparagraph essay.

You may want to begin your concluding sentence with one of the signals in the list on page 14. You may also end a paragraph without a formal signal or perhaps by using an expression like those in the column on the right.

---

[3]**hypothesis:** theory that has not been proven
[4]**phenomenon:** thing or event (*plural:* phenomena)

End-of-Paragraph Signals Followed by a Comma		End-of-Paragraph Signals Not Followed by a Comma
Finally,	Lastly,	The evidence suggests that . . .
In brief,	Therefore,	There can be no doubt that . . .
In conclusion,	Thus,	These examples show that . . .
Indeed,	To sum up,	We can see that . . .
In short,		

Notes
1. Many writing teachers think *In conclusion* and *In summary* are overused and so will not want you to use them.
2. Do not use the phrase *At last* as an end-of-paragraph signal. *At last* means "at the end of a long period of time," as in this sentence: *At last, you've come home.*

The models that follow demonstrate the two ways of writing a concluding sentence. As you read them, determine which concluding sentence summarizes the main points and which concluding sentence repeats the topic sentence in different words.

MODELS

Concluding Sentences

Greeting Cards

Have you noticed how many different kinds of greeting cards you can buy these days? In the old days, the local drugstore had one rack displaying maybe five or six basic kinds of cards. You could walk into the store and choose an appropriate card in five minutes or less. Nowadays, however, the display space for greeting cards is as big as a soccer field, and it may take an hour or two to hunt down exactly the right card with exactly the right message. There are at least 30 categories of birthday cards alone: birthday cards for different ages, from different ages, for different relatives, from different relatives, for different genders, from different genders, from a couple, from the office, for dog owners, for cat owners, and so on. There are cards for getting a job, for retiring from a job, for acquiring a pet, for losing a pet, for becoming engaged, for breaking up. There are also greeting cards to send for no reason—"Thinking of you" or "Just because" cards. The newest type of card is the "encouragement card." An encouragement card offers comforting thoughts and helpful advice to someone who is sad or distressed in these troubled times. In short, there is now a greeting card for every possible life event and for a few nonevents as well.

A Hawaiian Legend

Native people create legends to explain unusual phenomena in their environment. A legend from the Hawaiian island of Kauai explains how the naupaka flower, a flower that grows on beaches there, got its unusual shape. The flower looks like half a small daisy—there are petals on one side only. The legend says that the marriage of two young lovers on the island was opposed by both sets of parents. The parents found the couple together on a beach one day, and to prevent them from being together, one of the families moved to the mountains, separating the young couple forever. As a result, the naupaka flower separated into two halves; one half moved to the mountains, and the other half stayed near the beach. This story is a good example of a legend invented by native people to interpret the world around them.

Writing Technique Questions

1. In which paragraph does the concluding sentence summarize the main points of the paragraph, which are not specifically stated in the topic sentence?
2. In which paragraph does the concluding sentence paraphrase (repeat in different words) the topic sentence?
3. Circle the conclusion signals in each paragraph.

Note: Never introduce a new idea in the concluding sentence.

INCORRECT   In conclusion, we now have more variety of greeting cards to choose from, but they are also <u>becoming very expensive</u>. (*This is a new idea.*)

INCORRECT   In conclusion, there are many <u>other legends</u> like this one in Hawaii. (*This is a new idea.*)

PRACTICE 5

Writing Concluding Sentences

Step 1 Underline the topic sentence in each paragraph.
Step 2 Add a good concluding sentence to each paragraph. You may either paraphrase the topic sentence or summarize the main points.
Step 3 Practice using end-of-paragraph signals by starting each concluding sentence with one.

Paragraph 1

You can be a good conversationalist by being a good listener. When you are conversing with someone, pay close attention to the speaker's words while looking at his or her face. Show your interest by smiling and nodding. Furthermore, do not interrupt while someone is speaking; it is impolite to do so. If you have a good story, wait until the speaker is finished. Also, watch your body language; it can affect your communication whether you are the speaker or the listener. For instance, do not sit slumped in a chair or make nervous hand and foot movements. Be relaxed and bend your body slightly forward to show interest in the person and the conversation.

Paragraph 2

    Modern communication technology is driving workers in the corporate world crazy. They feel buried under the large number of messages they receive daily. In addition to telephone calls, office workers receive dozens of e-mail and voice mail messages daily. In one company, in fact, managers receive an average of 100 messages a day. Because they do not have enough time to respond to these messages during office hours, it is common for them to do so in the evenings or on weekends at home.

_____

_____

_____

Review

These are the important points covered in this chapter:

1. A good topic sentence
   - is a complete sentence with a subject, a verb, and a controlling idea.
   - is neither too general nor too specific. It clearly states the main idea of the paragraph but does not include specific details.
   - is usually the first sentence in the paragraph.
2. Good supporting sentences
   - explain or prove the topic sentence.
   - are specific and factual.
   - can be examples, statistics, or quotations.
3. A good concluding sentence
   - signals the end of the paragraph.
   - summarizes the important points briefly or restates the topic sentence in different words.

Writing Practice

In the back of the book is an appendix outlining the steps in the writing process (Appendix A, pages 265–279). Following the writing process steps will help you write successfully. Your instructor may direct you to follow some or all of them.

PRACTICE 6

Writing a Paragraph

Choose one of the topics from Practice 3B or Practice 3C (page 11) and write a paragraph eight to ten sentences in length.

Step 1 Begin with a topic sentence that you wrote in Practice 3. Write several supporting sentences. **Include at least one specific example**. End with a concluding sentence.

Step 2 After you have completed the first draft of your paragraph, use Self-Editing Worksheet 1. It is on page 317 at the back of the book. Answer the questions on it and write a second draft if necessary. Tear the page out of the book and bring it with your paragraph to class.

Step 3 Exchange papers with a classmate and check each other's paragraph using Peer-Editing Worksheet 1 on page 318. It is on the back side of the Self-Editing Worksheet. After your classmate has completed the checklist, discuss it with him or her and decide what changes you should make.

Step 4 At home or in class (as your instructor directs), write a final copy of your paragraph, making any improvements you discussed with your peer editor.

Step 5 Hand in your first draft, your second draft, and the page containing the two editing worksheets. Your instructor may also ask you to hand in any prewriting (brainstorming and/or outline) that you did for this assignment.

PRACTICE 7

Writing under Pressure

These assignments give you practice in thinking and writing quickly, as you will have to do for essay examinations. Your instructor may choose to change the time limit or assign other topics depending on the needs and interests of the class.

Choose one of the suggested topics and write a well-organized paragraph. Your instructor will give you a time limit. Try to use a specific example to support your topic sentence.

- Spend 1 to 2 minutes at the beginning thinking of ideas and organizing them.
- Spend 1 to 2 minutes at the end checking your work for errors.
- Spend the remaining time writing.

Topic Suggestions
Why some children have imaginary friends
The difficulty of translating from one language to another
The dependence of humans on machines
Pets
Diamonds
Any topic sentence from Practice 2 on page 9

Unity and Coherence

Ancient Greek disk with hieroglyphs

Unity

An important element of a good paragraph is **unity**. Unity means that a paragraph discusses one and only one main idea from beginning to end. For example, if your paragraph is about the advantages of owning a compact car, discuss only that. Do not discuss the disadvantages. Furthermore, discuss only *one* advantage, such as gas economy, in each paragraph. If you begin to discuss another advantage, start a new paragraph. Sometimes it is possible to discuss more than one aspect of the same idea in one paragraph *if they are closely related to each other*. For example, you could discuss gas economy and low maintenance costs in the same paragraph because they are closely related, but you should not discuss both gas economy and easier parking in the same paragraph because they are not closely related.

The second part of unity is that every supporting sentence must *directly* explain or prove the main idea. For example, in a paragraph about the high cost of prescription drugs in the United States, you could mention buying drugs from pharmacies outside the United States as an alternative, but if you write several sentences about buying drugs outside the United States, you are getting off the topic, and your paragraph will not have unity.

PRACTICE 1

Unity

A. The three paragraphs that follow all discuss the same topic. Only one of them shows unity. First read the paragraphs. Then answer these questions.

1. Which paragraph has unity?
2. Which paragraph does not have unity because it discusses two different topics?
3. Which paragraph does not have unity because it has sentences that are not related to the main topic?

Paragraph 1

Effects of Color

Colors create biological reactions in our bodies. These reactions, in turn, can change our behavior. In one study, prisoners were put in a pink room, and they underwent a drastic and measurable decrease in muscle strength and hostility within 2.7 seconds. In another study, athletes needing short bursts of energy were exposed to red light. Their muscle strength increased by 13.5 percent, and electrical activity in their arm muscles increased by 5.8 percent. Athletes needing more endurance for longer performances responded best when exposed to blue light. Other studies have shown that the color green is calming. Green was a sacred color to the Egyptians, representing the hope and joy of spring. It is also a sacred color to Moslems. Many mosques and religious temples throughout the world use green (the color of renewal and growth) and blue (the color of heaven) to balance heavenly peace with spiritual growth. To sum up, color influences us in many ways (Daniels 10).[1]

Paragraph 2

Effects of Color

Colors create biological reactions in our bodies. These reactions, in turn, can change our behavior. In one study, prisoners were put in a pink room, and they underwent a drastic and measurable decrease in muscle strength and hostility within 2.7 seconds. In another study, athletes needing short bursts of energy were exposed to red light. Their muscle strength increased by 13.5 percent, and electrical activity in their arm muscles increased by 5.8 percent. Athletes needing more endurance for longer performances responded best when exposed to blue light. Other studies have shown that the color green is calming. After London's Blackfriars Bridge was painted green, the number of suicides decreased by 34 percent. These and other studies clearly demonstrate that color affects not only our moods but our behavior as well (Daniels 10).

[1]Daniels, Amanda. "Curing with Color." From House to Home Feb./Mar. 2004: 8–10. Published by the Marin Independent Journal, Novato, California.

Paragraph 3

Effects of Color

Colors create biological reactions in our bodies. These reactions, in turn, can change our behavior. In one study, athletes needing short bursts of energy were exposed to red light. Their muscle strength increased by 13.5 percent, and electrical activity in their arm muscles increased by 5.8 percent. Athletes needing more endurance for longer performances responded best when exposed to blue light. Blue is not a good color for dinnerware, however. Food looks less appetizing when it is served on blue plates, perhaps because very few foods in nature are of that color. Other studies have shown that the color green is calming. After London's Blackfriars Bridge was painted green, the number of suicides from it decreased by 34 percent. It is clear that color affects not just our moods, but our behavior as well (Daniels 10).

B. Both of the following paragraphs break the rule of unity because they contain one or more sentences that are off the topic.

Step 1 Locate and underline the topic sentence of each paragraph.
Step 2 Cross out the sentence or sentences that are off the topic.

Paragraph 1

Adventure travel is the hot trend in the tourism industry. Ordinary people are no longer content to spend their two weeks away from the office resting on a sunny beach in Florida. More and more often, they are choosing to spend their vacations rafting down wild rivers, hiking through steamy rain forests, climbing the world's highest mountains, or crossing slippery glaciers.[1] People of all ages are choosing educational study tours for their vacations.

Paragraph 2

Daredevil[2] sports are also becoming popular. Young people especially are increasingly willing to risk life and limb[3] while mountain biking, backcountry snowboarding, or high-speed skateboarding. Soccer is also popular in the United States now, although football is still more popular. One of the riskiest new sports is skysurfing, in which people jump out of airplanes with boards attached to their feet. Skysurfing rivals[4] skydiving and bungee jumping for the amount of thrills—and risk.

C. Both of the following paragraphs not only have sentences that are off the topic but also discuss two or more topics.

Step 1 Decide where each paragraph should be divided into two paragraphs. Underline the topic sentence of each.
Step 2 Find sentence(s) that are off the topic and cross them out.

---

[1]**glaciers:** slowly moving rivers of ice
[2]**daredevil:** very dangerous
[3]**life and limb:** death and injury (idiom)
[4]**rivals:** competes with

Paragraph 1

Because the Internet makes the world a smaller place, the value of having a common language is greatly increased. The question is—which language? Because the Internet grew up in the United States, the largest percentage of its content is now in English. Bill Gates, Microsoft's president, believes that English will remain valuable for a long time as a common language for international communication. His company spends $200 million a year translating software into other languages. He says, "Unless you read English passably well, you miss out on some of the Internet experience." Someday, software may be available to instantly translate both written and spoken language so well that the need for any common language could decline. That day is decades away, however, because flawless machine translation is a very tough problem. Computer spelling checkers also exist for various languages. Software that does crude[5] translations already exists. It is useful if all you are trying to do is understand the general idea of something you see on your computer screen. However, if you are trying to negotiate a contract or discuss a scientific subject where details are important, machine translation is totally useless (Gates).[6]

Paragraph 2

Even when you try to be polite, it is easy to do the wrong thing inadvertently[7] in a new culture. For example, when someone offers you food or a beverage in the United States, accept it the first time it is offered. If you say, "No, thank you" because it is polite to decline the first one or two offers in your culture, you could become very hungry and thirsty in the United States. There, a host thinks that "no" means "no" and will usually not offer again. Meals in the United States are usually more informal than meals in other countries, and the times of meals may be different. Although North Americans are usually very direct in social matters, there are a few occasions when they are not. If a North American says, "Please drop by sometime," he may or may not want you to visit him in his home. Your clue that this may not be a real invitation is the word "sometime." In some areas of the United States, people do not expect you to visit them unless you have an invitation for a specific day and time. In other areas of the United States, however, "dropping by" is a friendly, neighborly gesture. Idioms are often difficult for newcomers to understand.

Coherence

Another element of a good paragraph is coherence. The Latin verb *cohere* means "hold together." For coherence in writing, the sentences must hold together; that is, the movement from one sentence to the next must be logical and smooth. There must be no sudden jumps. Each sentence should flow smoothly into the next one.

---

[5]**crude:** rough, unfinished
[6]Gates, Bill. "One universal language for all on the Internet." Bill Gates: Technology. Syndicated column, 1977.
[7]**inadvertently:** accidentally

There are four ways to achieve coherence:

1. Repeat key nouns.
2. Use consistent pronouns.
3. Use transition signals to link ideas.
4. Arrange your ideas in logical order.

Repetition of Key Nouns

The easiest way to achieve coherence is to repeat key nouns frequently in your paragraph. Read the model paragraph about gold to see how it uses this technique to smooth the flow of sentences. The key noun in this paragraph is *gold*. Circle the word *gold* and all pronouns that refer to it.

MODEL

Paragraph with Coherence

Gold

[1]Gold, a precious metal, is prized for two important characteristics. [2]First of all, gold has a lustrous beauty that is resistant to corrosion. [3]Therefore, it is suitable for jewelry, coins, and ornamental purposes. [4]Gold never needs to be polished and will remain beautiful forever. [5]For example, a Macedonian coin remains as untarnished today as the day it was made 25 centuries ago. [6]Another important characteristic of gold is its usefulness to industry and science. [7]For many years, it has been used in hundreds of industrial applications, such as photography and dentistry. [8]The most recent use of gold is in astronauts' suits. [9]Astronauts wear gold-plated heat shields for protection when they go outside spaceships in space. [10]In conclusion, gold is treasured not only for its beauty but also for its utility.

You should have circled the noun *gold* seven times, the pronoun *it* twice, and the pronoun *its* three times. (The word *it* in sentence 5 refers to *coin*, not *gold*, so you should not have circled it.)

There is no fixed rule about how often to repeat key nouns or when to substitute pronouns. You should repeat a key noun instead of using a pronoun when the meaning is not clear.

Throughout the following paragraph, the word *gold* has been replaced by pronouns, making the paragraph much less coherent.

MODEL

Paragraph without Coherence

Gold

Gold, a precious metal, is prized for two important characteristics. First of all, it has a lustrous beauty that is resistant to corrosion. Therefore, it is suitable for jewelry, coins, and ornamental purposes. It never needs to be polished and will remain beautiful forever. For example, a Macedonian coin remains as untarnished today as the day it was made 25 centuries ago. Another of its important characteristics is its usefulness to industry and science. For many years, it has been used in hundreds of industrial applications, such as photography and dentistry. Its most recent use is in astronauts' suits. Astronauts wear heat shields made from it for protection when they go outside spaceships in space. In conclusion, it is treasured not only for its beauty but also for its utility.

PRACTICE 2

*Repetition
of Key Nouns*

A. In the following paragraph, the key noun is never repeated. Replace the pronoun *it* with the key noun *English* wherever you think doing so would make the paragraph more coherent.

English

[1]English has almost become an international language. [2]Except for Chinese, more people speak it than any other language. [3]Spanish is the official language of more countries in the world, but more countries have it as their official or unofficial second language. [4]More than 70 percent of the world's mail is written in it. [5]It is the primary language on the Internet. [6]In international business, it is used more than any other language, and it is the language of airline pilots and air traffic controllers all over the world. [7]Moreover, although French used to be the language of diplomacy, it has displaced it throughout the world. [8]Therefore, unless you plan to spend your life alone on a desert island in the middle of the Pacific Ocean, it is a useful language to know.

B. In the following passage about dolphins, replace some of the pronouns with appropriate singular or plural nouns.

Dolphins

[1]Dolphins are interesting because they display almost human behavior at times. [2]For example, they display the human emotions of joy and sadness. [3]During training, when they do something correctly, they squeal excitedly and race toward their trainer. [4]When they make a mistake, however, they droop[1] noticeably and mope[2] around their pool. [5]Furthermore, they help each other when they are in trouble. [6]If one is sick, it sends out a message, and others in the area swim to help it. [7]They push it to the surface of the water so that it can breathe. [8]They stay with it for days or weeks until it recovers or dies. [9]They have also helped trapped or lost whales navigate their way safely out to the open sea. [10]They are so intelligent and helpful, in fact, that the U.S. Navy is training them to become underwater bomb disposal experts.

**Key Noun
Substitutes**

If you do not wish to repeat a key noun again and again, you can use synonyms or expressions with the same meaning. For example, in sentence 8 of the first paragraph about gold, the writer substituted the noun *use* as a synonym for *application* in sentence 7, thereby smoothing the flow of thought from one sentence to the next.

---

[1]**droop:** sink down
[2]**mope:** act depressed

PRACTICE 3

*Key Noun
Substitutes*

Step 1 In the topic sentence of the following paragraph, underline the key noun that names the topic.

Step 2 Then circle (a) repetitions of the key nouns, (b) pronouns that refer to them, and (c) synonyms that are substitutes for them. You should have a total of 10 circles: 3 circles around key nouns, 3 around pronouns, and 4 around synonyms.

A Mardi Gras Custom

[1]"Throw me something, mister," is the customary plea for a Mardi Gras "throw." [2]In the final days of Mardi Gras, the season of parties, parades, and revelry[1] that precedes the Christian period of fasting and penance[2] called Lent, crowds of spectators line the streets of New Orleans. [3]They hope to catch a Mardi Gras souvenir tossed from parading floats. [4]Mardi Gras organizations called "krewes" build the floats and sponsor the parades, and while cruising along parade routes, costumed krewe members throw plastic trinkets to the crowds below. [5]The trinkets, which are called "throws," consist of bead necklaces, coins, cups, toys, Frisbees, and figurines stamped with the krewe's symbol or the parade theme. [6]Mardi Gras throws are big business for the companies that supply them. [7]Krewe members spend an average of $800 on them, and some spend $2,000 or more. [8]By far the most treasured of the Mardi Gras mementos are gaudy bead necklaces. [9]Originally made of glass, they are now made of plastic (Roach).[3]

Consistent Pronouns

When you use pronouns, make sure that you use the same person and number throughout your paragraph. Don't change from *you* to *he* or *she* (change of person) or from *he* to *they* (change of number). Notice the changes the writer made for consistency in the following example.

       Students   Know   have

~~A student~~ who ~~knows~~ a few Latin and Greek roots and prefixes ~~has~~ an

                students   do not

advantage over ~~a student~~ who ~~does not~~ know them. They can often guess the

                               students

meaning of new words. If, *for* example, ~~you~~ know that the prefix *omni* means

    they

"all," ~~you~~ have a better chance of guessing the meanings of words such as

                               students   Know

omnibus, *omnipresent*, and *omnidirectional*. Furthermore, ~~a student~~ who ~~knows~~

that the root *sci-* comes from *scire*, "to know," can guess that *omniscient* means

"all-knowing."

---

[1]**revelry:** celebration, festivities
[2]**penance:** punishment that you accept to say that you are sorry for misbehavior
[3]Roach, John. "The Rich History of Mardi Gras's Cheap Trinkets." National Geographic.com 20 Feb. 2004. 24 Feb. 2004 <http://news.nationalgeographic.com/news/2004/02/0220_040220_mardigras.html>.

<table>
<tr><td>

PRACTICE 4

Using Consistent Pronouns

</td><td>

In the following paragraph, the pronouns are not consistent. Correct them to make this paragraph more coherent.

</td></tr>
</table>

Olympic Athletes

Olympic athletes must be strong both physically and mentally. First of all, if you hope to compete in an Olympic sport, you must be physically strong. Furthermore, aspiring[4] Olympians must train rigorously[5] for many years. For the most demanding sports, they train several hours a day, five or six days a week, for ten or more years. In addition to being physically strong, athletes must also be mentally tough. This means that you have to be totally dedicated to your sport, often giving up a normal school, family, and social life. Being mentally strong also means that he or she must be able to withstand the intense pressure of international competition with its accompanying media[6] coverage. Finally, not everyone can win a medal, so Olympians must possess the inner strength to live with defeat.

Transition Signals

Transition signals are expressions such as *first, finally*, and *however*, or phrases such as *in conclusion, on the other hand*, and *as a result*. Other kinds of words such as subordinators (*when, although*), coordinators (*and, but*), adjectives (*another, additional*), and prepositions (*because of, in spite of*) can serve as transition signals.

Transition signals are like traffic signs; they tell your reader when to go forward, turn around, slow down, and stop. In other words, they tell your reader when you are giving a similar idea (*similarly, and, in addition*), an opposite idea (*on the other hand, but, in contrast*), an example (*for example*), a result (*therefore, as a result*), or a conclusion (*in conclusion*).

Transition signals give a paragraph coherence because they guide your reader from one idea to the next.

<table>
<tr><td>

PRACTICE 5

Transition Signals

</td><td>

Compare paragraphs 1 and 2 that follow. Which paragraph contains transition signals and is more coherent? Circle all the transition signals you can identify.

</td></tr>
</table>

Paragraph 1

One difference among the world's seas and oceans is that the salinity[7] varies in different climate zones. The Baltic Sea in northern Europe is only one-fourth as salty as the Red Sea in the Middle East. There are reasons for this. In warm climates, water evaporates[8] rapidly. The concentration[9] of salt is greater. The surrounding land is dry and does not contribute much freshwater to dilute[10] the salty seawater. In cold climate zones, water evaporates slowly. The runoff created by melting snow adds a considerable amount of freshwater to dilute the saline seawater.

---

[4]**aspiring:** hopeful
[5]**rigorously:** strictly, without weakness
[6]**media:** radio, television, newspapers, magazines
[7]**salinity:** salt content
[8]**evaporates:** dries up
[9]**concentration:** percentage (of salt)
[10]**dilute:** reduce the concentration

Paragraph 2

One difference among the world's seas and oceans is that the salinity varies in different climate zones. For example, the Baltic Sea in northern Europe is only one-fourth as saline as the Red Sea in the Middle East. There are two reasons for this. First of all, in warm climate zones, water evaporates rapidly; therefore, the concentration of salt is greater. Second, the surrounding land is dry; consequently, it does not contribute much freshwater to dilute the salty seawater. In cold climate zones, on the other hand, water evaporates slowly. Furthermore, the runoff created by melting snow adds a considerable amount of freshwater to dilute the saline seawater.

Paragraph 2 is more coherent because it contains transition signals. Each transition signal has a special meaning; each shows how the following sentence relates to the preceding one.

For example tells you that an example of the preceding idea is coming.
Two tells you to look for two different reasons.
First of all tells you that this is the first reason.
Second and *furthermore* indicate that additional ideas are coming.
Therefore and *consequently* indicate that the second statement is a result of the first statement.
On the other hand tells you that an opposite idea is coming.

There are different kinds of transition signals. Some of them are listed in the chart on page 27. You will find a more complete list in Appendix C, pages 297–299. Each group has different rules for position in a sentence and punctuation.

Transition Words and Phrases and Conjunctive Adverbs

Most words and phrases in the first two columns of the chart can appear at the beginning, in the middle, or at the end of one independent clause[1] and are usually separated by commas.

For example, the Baltic Sea in northern Europe is only one-fourth as saline as the Red Sea in the Middle East.

The runoff created by melting snow, **furthermore,** adds a considerable amount of freshwater to dilute the saline seawater.

The Mediterranean Sea is more saline than the Red Sea, **however.**

EXCEPTIONS

1. The words and phrases in the last four groups in the chart (for listing ideas and time sequences, for emphasizing, for giving reasons, and for conclusions) usually appear only at the beginning of a sentence, not in the middle or at the end.
2. *Too* usually appears only at the end of a sentence, sometimes preceded by a comma.
3. The short time words *then, now,* and *soon* usually do not need commas.

---

[1]**independent clause:** group of words containing a subject and a verb that expresses a complete thought

Transition Signals

Meaning/ Function	Transition Phrases	Conjunctive Adverbs	Coordinating Conjunctions	Subordinating Conjunctions	Others
To introduce an **additional** **idea**	in addition	furthermore moreover besides also too	and		another (+ noun) an additional (+ noun)
To introduce an **opposite** **idea** or **contrast**	on the other hand in contrast	however nevertheless instead still nonetheless	but yet	although though even though whereas while	in spite of (+ noun) despite (+ noun)
To introduce a **choice** or **alternative**		otherwise	or	if unless	
To introduce a **restatement** or **explanation**	in fact indeed	that is			
To list in **order**	first, second, third next, last, finally				the first, second, third, etc. the next, last, final
To introduce an **example**	for example for instance				an example of (+ noun) such as (+ noun)
To introduce a **conclusion** or **summary**	clearly in brief in conclusion indeed in short in summary				
To introduce a **result**	accordingly as a result as a consequence	therefore consequently hence thus	so		

The words and phrases in the first two columns of the chart can also connect two independent clauses. In this case, we use them with a semicolon and a comma.

———— INDEPENDENT CLAUSE ————   — INDEPENDENT CLAUSE ——
In warm climate zones, water evaporates rapidly; **therefore,** the concentration of salt is greater.

——————— INDEPENDENT CLAUSE ———————
Both the Red Sea and the Mediterranean have narrow outlets to the ocean;
—————— INDEPENDENT CLAUSE ——————
however, the Mediterranean's is narrower.

———— INDEPENDENT CLAUSE ————   ———— INDEPENDENT CLAUSE ————
A few societies in the world are matriarchal; **that is,** the mother is head of the family.

——————— INDEPENDENT CLAUSE ———————
Some English words have no exact equivalents in other languages; **for example,**
—————— INDEPENDENT CLAUSE ——————
there is no German word for the adjective *fair*, as in *fair play*.

Look at Compound Sentences with Conjunctive Adverbs on pages 168–170 for more examples.

Coordinators

This group includes the seven coordinating conjunctions *and, but, so, or, nor, for,* and *yet* and the five correlative ("paired") conjunctions *both . . . and, not only . . . but also, neither . . . nor, either . . . or*, and *whether . . . or*. Coordinators may or may not have commas. When they connect two independent clauses, use a comma.

———— INDEPENDENT CLAUSE ————   —— INDEPENDENT CLAUSE ——
In a matriarchy, the mother is the head of the family, **and** all the children belong to her clan.[1]

———— INDEPENDENT CLAUSE ————   —— INDEPENDENT CLAUSE ——
In warm climate zones, water evaporates rapidly, **so** the concentration of salt is greater.

—— INDEPENDENT CLAUSE ——   —— INDEPENDENT CLAUSE ——
Children **not only** need love, **but** they **also** need discipline.

When coordinators connect two words or phrases, do not use a comma.

Would you rather take a written **or** an oral exam?

Children need **not only** love **but also** discipline.

Exception: Some writers use a comma before *but* and *yet* even when they do not connect independent clauses to emphasize the contrast of the connected ideas.

The poem is solemn, **yet** optimistic in tone.

Look at Compound Sentences with Coordinators on pages 165–167 and the section on Parallelism Correlative (Paired) Conjunctions on pages 181–183 for more examples.

---

[1]**clan:** extended family group

Subordinators

A subordinator (subordinating conjunction) is the first word in a dependent clause.[2] A dependent clause is always connected to an independent clause to make a sentence. The sentence may or may not have a comma. The general rule is this: Put a comma after a dependent clause but not in front of one.

┌─────────────── DEPENDENT CLAUSE ───────────────┐ ┌─── INDEPENDENT CLAUSE ───┐
Although the company's sales increased last year**,** its net profit declined.

┌─────────────── INDEPENDENT CLAUSE ───────────────┐ ┌─────── DEPENDENT CLAUSE ───────┐
The company's net profit declined last year **although** its sales increased.

For information about subordinators, see Chapter 13.

Others

The transition signals in this group include nouns such as *example*, adjectives such as *additional*, prepositions such as *in addition to*, verbs such as *cause*, and adverbs such as *too*. There are no punctuation rules for this group, but it is important to notice what kinds of words follow these signals.

An **additional** reason for the company's bankruptcy was the lack of competent management. (**Additional** *is an adjective, so it is followed by a noun.*)

In addition to increased competition, the lack of competent management caused the company's bankruptcy. (**In addition to** *is a preposition, so it is followed by a noun or noun phrase.*)

Vocabulary differences between British and American English include words **such as** *bonnet/hood, petrol/gasoline, windscreen/windshield*, and *lorry/truck*. (**Such as** *is followed by a noun or noun phrase.*)

Step 1 Circle all the transition signals in the following paragraphs.
Step 2 Punctuate the transition signals if necessary.

PRACTICE 6

Recognizing Transition Signals

Genetic[3] Engineering

Genetic research has produced both exciting and frightening possibilities. Scientists are now able to create new forms of life in the laboratory because of the development of gene splicing.[4] On the one hand, the ability to create life in the laboratory could greatly benefit humankind. One beneficial application of gene splicing is in agriculture. For example, researchers have engineered a more nutritious type of rice that could help alleviate the serious problem of vitamin A deficiency. It is estimated that 124 million children worldwide lack vitamin A, putting them at risk of permanent blindness and other health issues. In addition genetic engineers have created larger fish, frost-resistant strawberries, and cows that produce more milk. Indeed agriculture has already benefited from the promise of genetic engineering.

---

dependent clause: group of words containing a subject and a verb that does *not* express a complete thought. A dependent clause always begins with a subordinator.
[3] **genetic:** from *gene*, the unit of heredity
[4] **gene splicing:** gene joining

On the other hand not everyone is positive about gene-splicing technology. Some people feel that it could have terrible consequences. In fact a type of corn engineered to kill a certain insect pest also threatened to annihilate[1] desirable monarch butterflies. In another accident, a genetically engineered type of corn that was approved only for animal consumption because it was toxic to humans accidentally cross-pollinated with corn grown for humans. As a result many countries banned imports of genetically modified corn for several years. Furthermore the ability to clone human beings is a possibility that frightens many people. In 2004, two South Korean scientists reported that they had successfully cloned a human embryo (Dreifus).[2] The embryo did not develop into a baby however it is possible that one could do so in the future, a possibility that not everyone is comfortable with.

I don't give adam shit

PRACTICE 7

Choosing Transition Signals

A. From the choices given in parentheses, choose the transition signal that best shows the relationship between the sentences in each group. Write the signal in the space. Add punctuation and change capital letters to small letters if necessary. The first one has been done for you as an example.

Note: All the transition signals in this practice are transition phrases and conjunctive adverbs. This is to give you more practice in using and punctuating these types of transition signals correctly.

1. A recent article in *Era* magazine suggested ways to reduce inflation. The article suggested that the president reduce the federal budget ___; furthermore___, it suggested that the government reduce federal, state, and local taxes. (**however, in contrast, furthermore**)

2. The same article said that the causes of inflation were easy to find ___However___ the cure for inflation was not so easy to prescribe. (**however, for example, therefore**)

3. *Era* also suggested that rising wages were one of the primary causes of inflation ___therefore___ the government should take action to control wages. (**however, therefore, for example**)

4. In physics, the weight of an object is the gravitational force[3] with which Earth attracts it; ___For example___, if a man weighs 150 pounds, this means that Earth pulls him down with a force of 150 pounds. (**moreover, therefore, for example**)

5. The farther away from Earth a person is, the less the gravitational force of Earth. ___Therefore___ a man weighs less when he is 50,000 miles from Earth than when he is only 5,000 miles away. (**in conclusion, therefore, however**)

---

[1]**annihilate:** wipe out, destroy completely
[2]Dreifus, Claudia. "2 Friends, 242 Eggs and a Breakthrough." <u>New York Times</u> 17 Feb. 2004: F1–2.
[3]**gravitational force:** the force that pulls things toward Earth

6. A **tsunami** is a tidal wave produced by an earthquake on the ocean floor. The waves are very long and low in open water, but when they get close to land, they encounter friction[4] because the water is shallow ⟨As a result⟩ the waves increase in height and can cause considerable damage when they finally reach land. (**on the other hand, as a result, for example**)

B. Fill in each blank with an appropriate transition signal from the list provided. Use each signal only once. Add punctuation if necessary.

for example   in fact   similarly   also
indeed   third   second   final and most convincing

Time

One stereotype about North Americans says that they are obsessed with[5] time. It sometimes seems true that for North Americans, time seems as valuable as money. (1) _____ they even say, "Time is money." (2) _____ have you noticed how many verbs can be followed by both time and money? (3) _____ you can *spend time, save time, lose time, find time, make time, waste time*, and *run out of time*. (4) _____ you can spend, save, lose, find, make, waste, and run out of money. (5) _____ North Americans seem to regard time as a "thing" that one can own. You can *have time, buy time*, and *take time*. (One wonders how much it costs and where it is taken.) A (6) _____ piece of evidence that North Americans are obsessed with time is their fanaticism about always being on time. (7) _____ people who are habitually late risk punishment ranging from frowning disapproval to losing their jobs. The (8) _____ proof is that these poor people sometimes take courses in time management! That is really overdoing it, don't you agree?

C. Improve the coherence of the following paragraph by adding transitions in the blank spaces. Use the hints provided in parentheses to help you choose a transition.

Move Over, DVD. Here Comes BD!

First, CDs brought digital sound into our homes. Then DVD technology brought digital sound and video and revolutionized the movie industry. Soon there will be (1) _____ (*additional idea*) revolution: Blu-ray discs (BDs). A Blu-ray disc will have several advantages. (2) _____ (*list in order*) it has an enormous data storage capacity. A single-sided DVD can hold 4.7 gigabytes of information, about the size of an average 2-hour movie. A single-sided BD, (3) _____ (*contrast*), can hold up to 27 gigabytes, enough for 13 hours of standard video. A (4) _____ (*list in order*)

---

[4]**friction:** resistance
[5]**obsessed with:** fanatical about

advantage is that a BD can record, store, and play back high-definition video because of its larger capacity. A double-layer BD can store about 50 gigabytes, enough for 4.5 hours of high-definition video. The cost will be about the same. (5) _____ (*additional idea*), a BD has a higher date transfer rate— 36 megabits per second—than today's DVDs, which transfer at 10 megabits per second. (6) _____ (*result*) a BD can record 25 gigabytes of data in just over an hour and a half. (7) _____ (*conclusion*) because of their large storage capacity and comparable cost, BDs will probably take over the market when they become widely available.

PRACTICE 8

Using Transition Signals

Choose one of the two topic sentences that follow and write a paragraph that develops it. Use transition signals to connect the supporting sentences smoothly. You may use the transition signals suggested for each topic, or you may use others not listed. Add other sentences without transitions if you need to in order to explain the topic completely.

Sentence 1. There are four noticeable differences between British and American English.

the most noticeable difference	such as
for example	finally
another difference	for instance
for example	in conclusion
a third difference	

Here are some possible subtopics for your paragraph. You may, of course, use your own if you wish.

Subtopics	Examples
Pronunciation	Speakers of British English do not always pronounce *r*. *schedule*: In British English it is pronounced [shed-u-al]; in American English it is pronounced [sked-u-al]
Spelling	colour/color; realise/realize; defence/defense
Vocabulary	petrol/gas; biscuit/cookie; pocket money/allowance; bonnet/hood

Sentence 2. Sometimes I enjoy being alone.

for instance	on the other hand
moreover	therefore

Don't Overuse Transition Signals

Read your paragraph aloud and pay attention to your own language. Are you using too many transition signals? Too many can be distracting rather than helpful. There is no rule about how many to use in one paragraph. Use them only when they will help your reader follow your ideas.

PRACTICE 9

*Too Many
Transition
Signals*

The following paragraph has too many transition signals. Which ones are helpful to the reader? Which transition signals are an unnecessary distraction?

Step 1 Improve the paragraph by deleting some transition signals. You may want to rewrite sentences, and you may have to change the capitalization and punctuation.

Step 2 There are many possible ways to do this assignment. Discuss your changes with a partner or in a group.

How to Grow an Avocado Tree[1]

After you have enjoyed the delicious taste of an avocado, do not throw out the seed! You can grow a beautiful houseplant or even your own tree by following these simple steps. **First,** wash the seed. **Second,** dry it. **Third,** insert three toothpicks into its thickest part. **Then** fill a glass or empty jar with water. **After that,** suspend the seed in the water with the pointed end up and the broad end down. The water should cover about an inch of the seed. **Next,** put the glass in a warm place, but not in direct sunlight. Add water when necessary to keep the bottom of the seed under water at all times. In two to six weeks, you should see roots begin to grow. **Furthermore,** the seed will crack open, and **then** a stem will emerge from the top. **However,** wait until the stem is 6 to 7 inches long. **Then** cut it back to about 3 inches. **Now** wait until the roots are thick and the stem has leafed out again. **Then** fill an 8- to 10-inch diameter clay pot with enriched potting soil. Plant the seed, leaving the top half exposed. **Then** water it well. **After that,** water frequently but lightly; **also** give the plant an occasional deep soaking. **However,** do not overwater your little tree. Yellow leaves are a sign of too much water. **Then** place the potted plant in a sunny window and watch it grow. The more sunlight, the better. **Then, when** the stem is 12 inches high, cut it back to 6 inches to encourage the growth of side branches. In just a few more weeks, you will have a beautiful indoor plant. **In conclusion,** enjoy your new plant, but do not expect it to bear fruit. Avocados grown from seed occasionally flower and bear fruit; **however, first** you will have to plant it outside and **then** wait anywhere from five to thirteen years.

---

[1]"Grow Your Own Tree." California Avocado Commission. 6 Dec. 2004 <http://www.avocado.org/avocado-facts/growing-avocado.php>.

Logical Order

In addition to using transition signals and repeating key nouns and pronouns, a fourth way to achieve coherence is to arrange your sentences in some kind of logical order.

Your choice of one kind of logical order over another will, of course, depend on your topic and your purpose. You may even combine two or more different logical orders in the same paragraph. The important point to remember is to arrange your ideas in some kind of order that is logical to a reader accustomed to the English way of writing.

Some common kinds of logical order in English are *chronological order*, *logical division of ideas*, and *comparison/contrast*.

- *Chronological order* is order by time—a sequence of events or steps in a process. The model paragraph on how to grow an avocado tree (page 33) uses time order to organize the steps.
- In *logical division of ideas*, a topic is divided into parts, and each part is discussed separately. The model paragraph about gold on page 3 uses logical division. First, it discusses gold's beauty, and second its utility.
- In a *comparison/contrast* paragraph, the similarities and/or differences between two or more items are discussed. The paragraph about synonyms on page 5 compares and contrasts word meanings.

PRACTICE 10

Recognizing Kinds of Logical Order

Read the following paragraphs and decide which kind of logical order is used in each: comparison/contrast, chronological order, or logical division of ideas. Be able to discuss the reasons for your choice. Circle all transition signals.

Paragraph 1

The process of machine translation of languages is complex. To translate a document from English into Japanese, for example, the computer first analyzes an English sentence, determining its grammatical structure and identifying the subject, verb, objects, and modifiers. Next, the words are translated by an English-Japanese dictionary. After that, another part of the computer program analyzes the resulting awkward jumble[1] of words and meanings and produces an intelligible sentence based on the rules of Japanese syntax[2] and the machine's understanding of what the original English sentence meant. Finally, a human bilingual editor polishes the computer-produced translation.

Kind of logical order: _____

---

[1]**jumble:** confused mixture
[2]**syntax:** sentence structure, grammar

Paragraph 2

French and U.S. business managers have decidedly different management styles. French meetings, for example, are long and rambling[3] and rarely end on time. Furthermore, meetings often end without closure.[4] Managers in the United States, on the other hand, make an effort to start and stop a meeting on time, and North American business meetings typically end with decisions and action plans. Another difference involves documentation. North Americans adore documentation; they have a procedure manual for everything. The French, in contrast, think this is childish. French managers find it difficult to stick to a schedule, but U.S. managers are intolerant of delays. In addition, the French prefer to work alone, whereas North Americans like to work in teams. Another major difference in management style is that in French companies, authority comes from the top; French managers do not share information with subordinates and make decisions with little participation by employees beneath them. In U.S. companies, however, top managers share information and frequently solicit[5] input from subordinates ("How French Managers").[6]

Kind of logical order: _____

Paragraph 3

It took more than 2,500 years to develop the calendar used in most Western countries today. In about 700 B.C.E.,[7] the ancient Romans used a calendar that had 304 days divided into 10 months; March was the beginning of each year. There were more than 60 days missing from the calendar, so very soon the calendar did not match the seasons at all. Spring arrived when the calendar said that it was still winter. A few decades later, the Romans added the months of January and February to the end of the year. This calendar lasted about 600 years. Then in 46 B.C.E., Julius Caesar, the Roman ruler, made a new calendar. His calendar had 365 days, with one day added every fourth year. He also moved the beginning of the year to January 1, and he renamed a month for himself: Julius (July). In Caesar's calendar, February had 29 days. The very next emperor, Augustus, not only renamed a month for himself (August), but he also took one day from February and added it to August so that "his" month would be just as long as Caesar's. This calendar worked better than the previous ones, but it still was not perfect. By 1580, the first calendrical day of spring was 10 days too early, so in 1582, Pope Gregory XIII, the leader of the Roman Catholic religion, made a small change to make the calendar more accurate. In the Gregorian calendar, the year is still 26.3 seconds different from the solar year, but it will be a long time before this causes a problem.

Kind of logical order: _____

---

[3] **rambling:** not focused on a specific goal
[4] **closure:** decisions about points discussed
[5] **solicit:** ask for
[6] "How French Managers Compare to Americans." Money Beat. <u>Marin Independent Journal</u> 30 Nov. 1993: B7.
[7] **B.C.E.:** Before the Common Era (The Common Era began in the year 1.)

Paragraph 4

The many different calendars used throughout the world are all based on the phases of the moon, on the revolution of Earth around the sun, or on a combination of the two. The first kind of calendar is the lunar calendar, based on the phases of the moon. A month is calculated as the time between two full moons, 29.5 days, and a year has 354 days. The Islamic calendar used in Muslim countries is a lunar calendar. It has 12 months and a cycle of 30 years in which the 2nd, 5th, 7th, 10th, 13th, 16th, 18th, 21st, 24th, 26th, and 29th years have 355 days, and the others 354 days. A second kind of calendar is the solar calendar, which is based on the revolution of Earth around the sun. The ancient Egyptians used a solar calendar divided into 12 months of 30 days each, which left 5 uncounted days at the end of each year. A very accurate calendar developed by the Mayan Indians in North America was also a solar calendar. It had 365 days, 364 of which were divided into 28 weeks of 13 days each. The new year began on the 365th day. Because the solar year is exactly 365 days, 5 hours, 48 minutes, and 46 seconds long, however, a solar calendar is not totally accurate, so many cultures developed a third kind of calendar, the lunisolar calendar. In a lunisolar calendar, extra days are added every so often to reconcile[1] the lunar months with the solar year. The Chinese, Hebrew, and Gregorian calendars used today are lunisolar calendars.

Kind of logical order: _____

Review

These are the important points covered in this chapter.

1. Every good paragraph has both unity and coherence.
2. You achieve unity by
   - discussing only one idea in a paragraph.
   - always staying on the topic in your supporting sentences.
3. You achieve coherence by
   - repeating key nouns.
   - using consistent pronouns.
   - using transition signals.
   - arranging your ideas in some kind of logical order.
4. There are different types of transition signals. Each type is punctuated differently.

---

[1]**reconcile:** bring into agreement

In the following paragraph, notice how the four elements work together to create a unified and coherent paragraph.

A Leap Year Custom Lives On

ALL SENTENCES ARE RELATED TO THE TOPIC.

KEY NOUNS ARE REPEATED, AND SYNONYMS ARE USED.

PRONOUNS ARE CONSISTENT.

TRANSITION SIGNALS HELP THE READER FOLLOW THE PROGRESSION OF IDEAS.

IDEAS ARE PRESENTED IN LOGICAL ORDER.

No one knows for certain the origin of the custom that allows women to propose marriage on Leap Day. Leap Day is February 29th, the extra day added every four years to put the calendar year in synch with the solar year. One explanation for the custom comes from Ireland. According to Irish legend, Saint Brigid, an Irish holy woman who lived in the fifth century, complained to Saint Patrick about women having to wait for men to propose. Saint Patrick agreed that this practice was unfair, so he decided that eager females could propose on this one day. A different explanation of the custom comes from medieval England. According to this explanation, people there thought that because Leap Day existed to fix a problem in the calendar, it could also be used to fix an old and unjust practice. In 1288, the custom became an actual law in Scotland. Not only did the Scottish law allow women to propose on any day during a Leap Year, but it also said that any man who declined a woman proposal had to pay a fine! Whatever its origins, the tradition of women taking the initiative one day a year lives on in Sadie Hawkins Day celebrations held in many communities in the United States even today.

PRACTICE 11

Review of Coherence

Step 1 Turn back to Practice 1B on page 7, in which you selected the topic sentence in each group and marked it *TS*.

Step 2 Now put the supporting sentences of Paragraphs 2, 3, and 4 in order and mark them *SS1, SS2, SS3*, and so on.
- Skip Paragraph 1, for it lacks transition words or other clues.
- Use your knowledge of coherence—especially transition signals and repetition of key nouns—to determine the correct order.

Writing Practice

PRACTICE 12

Unity and Coherence

Step 1 Choose one of the topics suggested and write a paragraph that is 10 to 15 sentences in length. Focus on giving your paragraph unity and coherence. Follow the steps in the writing process. (See Appendix A.)

Step 2 After you have completed your first draft, use Self-Editing Worksheet 2 on page 319. Revise your paragraph and write a second draft if necessary.

Step 3 Exchange papers with a classmate and check each other's paragraph using Peer-Editing Worksheet 2 on page 320. After your classmate has completed the checklist, discuss it and decide what changes you should make.

Step 4 Revise your paragraph and write a final copy to hand in, making any improvements you discussed with your peer editor.

Step 5 Hand in your first draft, your second draft, your final copy, and the page containing the two editing worksheets. Your instructor may also ask you to hand in any prewriting (brainstorming and/or outline) that you did for this assignment.

Topic Suggestions

The influence of birth order on personality

One (or two) place(s) a visitor to your country should not miss

The disadvantages of being left-handed

A fad, fashion, or activity of your generation that drives an older generation crazy

An interesting custom or special celebration from your culture

PRACTICE 13

Writing under Pressure

Choose one of the topics listed below and write a well-organized paragraph. Your instructor will give you a time limit. Try to use a specific example to support your topic sentence.

• Spend 1 or 2 minutes at the beginning thinking of ideas and organizing them.
• Spend 1 minute at the end checking your work for errors.
• Spend the remaining time writing.

Topic Suggestions

Why you do a certain sport

Why you don't like to do sports

Why you are a morning person (or a night person)

Your opinion about genetic engineering

Supporting Details: Facts, Quotations, and Statistics

Egyptian hieroglyphs

Academic writing normally requires that you support your ideas and opinions with facts, statistics, quotations, and similar kinds of information. You get these kinds of supporting details from outside sources such as books, magazines, newspapers, Web sites, personal interviews, and so on.

Facts versus Opinions

First, it is important to distinguish between facts and opinions. **Opinions** are subjective statements based on a person's beliefs or attitudes.

> Men are better drivers than women.
>
> Smoking is a bad habit.
>
> English is an easy language to learn.

Opinions are not acceptable as support. It is certainly acceptable to express opinions in academic writing. In fact, most professors want you to express your own ideas. However, you may not use an opinion as support, and if you express an opinion, you must support it with facts. **Facts** are objective statements of truths.

At sea level, water boils at 100 degrees Celsius.

Women live longer than men.

Cigarettes are addictive.

Sometimes even facts need proof. While all three statements above are facts, the last two need proof. Your readers may not believe that women live longer than men, or they may not agree that cigarettes are addictive. You have to use specific supporting details to prove that these statements are true facts. Kinds of specific supporting details include examples, statistics, and quotations.

OPINION | Photographs of ultrathin fashion models send the wrong message to girls and young women.

FACT, BUT NEEDS PROOF | Fashion models are unnaturally thin.

SPECIFIC SUPPORTING DETAIL | The average model weighs 25 percent less than the average woman of the same height.

PRACTICE 1

Specific Supporting Details

Step 1 Decide which of the following statements is an opinion, a fact that needs proof, or a specific supporting detail. Write
   • *O* for opinion
   • *F-NP* for fact that needs proof
   • *SSD* for specific supporting detail
Step 2 Discuss with your classmates what specific supporting details you might use to support the sentences you marked *O* and *F-NP*.

The first three have been done for you as examples.

   __F-NP__ 1. People who steal identities do a lot of damage before their victims become aware of it. *(The writer could give an example of a person who was victimized before noticing it.)*
   ___O___ 2. Punishment for identity thieves is not severe enough. *(The writer could give an example of a typical punishment.)*
   __SSD__ 3. Last year, the losses of victims totaled more than $7 billion.
   _____ 4. Identity theft is more serious than any other type of theft.
   _____ 5. Identity theft is increasing at a rapid pace.
   _____ 6. In 2000, 31,000 cases of identity theft were reported to the Federal Trade Commission (FTC); in 2003, the number was 210,000.
   _____ 7. Most people do not report identity theft to the police.
   _____ 8. In 2003, 60 percent of identity theft victims did not notify the police, according to the FTC.
   _____ 9. Identity theft happens to ordinary people, not just to the wealthy.

_____ 10. As grocery clerk Sue Jamison reported, "My wallet was stolen, and within a week, the thieves had ordered an expensive cell phone package, applied for a VISA credit card, and received a PIN from the Department of Motor Vehicles to change my driving record online."

_____ 11. It is easy for a thief to use the U.S. Postal Service to steal identities.

_____ 12. For example, thieves steal credit card statements from mailboxes, and then send a change-of-address card to the postal service to have future statements sent to a different address.

_____ 13. Most victims of identity theft are young adults.

_____ 14. The Federal Trade Commission reports that there were more victims in the age group 18–29 than in any other group.

_____ 15. The police should do more to protect citizens from identity theft.

_____ 16. "You cannot prevent identity theft entirely, but you can minimize your risk," according to the Federal Trade Commission booklet "Facts for Consumers."

_____ 17. Most identity thieves operate in large, organized gangs.

Using Outside Sources

Where can you find specific supporting details to support your ideas? For some assignments, you may be able to use examples from your own personal experience, or you may be able to gather quotations and statistics by performing an experiment, taking a survey, or interviewing people. For other assignments, you may have to look for outside sources by researching your topic in a library or on the Internet.

For basic information on doing research, see Appendix E: Research and Documentation of Sources.

There are three ways to insert outside information into your own writing: (1) You can quote it, (2) you can summarize it, or (3) you can paraphrase it. You will learn to use quotations in this chapter. In Chapter 8, you will learn to summarize and paraphrase.

Plagiarism   It is important to learn how to use information from outside sources without committing plagiarism. Plagiarism is using someone else's words or ideas as if they were your own, and it is a serious offense. Students who plagiarize may fail a class or even be expelled from school. When you use information from an outside source without acknowledging that source, you are guilty of plagiarism.

One way to avoid plagiarism is to always put quotation marks around words that you copy exactly. (You do not need to use quotation marks if you change the words.) You are also guilty of plagiarism if you fail to cite the source of outside information—words or ideas—that you use. To cite a source means to tell where you got the information.

Citing Sources

Citing a source is a two-step process.

1. Insert a short reference in parentheses at the end of each piece of borrowed information. This short reference is called an *in-text citation.*
2. Prepare a list describing all your sources completely. This list is titled "Works Cited" and appears as the last page of your paper.

Here is an example of an in-text citation and of its corresponding entry in a works-cited list. Notice the position and punctuation of the citation—at the end of the last sentence of the borrowed information, before the final period.

IN-TEXT CITATION

According to the Insurance Institute for Highway Safety, "Communities don't have the resources to allow police to patrol intersections as often as would be needed to ticket all motorists who run red lights" ("Q&A").

The abbreviation "Q&A" in parentheses at the end of this sentence is the first element of the title of an article from which the words in quotation marks were copied. There was no author.

If readers want more information about this source, they can turn to the works-cited list at the end of the essay, report, or paper and find this entry:

ENTRY IN WORKS-CITED LIST

"Q&A: Red Light Running." Insurance Institute for Highway Safety June 2003. 26 Feb. 2004 <http://www.hwysafety.org/safety_facts/quanda/rlc.htm>.

This entry tells us that the complete title of the article is "Q&A: Red Light Running." It was published online in June 2003 by the Insurance Institute for Highway Safety. The date 26 Feb. 2004 is the date the writer found the article while researching the topic. The information in angle brackets < > is the Web site address (URL) where the article can be found.

More complete information on how to write in-text citations and works-cited lists is found in Appendix E: Research and Documentation of Sources.

Quotations

Quotations from reliable and knowledgeable sources are good supporting details. There are two kinds of quotations: direct and indirect. In a direct quotation, you copy another person's exact words (spoken or written) and enclose them in quotation marks. In an indirect quotation, you report the person's words without quotation marks, but with a reporting expression such as *according to XYZ . . .* or *XYZ believes that . . . .*

Direct Quotations

Read the following model and notice how direct quotations are used to support the topic sentence. Notice that a quotation can be a complete sentence (or several sentences) or a short phrase. Also notice the punctuation of each quotation.

MODEL

Direct Quotations

Drugs and the Olympic Games 1

¹It is no secret that performance-enhancing drugs have been used by Olympic athletes for decades. ²According to an article in *Forbes* magazine, "From the brute steroids the East Germans reportedly used on their Olympians during the Cold War to today's man-made versions of natural human proteins, drugs have been as much a staple of the Games as gold, silver, and bronze" (Herper, par. 4).¹ ³Despite rigorous drug testing, the use of banned performance-enhancing substances has become more widespread than ever. ⁴The disqualification of athletes from the most recent Olympic Games because of illegal drug use shows that the problem is ongoing.

⁵It seems apparent that if athletes want to win, they must consider using drugs. ⁶Dr. Michael Karsten, a Dutch physician who said he had prescribed anabolic steroids to hundreds of world-class athletes, states, "If you are especially gifted, you may win once, but from my experience you can't continue to win without drugs. ⁷The field is just too filled with drug users" (qtd. in Bamberger and Yaeger 62).² ⁸In fact, some people claim that record-breaking performances of Olympic athletes may be directly due to drugs. ⁹Charles Yesalis, a Pennsylvania State University professor who has studied the use of drugs in sports, believes "a large percentage" of athletes who have set new records have done so with the help of performance-enhancing drugs. ¹⁰"A lot of experts, at least in private, feel that way," he claims (qtd. in Herper, par. 6).

Writing Technique Questions
1. Which sentence states the main idea of the first paragraph?
2. What direct quotation supports it? What phrase introduces the quotation?
3. What is the main idea in the second paragraph? What three direct quotations support it?
4. What verbs introduce the quotations in the second paragraph?
5. Explain the in-text citation at the end of the second paragraph.
   • Who spoke the words in quotation marks?
   • Who wrote the article in which the words in quotation marks appear?
   • Is the source a printed article or an online article? How can you tell?

Reporting Verbs and Phrases

To introduce borrowed information—direct quotations, indirect quotations, or statistics—use the phrase *according to* or a reporting verb such as the following:

assert	insist	report	suggest
claim	maintain	say	write
declare	mention	state	

---

¹Herper, Matthew. "Olympics: Performance Drugs Outrun Olympics." <u>Forbes</u> 15 Feb. 2002. 30 Mar. 2004 <http://www.forbes.com/2002/02/15/0215ped.html>.

The form of this in-text citation shows that the words in quotation marks are from paragraph 4 of an online article written by a person whose last name is Herper.

²Bamberger, Michael, and Don Yaeger. "Over the Edge." <u>Sports Illustrated</u> 14 Apr. 1997: 60–86.

The form of this citation means that the words in quotation marks were spoken by Dr. Michael Karsten and were quoted on page 62 of an article written by two people named Bamberger and Yaeger.

Here are some rules for their use.

1. Reporting verbs can appear before, in the middle of, or after borrowed information. The reporting phrase *according to* usually appears before or after but not in the middle.

    One young bicyclist **says**, "To win in world-class competition, you have to take drugs" (Jones).

    "To win in world-class competition," **says** one young bicyclist, "you have to take drugs" (Jones).

    "To win in world-class competition, you have to take drugs," **says** one young bicyclist (Jones).

    According to one young bicyclist, athletes have to take drugs to win (Jones).

    Athletes have to take drugs to win, **according to** one young bicyclist (Jones).

2. Reporting verbs can be used either with or without the subordinator *as*.

    As one writer **says** when discussing the case of an Olympic medallist who unknowingly took a banned drug, "The human body, of course, doesn't distinguish intentional use from inadvertent exposure. Neither does the IOC [International Olympic Committee]" (Kidder, par. 5).

    One writer **says** when discussing the case of an Olympic medallist who unknowingly took a banned drug, "The human body, of course, doesn't distinguish intentional use from inadvertent exposure. Neither does the IOC [International Olympic Committee]" (Kidder, par. 5).

3. Reporting verbs can be in any tense. However, be aware that a past tense reporting verb may cause changes in verbs, pronouns, and time expressions in an indirect quotation. (See Sequence of Tenses Rules on page 48.)

    Some critics **claim/have claimed** that the International Olympic Committee has been lax on enforcement of drug bans ("2000 Olympics," par. 6).

    Some critics **claimed** that the International Olympic Committee had been lax on enforcement of drug bans ("2000 Olympics," par. 6).

4. Including the source of the borrowed information with the reporting expression gives authority to your writing because it lets your reader know immediately that your information is from a credible source.

    The Institute of Global Ethics warns, "The Olympics could well become just another money-drenched media promotion in which contestants will be motivated less by athletic glory than by lucrative future contracts" (Kidder, par. 7).

Punctuating Direct Quotations

Follow these general rules for punctuating direct quotations.

1. Put quotation marks around information that you copy word for word from a source. Do not use quotation marks with paraphrases, summaries, or indirect quotations.

2. Normally, place commas (and periods) before the first mark and also before the second mark in a pair of quotation marks.

    According to *Sports Illustrated,* "Eliminating drug use from Olympic sports would be no small challenge."

    "Eliminating drug use from Olympic sports would be no small challenge," according to *Sports Illustrated.*

    There are two important exceptions:

    - If you insert only a few quoted words into your own sentence, don't use commas.

        Charles Yesalis believes that "a large percentage" of athletes who have set new records have done so with the help of performance-enhancing drugs (qtd. in Herper, par. 6).

    - When you add an in-text citation after a quotation, put the period after the closing parenthesis mark.

        The Institute of Global Ethics warns, "The Olympics could well become just another money-drenched media promotion in which contestants will be motivated less by athletic glory than by lucrative future contracts" (Kidder, par. 7).

3. Capitalize the first word of the quotation as well as the first word of the sentence.

    Dr. Donald Catlin, director of a drug-testing lab at UCLA, stated, "The sophisticated athlete who wants to take drugs has switched to things we can't test for" (qtd. in Bamberger and Yaeger 62).

4. If you break a quoted sentence into two parts, enclose both parts in quotation marks and separate the parts with commas. Capitalize only the first word of the sentence.

    "The sophisticated athlete who wants to take drugs," stated Dr. Donald Catlin, director of a drug-testing lab at UCLA, "has switched to things we can't test for" (qtd. in Bamberger and Yaeger 62).

5. If you omit words, use an ellipsis (three spaced periods).

    According to a 1997 article in *Sports Illustrated,* "The use of steroids . . . has spread to almost every sport, from major league baseball to college basketball to high school football" (Bamberger and Yaeger 62).

6. If you add words, put square brackets around the words you have added.

> One athlete declared, "The testers know that the **[drug]** gurus are smarter than they are" (qtd. in Bamberger and Yaeger 62).

7. Use single quotation marks to enclose a quotation within a quotation.

> A young athlete openly admitted, "My ethical inner voice tells me, 'Don't use drugs,' but my competitive inner voice says, 'You can't win if you don't'" (Jones).

8. If your quotation is four lines or longer, do not use quotation marks. Introduce this type of quotation with a colon and indent it one inch from the left-hand margin.

> A national news agency reported these shocking survey results:

>> Several years ago [when] 198 athletes were asked if they would take a performance-enhancing drug if they knew they would NOT be caught and they would win, 195 said they would take the drug. The second question revealed a more frightening scenario. The athletes were asked if they would take a drug that would ensure they would win every competition for five years and wouldn't get caught, but the side effects would kill them—more than HALF said they would take the drug ("2000 Olympics," par. 12).

For more examples showing the use of quotation marks, see pages 288–289 in Appendix B.

PRACTICE 2

*Punctuating
Direct Quotations*

Add punctuation to the following direct quotations, and change the capitalization if necessary.

1. Dr. Yixuan Ma, a well-known astrophysicist who has been studying black holes, said they are the most interesting phenomena we astrophysicists have ever studied.

2. As she explained in black holes the laws of nature do not seem to apply.

3. A black hole is a tiny point with the mass 25 times the mass of our sun explained Ma's associate, Chun-Yi Su. Black holes are created by the death of a very large star she stated.

4. It is an invisible vacuum cleaner in space she added with tremendous gravitational pull.

5. According to Dr. Su, if a person falls into a black hole, he will eventually be crushed due to the tremendous gravitational forces.

6. Time will slow down for him as he approaches the point of no return she said and when he reaches the point of no return, time will stand still for him.

Indirect Quotations

In indirect quotations, the speaker's or writer's words are reported indirectly, without quotation marks. For this reason, indirect quotations are sometimes called reported speech. Indirect quotations are introduced by the same reporting verbs used for direct quotations, and the word *that* is often added for clarity. The tense of verbs in indirect quotations is affected by the tense of the reporting verb.

Compare the following model with the second paragraph of the model for direct quotations on page 43. Notice the changes that occur when you rewrite direct quotations as indirect quotations.

Note: The same sentence numbers are used to help you compare the two paragraphs.

MODEL

Indirect Quotations

> **Drugs and the Olympic Games 2**
> [5]It seems apparent that if athletes want to win, they must consider using drugs. [6]Dr. Michael Karsten, a Dutch physician who said he had prescribed anabolic steroids to hundreds of world-class athletes, stated that if [athletes] were especially gifted, [they] might win once, but from his experience [they] couldn't continue to win without drugs. [7]He asserted that the field was just too filled with drug users (qtd. in Bamberger and Yaeger 62). [8]In fact, some people claim that record-breaking performances of Olympic athletes may be directly due to drugs. [9]Charles Yesalis, a Pennsylvania State University professor who has studied the use of drugs in sports believes that "a large percentage" of athletes who have set new records have done so with the help of performance-enhancing drugs. [10]He claims that a lot of experts, at least in private, feel that way (qtd. in Herper, par. 6).

Writing Technique Questions

1. Underline the verbs *said* and *stated* in sentence 6. What tense are these verbs?
2. Underline the verbs in the indirect quotations following these two verbs. Compare them with the same verbs in the model on page 43. Are they in the same or a different tense?
3. Compare sentence 7 in both models. What has been added to sentence 7 in the model for indirect quotations? How did the verb in the quotation change?
4. In sentence 6, why are the words *athletes* and *they* in square brackets?
5. Compare sentence 9 in both models. Did any words change?

Changing Direct Quotations to Indirect Quotations

To change a direct quotation to an indirect quotation:

1. Omit the quotation marks.
2. Add the subordinator *that*. (You may omit *that* if the meaning is clear without it.)
3. Change the verb tense if necessary. Follow the sequence of tenses rules.
4. Change pronouns (and time expressions if necessary) to keep the sense of the original.

Sequence of Tenses Rules

If the reporting verb is in a past tense, the verbs in an indirect quotation may change tense according to the following rules. Also, pronouns (and sometimes time expressions) may change.

Tense Change	Direct Quotation	Indirect Quotation
Simple present changes to simple past.	Susan said, "The exam **is** at eight o'clock."	Susan said (that) the exam **was** at eight o'clock.
Simple past and present perfect change to past perfect.	She said, "We **didn't have** time to eat breakfast." He said, "The exam **has** just **started**."	She said (that) they **hadn't had** time to eat breakfast. He said (that) the exam **had** just **started**.
Will changes to *would*, *can* to *could*, *may* to *might*, and *must* to *had to*.	Sam mentioned, "Today I **will eat** Chinese food, and tomorrow I'**ll eat** French food if I **can find** a good restaurant."	Sam mentioned that today he **would eat** Chinese food and that tomorrow he'**d eat** French food if he **could find** a good restaurant.
Time expressions may change if the meaning requires it.	The teacher said, "You must finish the test right **now**."	The teacher said that we had to finish the test right **then**."

There are three exceptions:

- When the reporting verb is simple present, present perfect, or future, the verb tense in the quotation does not change.

  He says, "I **can finish** it today."

  He says that he **can finish** it today.

- When the reporting phrase is *according to*, the verb tense does not change.

  The lawyer said, "My client **is** innocent."

  According to the lawyer, his client is innocent.

- When the quoted information is a fact or a general truth, the verb tense in the quotation does not change.

  He said, "Water **boils** at a lower temperature in the mountains."

  He said that water **boils** at a lower temperature in the mountains.

For additional examples of indirect quotations, look at Chapter 12: Noun Clauses.

PRACTICE 3

Changing Direct Quotations to Indirect Quotations

Rewrite the following direct quotations as indirect quotations.

1. Television channel KSA General Manager Jim Burns said, "Not everyone can attend college in the traditional way; therefore, taking courses via television will offer many more students the chance to earn a college degree."

   _____

   _____

   _____

2. Pre-med student Alma Rodriguez said, "I miss being on campus, but I have to work and take care of my family."

   _____

   _____

   _____

3. Other students said, "Last year, we spent several hours a day commuting to and from school. Now we don't have to do that."

   _____

   _____

   _____

4. Computer engineering student Amir Mehdizadeh stated, "I can choose when to study and how to study without pressure." He also said, "I will take two more telecourses in the fall."

   _____

   _____

   _____

Writing Practice

PRACTICE 4

Using Quotations as Support

Write a short paragraph that develops the topic you are given after the example. Use the quotations for support. You may use them either as direct or as indirect quotations. Include some additional supporting sentences and transition signals to connect the ideas and make your paragraph flow smoothly.

Step 1 Copy the topic sentence exactly as it is given.

Step 2 Write several supporting sentences, using the main points and quotations supplied. Add supporting details such as examples if you can. Use the techniques and rules you have learned for direct and indirect quotations.

Step 3 Add an in-text citation in the proper format after each direct and indirect quotation.

Example

TOPIC SENTENCE	The increased use of computers in business has been accompanied by a costly increase in computer crime.
MAIN POINT A	Computer criminals cost business a lot of money.
QUOTATION	"The financial losses to business from computer thefts will exceed $25 billion in 2005."
MAIN POINT B	Computer criminals steal not only money but also information.
QUOTATION	"It is not just the money they steal; they steal data, and data is power."
SOURCE	A book written by Meredith Bruce, *Cybercrime*, page 185. The book was published in New York by a company named Wexler in 2004.

Completed Paragraph

The increased use of computers in business has been accompanied by a costly increase in computer crime. The losses to victims of computer crimes are very high. In her book <u>Cybercrime</u>, author Meredith Bruce claimed that the financial losses to business from computer thefts would exceed $25 billion in 2005 (185). Computer criminals steal not only money but also information. For example, they steal confidential business records, customer lists, and corporate plans. As Bruce stated, "It is not just the money they steal; they steal data, and data is power" (185).

Topic for Your Paragraph

TOPIC SENTENCE	Computers cannot be compared to human brains.
MAIN POINT A	The human brain is more powerful than any computer.
QUOTATION	"It has been estimated that the information-processing capacity of even the most powerful supercomputer is equal to the nervous system of a snail—a tiny fraction of the power available to the supercomputer inside the human skull."
MAIN POINT B	The kinds of processing in a human brain and a computer are different, too.
QUOTATION	"Computers find it easy to remember a 25-digit number but find it hard to summarize the gist[1] of [children's story] 'Little Red Riding Hood,' and humans find it hard to remember the number but easy to summarize the story."
SOURCE	Both quotations are on page 64 of a magazine article titled "Can a Computer Be Conscious?" by Steven Pinker. The article appeared on pages 63–65 of the news magazine *U.S. News & World Report* on August 18, 1997.

---

[1]**gist:** the main point

Statistics

Like quotations, statistics are good supporting details. Study the graph and then read the paragraph that uses data from it. Notice the reporting verb that gives the source of information. As you do with quotations, you must also cite the source of statistical data.

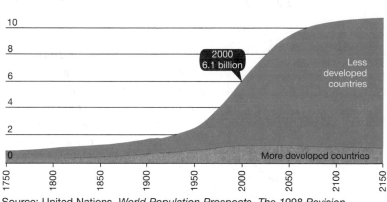

World Population Growth, 1750–2150

Population (in billions)

Source: United Nations, *World Population Prospects, The 1998 Revision*, and estimates by the Population Reference Bureau.

MODEL

Statistics

World Population Growth

According to statistics from the Population Reference Bureau, the world's population is increasing at a geometric rate. World population first reached 1 billion back in 1804. It took 123 years for it to reach 2 billion in 1927. By 1960, a period of just 32 years, it had added another billion. Just 15 years later, we were at 4 billion, 12 years later at 5 billion, and 11 years after that at 6 billion. The United Nations has projected an increase to 9 billion by the year 2050. Most of the increase will be in the world's less developed countries ("World" 1).[2]

Writing Technique Questions
1. Underline the topic sentence of the paragraph.
2. What is the source of the statistics that are used to support this idea?
3. What reporting expression is used to identify this source?

---

[2]"World Population Growth, 1750–2150." Chart. Population Reference Bureau. 20 Oct. 2004 <http://www.prb.org//Content//NavigationMenu//PRB//Educators//Human_Population//Population Growth//Population_Growth.htm>. (The graph appeared on page 1.)

PRACTICE 5

Using Statistics

Study the graphs that follow. Then complete the paragraph about world energy consumption by filling in the blanks with information from the graphs.

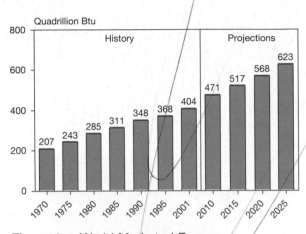

Quadrillion Btu

Figure 1. World Marketed Energy Consumption, 1970–2025

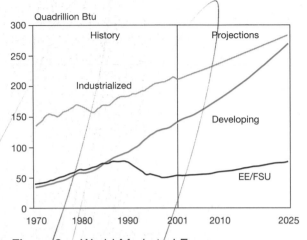

Quadrillion Btu

Figure 2. World Marketed Energy Consumption by Region, 1970–2025

World Energy Consumption[1]

According to (1) _____, world energy consumption has been steadily (2) _____. Currently, the nations of the world use between (3) _____ and (4) _____ quadrillion Btu (British thermal units) annually. By the year 2025, consumption is projected to increase to (5) _____ Btu, an increase of (6) _____ percent from the year (7) _____. The largest consumers are the (8) _____ countries, and the nations who consume the least energy belong to the EE/FSU (Eastern Europe/Former Soviet Union) group. Developing nations consumed approximately the same amount of energy as (9) _____ until (10) _____, when the energy use of developing nations began to (11) _____. By (12) _____, it is projected that their use will nearly equal that of (13) _____ ("International" 10).

---

[1]"International Energy Outlook 2004: Highlights." Graphs. Energy Information Administration. 21 Oct. 2004 <http://www.eia.doe.gov/oiaf/ieo/highlights.html>. (Both graphs appeared on page 10.)

Writing Practice

PRACTICE 6

Using Statistics as Support

Choose one of the graphs that follow below and on page 54, and write a paragraph explaining its significance.

Step 1 Decide what main idea the graph illustrates, and write this idea as a topic sentence.

Step 2 Write five to ten supporting statements, using the statistical information shown in the graphs.

Step 3 Use a reporting verb or phrase to identify the source of your statistics.

Step 4 Write an in-text citation in the proper form at the end of your paragraph.

Graph 1. Median Earnings and Tax Payments by Level of Education, 2003[2]

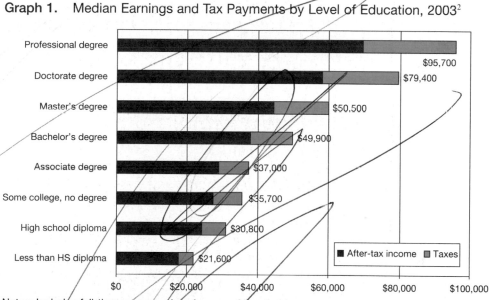

Notes: Includes full-time year-round workers age 25 and older.
Tax payments are based on 2002 tax rates and do not incorporate the 2003 federal income reductions.
Source: U.S. Census Bureau, 2004, PINC-03; Internal Revenue Service, 2003, Table 3; McIntyre, et al, 2003; Calculations by the authors.

The bars in this graph show median earnings at each level of education. The color segments represent the average federal, state, and local taxes paid at these income levels. The black segments show after-tax income.

---

[2]"Education, Earnings, and Tax Payments." Graph. Baum, Sandy, and Kathleen Payea. <u>Education Pays: The Benefits of Higher Education for Individuals and Society</u>. College Board Online. 21 Oct. 2004 <www.collegeboard.com/prod_downloads/press/cost04/EducationPays2004.pdf>. (The graph appeared on page 10.)

Graph 2. Cost of a Double Cappuccino at Specialty Coffee Shops[1]

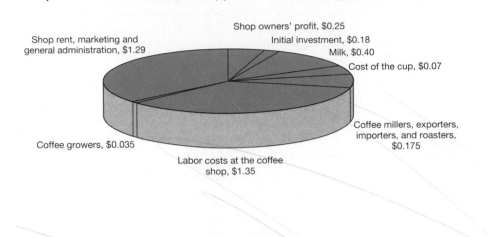

Shop owners' profit, $0.25

Initial investment, $0.18

Milk, $0.40

Cost of the cup, $0.07

Shop rent, marketing and general administration, $1.29

Coffee millers, exporters, importers, and roasters, $0.175

Coffee growers, $0.035

Labor costs at the coffee shop, $1.35

Review

These are the important points covered in this chapter:

1. In academic writing, you are expected to use information from outside sources to support your ideas. Keep in mind that the U.S. system of education values students' original thinking and writing. Use outside sources *to support your own ideas.* Don't write a paper that contains *only* the ideas of others.
2. Search for specific supporting details in the library or on the Internet.
   • Direct quotations: Repeat the writer's or speaker's exact words, and place them inside quotation marks.
   • Indirect quotations: Report the author's words, making changes in pronouns and verb tenses as necessary. Do not use quotation marks.
   • Use appropriate statistics to support your points.
3. Don't just drop a quotation or a statistic into your paper. Make the connection between the borrowed information and your idea clear.
4. Cite your sources to avoid plagiarizing.

[1]*Source of data:* Day, Sherri. "Move Over Starbucks, Juan Valdez Is Coming." <u>New York Times</u> 29 Nov. 2003: B1.

Writing an Essay

From Paragraph to Essay

Egyptian hieroglyphs

An **essay** is a piece of writing several paragraphs long. It is about one topic, just as a paragraph is. However, because the topic of an essay is too complex to discuss in one paragraph, you need to divide it into several paragraphs, one for each major point. Then you need to tie the paragraphs together by adding an introduction and a conclusion.

Writing an essay is no more difficult than writing a paragraph except that an essay is longer. The principles of organization are the same for both, so if you can write a good paragraph, you can write a good essay.

The Three Parts of an Essay

An essay has three main parts: an **introduction** (introductory paragraph), a **body** (at least one, but usually two or more paragraphs), and a **conclusion** (concluding paragraph).

The following chart shows you how the parts of a paragraph correspond to the parts of an essay.

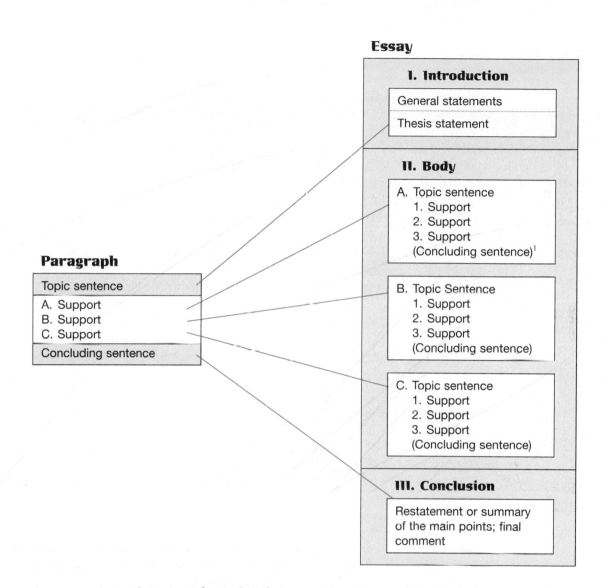

An essay **introduction** consists of two parts: a few general statements to attract your reader's attention and a **thesis statement** to state the main idea of the essay. A thesis statement for an essay is like a topic sentence for a paragraph: It names the specific topic and gives the reader a general idea of the contents of the essay. The **body** consists of one or more paragraphs. Each paragraph develops a subdivision of the topic, so the number of paragraphs in the body will vary with the number of subdivisions or subtopics. The **conclusion**, like the concluding sentence in a paragraph, is a summary or review of the main points discussed in the body.

An essay has **unity** and **coherence**, just as a paragraph does. **Transition signals** and the **repetition of key nouns** link the paragraphs into a cohesive whole.

---

[1]Concluding sentences for body paragraphs in an essay are not always necessary, especially when the ideas in consecutive paragraphs are closely related.

Study the model essay about the influence of Native Americans[1] on modern U.S. culture and notice its structure.

MODEL

Essay Structure

INTRODUCTORY PARAGRAPH

THESIS STATEMENT

BODY PARAGRAPH 1

BODY PARAGRAPH 2

BODY PARAGRAPH 3

BODY PARAGRAPH 4

Native American Influences on Modern U.S. Culture

When the first Europeans came to the North American continent, they encountered the completely new cultures of the Native American peoples of North America. Native Americans, who had highly developed cultures in many respects, must have been as curious about the strange European manners and customs as the Europeans were curious about them. As always happens when two or more cultures come into contact, there was a cultural exchange. Native Americans adopted some of the Europeans' ways, and the Europeans adopted some of their ways. As a result, Native Americans have made many valuable contributions to modern U.S. culture, particularly in the areas of language, art, food, and government.

First of all, Native Americans left a permanent mark on the English language. The early English-speaking settlers borrowed from several different Native American languages words for places in this new land. All across the country are cities, towns, rivers, and states with Native American names. For example, the states of Delaware, Iowa, Illinois, and Alabama are named after Native American tribes,[2] as are the cities of Chicago, Miami, and Spokane. In addition to place names, English adopted from various Native American languages the words for animals and plants found in the Americas. *Chipmunk, moose, raccoon*, *skunk, tobacco*, and *squash* are just a few examples.

Although the vocabulary of English is the area that shows the most Native American influence, it is not the only area of U.S. culture that has been shaped by contact with Native Americans. Art is another area of important Native American contributions. Wool rugs woven by women of the Navajo tribe in Arizona and New Mexico are highly valued works of art in the United States. Native American jewelry made from silver and turquoise is also very popular and very expensive. Especially in the western and southwestern regions of the United States, native crafts such as pottery, leather products, and beadwork can be found in many homes. Indeed, native art and handicrafts are a treasured part of U.S. culture.

In addition to language and art, agriculture is another area in which Native Americans had a great and lasting influence on the peoples who arrived here from Europe, Africa, and Asia. Being skilled farmers, the Native Americans of North America taught the newcomers many things about farming techniques and crops. Every U.S. schoolchild has heard the story of how Native Americans taught the first settlers to place a dead fish in a planting hole to provide fertilizer for the growing plant. Furthermore, they taught the settlers irrigation methods and crop rotation. Many of the foods people in the United States eat today were introduced to the Europeans by Native Americans. For example, corn and chocolate were unknown in Europe. Now they are staples in the U.S. diet.

Finally, it may surprise some people to learn that citizens of the United States are also indebted[3] to the native people for our form of government. The Iroquois, who were an extremely large tribe with many branches called "nations," had

[1]**Native Americans:** American Indians
[2]**tribes:** groups of native people
[3]**indebted:** owing gratitude

developed a highly sophisticated system of government to settle disputes that arose between the various branches. Five of the nations had joined together in a confederation called "The League of the Iroquois." Under the league, each nation was autonomous[4] in running its own internal affairs, but the nations acted as a unit when dealing with outsiders. The league kept the Iroquois from fighting among themselves and was also valuable in diplomatic relations with other tribes. When the 13 colonies were considering what kind of government to establish after they had won their independence from Britain, someone suggested that they use a system similar to that of the League of the Iroquois. Under this system, each colony or future state would be autonomous in managing its own affairs but would join forces with the other states to deal with matters that concerned them all. This is exactly what happened. As a result, the present form of government of the United States can be traced directly back to a Native American model.

CONCLUDING PARAGRAPH   In conclusion, we can easily see from these few examples the extent of Native American influence on our language, our art forms, our eating habits, and our government. The people of the United States are deeply indebted to Native Americans for their contributions to U.S. culture.

Writing Technique Questions

1. How many paragraphs does this essay contain? How many paragraphs are in the body?
2. Underline the topic sentence of each body paragraph, and double underline the topic. (*Note*: The topic sentence is not necessarily the first sentence in every paragraph.)
3. Notice which noun phrase appears four times in the introduction. Circle each repetition of this key noun in the other paragraphs of the essay.

Now let's examine the parts of an essay in more detail.

The Introductory Paragraph

An introductory paragraph has two parts, general statements and the thesis statement. **General statements**

- introduce the general topic of the essay.
- capture the reader's interest.

The **thesis statement**

- states the specific topic.
- may list subtopics or subdivisions of the main topic or subtopics.
- may indicate the pattern of organization of the essay.
- is normally the last sentence in the introductory paragraph.

---

[4]**autonomous**: independent, self-governing

Notice how the general statements in the introductory paragraph of the model essay introduce the topic. The first sentence is about the arrival of Europeans and their encounter with new cultures. The next sentence points out that there were large differences between European and Native Americans. The next two sentences say that two-way cultural exchange happened, but the direction of the exchange and the specific items are not identified.

> When the first Europeans came to the North American continent, they encountered the completely new cultures of the Native American peoples of North America. Native Americans, who had highly developed cultures in many respects, must have been as curious about the strange European manners and customs as the Europeans were curious about them. As always happens when two or more cultures come into contact, there was a cultural exchange. Native Americans adopted some of the Europeans' ways, and the Europeans adopted some of their ways.

The thesis statement is specific; it gives the direction of the exchange (Native American influences on modern U.S. culture) and lists the subtopics (language, art, food, and government).

> As a result, Native Americans have made many valuable contributions to modern U.S. culture, particularly in the areas of language, art, food, and government.

Funnel Introduction

The introductory paragraph of the model essay is a funnel introduction. This introduction is so called because it is shaped like a funnel—wide at the top and narrow at the bottom. It begins with one or two very general sentences about the topic. Each subsequent sentence becomes increasingly focused on the topic until the last sentence, which states very specifically what the essay will be about. Writing a funnel introduction is like focusing a camera with a telephoto lens. You start with a wide picture and gradually narrow the focus so that just one object appears in the camera's viewfinder: your thesis statement.

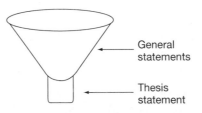

General statements

Thesis statement

MODEL

Funnel Introduction

> Moving to a new country can be an exciting, even exhilarating experience. In a new environment, you somehow feel more alive. Seeing new sights, eating new food, hearing the foreign sounds of a new language, and feeling a different climate against your skin stimulate your senses as never before. Soon, however, this sensory bombardment becomes sensory overload. Suddenly, new experiences seem stressful rather than stimulating, and delight turns into discomfort. This is the phenomenon known as culture shock. Culture shock is more than jet lag or homesickness, and it affects nearly everyone who enters a new culture—tourists, business travelers, diplomats, and students alike. Although not everyone experiences culture shock in exactly the same way, many experts agree that it has roughly five stages.

Attention-Getting Introduction

Other kinds of introductions are good for capturing your reader's attention.

MODEL

Dramatic, Interesting, or Funny Story

> On November 14, 1963, a few miles off the southern coast of Iceland, the crew of a fishing boat noticed smoke on the horizon. Thinking that another fishing boat was on fire, they went to investigate. When they got closer, they discovered that the smoke was not from a boat on fire; rather, it was from an undersea volcano about to erupt. The next day, ash, cinders, and pumice were blown 1,000 feet into the air. The fishermen had witnessed a rare event—the violent birth of an island. The volcano continued to erupt for about four years, eventually creating an island about 1 square mile in area and 560 feet in height. The birth of Surtsey, as the island is named, offered scientists an extraordinary opportunity to learn how life takes hold on a sterile landmass.

MODEL

Surprising Statistics or Facts

> Got high blood pressure? Try a truffle. Worried about heart disease? Buy a bon-bon. It's the best news in years! Studies in two prestigious scientific journals say dark chocolate is good for you. It seems that eating a small piece of dark chocolate regularly can reduce the risk of heart disease because dark chocolate—but not milk chocolate or white chocolate—contains high amounts of flavenoids, powerful cholesterol-fighting compounds. What is the next health food going to be? Ice cream? Sugar cookies? There are so many conflicting news stories about which foods are good for you that it is often difficult to make the right choices at the supermarket.

MODEL

Historical Background

> The Pilgrims who arrived in Massachusetts in 1620 came to find religious freedom. In the seventeenth and eighteenth centuries, large numbers of African men and women were brought as slaves to work on large plantations in the South. Immigrants from northern and southern Europe came in the early nineteenth century to escape poor economic conditions at home. Later in the nineteenth century, the first immigrants from China came as contract laborers to build the railroads connecting East and West. In the twentieth century, political and economic refugees arrived from Asia, Eastern Europe, and Latin America. Indeed, the United States has seen immigrants come from many different parts of the world, and they have come for many different reasons. Their ability to adjust to life in their adopted land has depended on several factors.

Writing Technique Questions
1. Underline the thesis statement in each example introductory paragraph.
2. In your opinion, which introduction captures the reader's interest the best? Why?

PRACTICE 1

Introductory Paragraphs

Step 1 Read each of the following sets of sentences. When put in the correct order, they will form introductory paragraphs.

Step 2 Write each paragraph, beginning with the most general statement first. Then add each sentence in the correct order until the introduction becomes more specific. Write the thesis statement last.

Step 3 Identify the type of introduction (funnel, dramatic/interesting/funny story, surprising statistics, historical).

Paragraph 1

1. If done properly, a handshake gives the impression of strength and honesty, and if done improperly, it conveys weakness and dishonesty.
2. In some cultures, people bow, and in others, they shake hands.
3. In English-speaking countries, shaking hands is the custom.
4. A proper handshake has four ingredients: pressure, pumps,[1] eye contact, and verbal message.
5. The way people greet each other when they meet for the first time varies from culture to culture.
6. How one shakes hands sends an important message about one's character.

Type of introduction: _____

Paragraph 2

1. To celebrate the occasion, Mr. X decided to throw a big party at the plant.
2. Mr. X went to Mexico from England to manage a milk pasteurization plant.
3. Then one day an impressive new pasteurization unit arrived and was installed.
4. The employees did most of the planning and draped the new unit with garlands.
5. During the party one of Mr. X's supervisors took him aside and said, "Now we see that you are *buena gente*[2]; from now on I am sure everyone will really try to do their best for you."
6. And so it was—neither punctuality nor quality checks were any longer needed.
7. This story illustrates the need to understand that doing business in a different culture demands an understanding of the culture.
8. The party was a great success and everybody had a good time.
9. For eight months, he tried every way possible to convince his workers of the importance of punctuality and of checking every detail of their work.
10. The response was always, "Yes, yes, we will do our best," but nothing ever changed.

Type of introduction: _____

---

[1]**pumps:** movements up and down
[2]***buena gente***: Spanish for "a good person"—someone you can trust and have as a friend

Paragraph 3

Note: The order of sentences 2, 3, and 4 can vary.

1. Currently under study are four main methods for predicting when and where the next Big One will occur.
2. In 1976, an earthquake in Tangshan, China, killed over 250,000 people.
3. In an average year, earthquakes kill 10,000 people worldwide and cause millions of dollars worth of property damage.
4. Iran suffered more than 80,000 deaths in two massive quakes in 1990 and 2003.
5. Scientists keep trying to find ways to predict earthquakes—so far without much success.

Type of introduction: _____

Thesis Statement

The thesis statement is the most important sentence in the introduction. It states the specific topic of the essay.

> Native Americans have made many valuable contributions to modern U.S. culture.

> Young people in my culture have less freedom than young people in the United States.

> The large movement of people from rural to urban areas has major effects on cities.

Sometimes a thesis statement lists the subtopics that will be discussed in the body.

> Native Americans have made many valuable contributions to modern U.S. culture, particularly in the areas of language, art, food, and government.

> Young people in my culture have less freedom than young people in the United States in their choice of where they live, whom they marry, and what their job is.

> The large movement of people from rural to urban areas has major effects on a city's ability to provide housing, employment, and adequate sanitation services.

Sometimes a thesis statement also indicates the pattern of organization that the essay will follow. Which of the following thesis statements indicates chronological order? Logical division of ideas? Comparison/contrast?

> When buying a used car, use these four strategies to get the best price.

> There are several differences between a nurse practitioner and a physician's assistant.

> My best friend and I spent an entire summer constructing a tree house in my grandmother's old apple tree.

PRACTICE 2

Thesis Statements

A. Study these thesis statements from two different essays on the topic of the status of women in Xanadu, an imaginary country. One of the essays uses a comparison/contrast pattern, the other a time sequence (chronological order) pattern. Which statement indicates which pattern?

1. Beginning in World War II and continuing through the period of economic boom, the status of women in Xanadu has changed remarkably.

   Pattern of organization:_____

2. Although the status of women in Xanadu has improved remarkably in recent years, it is still very low when compared to the status of women in the countries of the industrial world.

   Pattern of organization:_____

B. In each of the following two thesis statements, both the method of organization and the major subdivisions of the topic are indicated. Each subdivision will itself become the topic of a separate paragraph in the body of the essay. Underline the topics of each paragraph. How many paragraphs will the body of each essay probably contain?

1. The status of women in Xanadu has changed remarkably in recent years due to increased educational opportunities and changes in the country's laws.

   Probable number of body paragraphs: _____

2. The status of women in Xanadu has improved remarkably in recent years in the areas of economic independence, political rights, educational opportunities, and social status.

   Probable number of body paragraphs: _____

Body Paragraphs

The body paragraphs in an essay are like the supporting sentences in a paragraph. They are the place to develop your topic and prove your points. You should organize body paragraphs according to some sort of pattern, such as chronological order or comparison/contrast. Sometimes, depending on your topic, you will need to use a combination of patterns.

Logical Division of Ideas

A basic pattern for essays is logical division of ideas. In this pattern, you divide your topic into subtopics and then discuss each subtopic in a separate paragraph. Logical division is an appropriate pattern for explaining causes, reasons, types, kinds, qualities, methods, advantages, and disadvantages, as these typical college exam questions ask you to do.

Economics	Explain the three causes of inflation.
Agriculture/Landscape Design	Describe the basic types of soils and what additives are needed to prepare each type for planting.
U.S. History	Discuss the causes of the U.S. Civil War.
Business	Explain the three main forms of business organization.
Health Sciences	Describe the various classes of drugs used to treat depression.

Three Keys

Here are three keys to organizing a logical division essay.

1. Divide your topic into subtopics, and then discuss each subtopic in a separate paragraph.
2. Write a thesis statement that indicates logical division.
3. Use transitions between paragraphs to guide your reader from one subtopic to the next.

Thesis Statements for Logical Division of Ideas

The thesis statement of a logical division essay often indicates the number of subtopics:

Native Americans have made valuable contributions to modern U.S. culture in four main areas.

Inflation has three causes.

The thesis statement may even name the specific subtopics:

a. Native Americans have made many valuable contributions to modern U.S. culture, particularly in the areas of language, art, food, and government.

b. Inflation has three causes: excessive government spending, unrestrained consumer borrowing, and an increase in the supply of paper money.

Paired conjunctions (*both . . . and, not only . . . but also*) are an especially effective way to list two subtopics:

c. Young people in my culture have less freedom than young people in the United States **not only** in their choice of lifestyle **but also** in their choice of careers.

d. Puppies, like children, need **both** love **and** discipline to become responsible members of society.

A colon (:) is often useful before lists of two, three, or more subtopics in a thesis statement:

e. Young people in my culture have less freedom than young people in the United States in three areas: where they live, whom they marry, and what their job is.

f. The Father of Psychoanalysis, Sigmund Freud, believed that the human mind had three separate parts: the id, the ego, and the superego.

Notice that subtopics are in parallel form, which means that they have the same grammatical form: In examples *a*, *d*, and *f*, all are nouns; in example *b*, all are adjective + noun phrases; in example *c*, all are prepositional phrases; in example *e*, all are dependent noun clauses.

See the section Parallelism on pages 179–180 for information about parallel form. For colons, see pages 285–287, and for paired conjunctions, see page 181.

PRACTICE 3

Thesis Statements for Logical Division of Ideas

A. Check (✓) the thesis statements that suggest logical division as a method of organization.

_____ 1. Teenagers demonstrate their independence in several ways.

_____ 2. My eighteenth birthday was the most memorable day in my life so far.

_____ 3. On their eighteenth birthdays, U.S. citizens receive two important rights/responsibilities: They can vote, and they can sign legal contracts.

_____ 4. In most occupations, women are still unequal to men in three areas: salary, power, and status.

_____ 5. Living in a dormitory offers several advantages to first-year students.

_____ 6. Photosynthesis is the process by which plants manufacture their own food.

_____ 7. A college degree in international business requires (1) a knowledge of business procedures and (2) a knowledge of cultural differences.

_____ 8. A computer is both faster and more accurate than a human.

_____ 9. Giving a surprise birthday party requires careful planning.

_____ 10. Being an only child has both advantages and disadvantages.

B. Analyze the following thesis statements.

Note: You may want to use one of the topics in this practice or the next for your own essay at the end of the chapter.

Step 1 Locate the main topic and the subtopics in each of the following thesis statements.

Step 2 Draw a box around the topic.

Step 3 Underline the subtopics.

Step 4 Draw a circle around the words or punctuation marks that introduce the subtopics.

The first one has been done for you as an example.

1. Capital punishment should be abolished not only because it deprives another person of life but also because it does not stop crime.

2. Women generally live longer than men for two main reasons: They tend to take better care of their health and they have better resistance to stress.

3. Teenagers declare their separateness from their parents by the way they dress and by the way they talk.

4. In choosing a major, a student has to consider various factors, such as personal interest, job opportunities, and the availability of training institutions.

5. An architect should be both an artist and an engineer.
6. A healthy lifestyle involves eating a nutritious diet, exercising regularly, and getting enough sleep at night.

C. Complete the following thesis statements by adding subtopics to them. Be sure to check your sentences for parallel form.

1. A computer is necessary for college students for three reasons: _____
   _____

2. Students have a difficult time taking notes in class due to _____
   _____

3. Successful politicians have the following qualities: _____
   _____

4. A generation gap[1] exists in my home because of _____
   _____

5. To survive a major disaster such as an earthquake requires _____
   _____

6. My two sisters are as different as day and night not only in _____
   _____ but also in _____

7. Living in a large city has certain advantages over living in a small town:
   _____
   _____

8. Latino culture has enriched North American culture in several areas:
   _____
   _____

Thesis Statement Pitfalls

A thesis is the most important sentence in your essay, so write it with special thought and care. Avoid these common problems:

Problem 1: The thesis is too general.

TOO GENERAL	A college education is a good investment.
IMPROVED	A college education is a good investment for four reasons.
TOO GENERAL	Lasers are very useful.
IMPROVED	Lasers have several applications in industry and medicine.

Problem 2: The thesis makes a simple announcement.

ANNOUNCEMENT	I am going to write about sports injuries.
IMPROVED	Avoid sports injuries by taking a few simple precautions.

[1] **generation gap:** difference in attitudes and values between generations, especially between parents and children

Problem 3: The thesis states an obvious fact.

OBVIOUS FACT	The Internet is a communication superhighway.
IMPROVED	The explosion of the Internet has had both positive and negative consequences.

PRACTICE 4

Writing Logical Division Thesis Statements

Write a thesis statement for a logical division essay on each of the following topics. For items 1–3, suggestions for subtopics are given in parentheses, which you do not have to use if you have ideas of your own. For items 4 and 5, use your own ideas. *Note*: You may want to use one of these topics for your essay at the end of the chapter.

1. Clothing, hair, or shoe styles in your school (three styles)
2. Dangerous automobile drivers (speeders, cell-phone users, teens)
3. Disneyland's or Disney World's appeal (children and adults)
4. The advantages (or the disadvantages) of living in a large city/a small town
5. Kinds of appeals television advertisers use to sell automobiles/beer/any product or service

Transition Signals for Logical Division of Ideas

Transition signals for logical division essays include many that you may already know.

Transition Words and Phrases	
first, first of all, second, third, etc. next, last, finally also, in addition, moreover, furthermore	**First**, excessive government spending can lead to inflation. **In addition**, unrestrained consumer borrowing can cause inflationary tendencies. **Finally**, an increase in the supply of paper money gives rise to inflation.
Coordinators	
and both . . . and not only . . . but also	**Both** an increase in the supply of paper money **and** unrestrained consumer borrowing can cause inflationary tendencies. To lose weight, one must **not only** exercise regularly **but also** eat wisely.
Others	
the first *cause, reason, factor*, etc. the/a second *problem, result, advantage*, etc. one *problem, reason, important factor*, etc. another *way, reason, disadvantage*, etc. an additional *problem, result*, etc. in addition to *math and science*, . . .	A **second** cause is an increase in the supply of paper money. Regular exercise is **one** way to get fit and lose weight. **In addition to** government spending, unrestrained consumer borrowing can cause inflationary tendencies.

Transition Signals between Paragraphs

Linking paragraphs with transitions helps your reader see how the subtopics are related. Link one paragraph to the next by adding a transition to the topic sentence of the second paragraph. This transition may be a single word, a phrase, or a dependent clause that repeats or summarizes the main idea in the preceding paragraph.

Study the following model, and notice how the paragraphs are linked.

MODEL

Paragraph Transitions

INTRODUCTORY PARAGRAPH

Aggressive Drivers

The number of vehicles on freeways and streets is growing at an alarming rate. This increase of motor vehicles is creating hazardous conditions. Moreover, drivers are in such a rush to get to their destinations that many become angry or impatient with other motorists who are too slow or who are in their way. Aggressive drivers react foolishly toward others in several dangerous ways.

BODY PARAGRAPH 1

TRANSITION WORDS

One way an angry driver may react is to cut off[1] another motorist. (+ supporting sentences) _____ _____ _____

BODY PARAGRAPH 2

TRANSITION WORDS

Another way is to tailgate[2] the other car. (+ supporting sentences) _____ _____ _____

BODY PARAGRAPH 3

TRANSITION PHRASE

In addition to cutting off and tailgating other cars, aggressive drivers often use rude language or gestures to show their anger. (+ supporting sentences) _____ _____ _____

BODY PARAGRAPH 4

TRANSITION CLAUSE

Although law enforcement authorities warn motorists against aggressive driving, the number who act out their angry impulses has not declined. (+ supporting sentences)

_____ _____ _____

CONCLUDING PARAGRAPH

To conclude, aggressive drivers are endangering everyone because they create hazardous conditions by acting and driving foolishly. They should control their anger and learn to drive safely. After all, the lives they save could be their own.

---

[1]**cut off:** drive in front of
[2]**tailgate:** drive closely behind or on the tail of another car

PRACTICE 5

Transitions between Paragraphs

A. Circle the transition expressions that link paragraphs in the model essay on pages 58–59.

B. Connect the ideas in the following paragraphs by adding a transition word, phrase, or clause to the topic sentences of the third, fourth, and fifth paragraphs. Try to vary the transitional linking expressions you use. You may rewrite the topic sentences if necessary. The first one has been done for you as an example.

Icebergs: A Potential Source of Water

1   In countries where rainfall is very sparse,[1] scientists must constantly seek ways to increase supplies of water. One method being considered is the use of desalination plants, which would remove salt from seawater. Another method being considered is the towing of icebergs. According to this method, large icebergs from Antarctica would be wrapped in cloth or plastic, tied to powerful tugboats by strong ropes, and towed to the countries needing freshwater. While this plan may have some potential, there are certain practical problems that must be solved.

2   <u>The first problem</u> is the expense. According to estimates, it would cost between $50 million and $100 million to tow a single 100-million-ton iceberg from Antarctica to, for example, the coast of Saudi Arabia.

3   _____ is the possibility that the iceberg would melt en route.[2] No one knows if an iceberg could be effectively insulated for such a long journey. At the very least, there is the possibility that it would break up into smaller pieces, which would create still other problems.

4   _____ there is the danger that a huge block of ice floating off an arid[3] coast could have unexpected environmental effects. The ice could drastically[4] change the weather along the coast, and it would probably affect the fish population.

5   _____ the cost of providing freshwater from icebergs would be less than the cost of providing water by desalinization, according to most estimates. It would cost between 50 and 60 cents per cubic meter to get water from an iceberg, as opposed to the 80 cents per cubic meter it would cost to get the same amount by desalinization.

6   In conclusion, before icebergs can become a source of freshwater in the future, problems involving cost, overall practicality, and most important, environmental impact[5] must be solved.

---

[1] **sparse:** small in amount
[2] **en route:** during the journey
[3] **arid:** dry
[4] **drastically:** in an extreme way
[5] **impact:** effect

C. Add transition words, phrases, or clauses to the topic sentences of the paragraphs in this essay. Rewrite the topic sentences if necessary.

Medicine and Ethics[6]

1   Recent advances in the fields of medicine and biotechnology have brought about situations that could scarcely be imagined only a generation ago. Battery-operated plastic hearts can be implanted into[7] people. People can be kept alive indefinitely by machines. Exact duplicates of animals can be made. While such scientific achievements may ultimately benefit humankind, they have also created complex legal and ethical issues.

2   _____ involves doctors' ability to intervene in human reproduction. A well-known example is the case of Baby M. A man paid a woman to bear a child for him and his wife, who could not have children. They signed a contract, but after the baby was born, the woman wanted to keep the baby. The father said the baby was his, but the woman said it was hers. It took the courts many months to decide who was right.

3   _____ another ethical dilemma[8] has arisen because doctors are now able to keep people who are in comas[9] alive for years by attaching their bodies to machines. This gives great power and great responsibility to the people who control the machines. As a result of this power, society has had to develop a new definition of death. How does a person decide whether another person whose heart cannot beat on its own and whose lungs are pumped by a machine is still alive or not?

4   _____ the ability of biotechnologists to produce new forms of life in their laboratories is another area with profound[10] ethical consequences. Isn't a scientist who creates, for example, a new bacterium "playing God"? Furthermore, is it even safe to introduce new life forms into Earth's atmosphere? Is there a risk that such life forms could get out of control? Some people fear so.

5   _____ scientists are now able to duplicate living organisms, cell by cell, through a process called cloning. Recently, the world was stunned by the successful cloning of a human embryo. Should biotechnologists be allowed to clone people? Who should control human cloning?

6   _____ revolutions—political or technological—cause upheaval[11] and force change. Our new ability to create and prolong life is raising questions and forcing changes in our very concept of life, an issue involving not only legal but also profound moral considerations.

---

[6]**ethics:** the study of right and wrong
[7]**implanted into:** put into
[8]**dilemma:** difficult problem
[9]**comas:** states of unconsciousness (being unable to see, hear, or speak)
[10]**profound:** important; serious
[11]**upheaval:** social disturbance

The Concluding Paragraph

The conclusion is the final paragraph in an essay. It has three purposes.

1. It signals the end of the essay. To do so, begin your conclusion with a transition signal. See Transition Signals in Appendix C, pages 297–299.
2. It reminds your reader of your main points, which you can do in one of two ways: You can
   • summarize your subtopics.
   • paraphrase your thesis.
3. It leaves your reader with your final thoughts on the topic. This is your opportunity to convey a strong, effective message that your reader will remember.

Here are techniques that you can use to write a memorable conclusion.

Make a prediction.
We have seen how the costs of attending college have been rising while, at the same time, sources of financial aid for students have been disappearing. If this trend continues, fewer and fewer families will be able to send their children through four years of college.

Suggest results or consequences.
To sum up, the costs of attending college are up and financial aid for students is down. Fewer and fewer future members of the workforce are able to educate themselves beyond high school. As a result, the nation will waste the intelligence, imagination, and energy of a large segment of the present college-age generation.

Suggest a solution, make a recommendation, or call for action.
It is clear that the U.S. system of higher education is in trouble. For many students, four years of college is no longer possible because of increasing costs and decreasing financial aid. To reverse this trend, we must demand that government increase its financial support of colleges and universities and restore financial aid programs. Our future depends on it.

Quote an authority on the topic.
In conclusion, costs are rising and financial aid is declining, with the result that many can no longer afford to go to college. If our nation is to prosper, increased government funding for education is essential, even if it requires higher taxes. As Horace Mann[1] argued in his *Fifth Annual Report*, a nation's economic wealth will increase through an educated public. It is therefore in the self-interest of business to pay the taxation for public education.

---

[1]Horace Mann (1796–1859) is considered the father of public education in the United States.

PRACTICE 6

Concluding Paragraphs

Step 1 Read the following essay and the two possible concluding paragraphs.
Step 2 Then answer the questions.

Culture Shock

Moving to a new country can be an exciting, even exhilarating experience. In a new environment, you somehow feel more alive: seeing new sights, eating new food, hearing the foreign sounds of a new language, and feeling a different climate against your skin stimulate your senses as never before. Soon, however, this sensory bombardment becomes sensory overload. Suddenly, new experiences seem stressful rather than stimulating, and delight turns into discomfort. This is the phenomenon known as culture shock. Culture shock is more than jet lag or homesickness, and it affects nearly everyone who enters a new culture—tourists, business travelers, diplomats, and students alike. Although not everyone experiences culture shock in exactly the same way, many experts agree that it has roughly five stages.

In the first stage, you are excited by your new environment. You experience some simple difficulties such as trying to use the telephone or public transportation, but you consider these small challenges that you can quickly overcome. Your feelings about the new culture are positive, so you are eager to make contact with people and to try new foods.

Sooner or later, differences in behavior and customs become more noticeable to you. This is the second stage of culture shock. Because you do not know the social customs of the new culture, you may find it difficult to make friends. For instance, you do not understand how to make "small talk," so it is hard to carry on a casual, get-acquainted conversation. One day in the school cafeteria, you overhear a conversation. You understand all the words, but you do not understand the meaning. Why is everyone laughing? Are they laughing at you or at some joke that you did not understand? Also, you aren't always sure how to act while shopping. Is this store self-service, or should you wait for a clerk to assist you? If you buy a sweater in the wrong size, can you exchange it? These are not minor challenges; they are major frustrations.

In the third stage, you no longer have positive feelings about the new culture. You feel that you have made a mistake in coming here. Making friends hasn't been easy, so you begin to feel lonely and isolated. Now you want to be with familiar people and eat familiar food. You begin to spend most of your free time with students from your home country, and you eat in restaurants that serve your native food. In fact, food becomes an obsession, and you spend a lot of time planning, shopping for, and cooking food from home.

You know that you are in the fourth stage of culture shock when you have negative feelings about almost everything. In this stage, you actively reject the new culture. You become critical, suspicious, and irritable. You believe that people are unfriendly, that your landlord is trying to cheat you, that your teachers do not like you, and that the food is making you sick. In fact, you may actually develop stomachaches, headaches, sleeplessness, lethargy, or other physical symptoms.

Finally, you reach the fifth stage. As your language skills improve, you begin to have some success in meeting people and in negotiating situations. You are able to exchange the sweater that was too small, and you can successfully chat about the weather with a stranger on the bus. Your self-confidence grows. After realizing that you cannot change your surroundings, you begin to accept the differences and tolerate them. For instance, the food will never be as tasty as the food in your home country, but you are now able to eat and sometimes even enjoy many dishes. You may not like the way some people in your host country dress or behave in public, but you do not regard their clothes and behavior as wrong—just different.

Concluding Paragraph A

To sum up, culture shock is a very real phenomenon that has been studied for more than 30 years by psychologists and anthropologists. Its five phases are (1) positive feelings toward the new culture, (2) awareness of small differences, (3) growing discomfort and need for contact with home culture, (4) negative feelings, and (5) acceptance and adjustment. Symptoms may vary, and not all people experience all five phases. In the end, however, people who suffer culture shock are stronger from having overcome the difficulties and frustrations of adapting to life in a new land.

Concluding Paragraph B

In conclusion, nearly everyone moving to a new country feels some degree of culture shock. Symptoms may vary, and not all people experience all five stages. Newcomers with a strong support group may feel at home immediately in the new culture, while others may take months to feel comfortable. Staying in touch with friends and family, keeping a positive attitude, and, above all, learning the language as soon as possible are ways to overcome the difficulties and frustrations of adapting to life in a new land.

1. Which concluding paragraph is a summary of the subtopics? Which one paraphrases the thesis statement?
2. Which concluding paragraph gives suggestions? Which one makes a prediction?

PRACTICE 7

Writing Concluding Paragraphs

Step 1 Read the following "skeleton" essays. Only the introductory paragraph and topic sentences for the body paragraphs are given.
Step 2 Write a concluding paragraph for each essay.

Essay 1

Controlling Stress

Introductory Paragraph

The busy schedules that most adults face every day have created a growing health problem in the modern world. Stress affects almost everyone, from the highly pressured executive to the busy homemaker or student. It can cause a variety of physical disorders ranging from headaches to stomach ulcers and even alcoholism. Stress, like the common cold, is a problem that cannot be cured; however, it can be controlled. A person can learn to control stress in four ways.

Topic Sentences for Body Paragraphs
A. Set realistic goals.
B. Take up a hobby.
C. Exercise regularly.
D. Maintain close relationships with family and friends.

Concluding Paragraph

_____
_____
_____
_____
_____
_____
_____

Essay 2

Studying in Great Britain

Introductory Paragraph

People come from all over the world to the United Kingdom to pursue education. Some come for a year, while others may stay four years or longer to complete a program or earn a degree. Of course, the first few weeks in a new country are always a little stressful, but knowledge of a few British characteristics and customs can smooth the path for new arrivals.

Topic Sentences for Body Paragraphs

A. British people are usually reserved.[1]
B. British people are very orderly, so waiting in a queue[2] for a bus or in a shop is a must.
C. The weather is no joke—it rains a lot.
D. Cars drive on the left side of the road, and stepping off a curb can be dangerous if you are not used to looking to the right instead of to the left.

Concluding Paragraph

_____
_____
_____
_____
_____
_____
_____

Essay Outlining

Because an essay is long, it is important to organize and plan before you begin to write. The best way to do this is to make an outline. An outline not only organizes your thoughts, but it also keeps you on track once you begin to write.

---

[1]**reserved:** quiet, restrained, undemonstrative in words and actions
[2]**queue:** British English word for American English _line_. People in the United Kingdom stand in a _queue_; people in the United States stand in a _line_ to get service at a counter in a shop, to buy tickets, to wait for a bus, to board an airplane, and so on.

A formal outline has a system of numbers and letters such as the following. In other fields of study, different systems are used.

Roman numerals I, II, and III number the major sections of an essay (introduction, body, conclusion)
Capital letters A, B, C, D, and so on label the body paragraphs.
Arabic numerals 1, 2, 3, 4, and so on number the subpoints in each paragraph.
Small letters a, b, c, d, and so on label the specific supporting details.

To see an example of a complete essay outline, turn to pages 271–272 of Appendix A.

PRACTICE 8

Essay Outlining

A. Below is an incomplete outline of the model essay "Native American Influences on Modern U.S. Culture" on pages 58–59. Complete the outline by filling in the missing parts.

Native American Influences on Modern U.S. Culture

I. Introduction

Thesis statement: Native Americans have made many valuable contributions to modern U.S. culture, particularly in the areas of language, art, food, and government.

II. Body

A. Native Americans left a permanent mark on the English language.

　1. Names of places—cities, towns, rivers, and states

　　a. States: Delaware, Iowa, Illinois, Alabama

　　b. Cities: Chicago, Miami, Spokane

　2. Names of animals and plants

　　a. Animals: chipmunk, moose, raccoon, skunk

　　b. Plants: tobacco, squash

B. _____

　1. Navajo rugs

　2. Silver and turquoise jewelry

　3. _____

　　a. Pottery

　　b. _____

　　c. _____

C. _____

　1. Farming techniques

　　a. _____

　　b. _____

　2. _____

　　a. _____

　　b. _____

    D. _____

      1. Iroquois—large tribe with many branches ("nations")
         Needed to settle disputes among various branches
      2. Five nations formed League of Iroquois
        a. _____
        b. Acted together when dealing with outsiders
      3. After independence, 13 colonies adopted similar system.
        a. Each colony (future state) was autonomous in managing own affairs.
        b. _____

III. Conclusion

We can easily see from these few examples the extent of Native American influence on our language, our art forms, our eating habits, and our government.

B. Choose one thesis statement from Practices 3B, 3C, or 4 on pages 66–68. Follow the steps in the writing process, which you will find in Appendix A at the back of the book. Brainstorm for ideas, and then organize your ideas into a formal outline like the model.

Review

These are the important points covered in this chapter.

Main Parts of an Essay

1. An essay has three main parts: an introduction, a body, and a conclusion.
   - The introductory paragraph consists of two parts: a few general statements to attract your reader's attention and a thesis statement to state your main idea. A thesis statement may also name the major subdivisions of the topic, and it may indicate how you will organize the essay.
   - The body of an essay discusses the subtopics, one by one. It contains as many paragraphs as necessary to explain all subtopics.
   - The concluding paragraph reminds your reader of what you have said. In it, you summarize your main ideas or paraphrase your thesis. You may also make a final comment on the topic for your reader to remember.
2. Use the logical division of ideas pattern to divide a topic into separate paragraphs.
3. Link paragraphs with transitions; that is, show how one paragraph is related to the next by using appropriate transition words, phrases, or clauses.
4. Prepare an outline to organize your ideas before you begin to write.

Writing Practice

PRACTICE 9 *Writing an Essay*	**Step 1** Write an essay from the outline you prepared in Practice 8B on page 76. Follow the steps in the writing process. (See Appendix A.) **Step 2** After you have completed your first draft, use Self-Editing Worksheet 4 on page 321. Revise your essay and write a second draft if necessary. **Step 3** Exchange papers with a classmate and check each other's essays using Peer-Editing Worksheet 4 on page 322. After your classmate has completed the checklist, discuss it and decide what changes you should make. **Step 4** Revise your essay and write a final copy to hand in, making any improvements you discussed with your peer editor. **Step 5** Hand in your first draft, your second draft, and the page containing the two editing worksheets. Your instructor may also ask you to hand in any prewriting (brainstorming and/or outline) that you did for this assignment.
PRACTICE 10 *Writing under Pressure*	*Note*: These topics are intended to elicit a single paragraph, not an essay. Choose one of the topics suggested and write a well-organized paragraph. Be sure to use specific examples to support your ideas. Your instructor will give you a time limit. • Spend 1 or 2 minutes at the beginning thinking of ideas and organizing them. • Spend 1 minute at the end checking your work for errors. • Spend the remaining time writing.

Topic Suggestions

One area of influence from one culture on another (examples: food, language, music, art, political system, educational system)

Define one of the following. Use examples to support your definition.

friendship	an optimist
success	a pessimist
addiction	a good teacher
sports fanaticism	a good parent

Applying What You Have Learned

Logical Division of Ideas

Chapters 4–7 and 9 end with authentic readings that illustrate the rhetorical mode just studied. The writer of the following newspaper article, for example, uses logical division of ideas. As you read the article, notice the organization. Also look for words and phrases that the writer uses to introduce his examples.

At the Movies
You Are Where You Sit: Seating Choice Can Tell a Lot about a Person[1]

1   When he goes to the movies, Ravel Centeno likes to sit on the aisle and stretch his feet out—a fact that by itself speaks volumes about his personality, according to a new study. The study, commissioned by the British movie theater company Odeon, examined how theater seating habits reflect personality. And as the summer movie season reaches its zenith, the research says you are where you sit. Psychologist Donna Dawson divided moviegoers into four different personality types based on their seating preferences and cited examples of movie characters who fit those types.

2   Those who sit on the aisle, like Centeno, are "detached observers"—people who like to have their own space, who are observers and tend to be quieter. "That's funny, because I'm a writer," Centeno said Thursday as he waited to see *A.I.* at the Cineplex Odeon at Universal CityWalk. "So that's what I do (observe people)." One celluloid example of a detached observer, said Dawson, is Jack Nicholson's Melvin Udall character in *As Good as It Gets*.

3   Other personality types, according to Dawson:

4   The "front row film fanatic": Extroverted, assertive, and competitive, these are people who like to see movies with others, not on their own. An example from the movies might be Mike Meyers's Austin Powers or Julia Roberts's Erin Brockovich.

5   The "middle-of-the-roaders": These are the people who like to sit in the middle, fittingly. They are people who are flexible and try to get along with others, such as Gwyneth Paltrow's *Emma*. Gloria and Tom Candelaria of Redlands say that seems to fit them. "We like the middle because it's not too far back and not too close to the front," Gloria Candelaria said as she scanned the marquee at CityWalk. Tom Candelaria said the "middle-of-the-roader" label seems to fit them because "we're easygoing."

6   The "invisible rebels": Those who sit far in the back are people who are rebellious and like excitement but don't necessary seek the limelight, the study said. A typical example is Clint Eastwood's *Man with No Name* and Sigourney Weaver's Lt. Ripley in the *Alien* films. "The back row is where things happen; it's an exciting area of danger and lots of passionate smooching," Dawson said in the Odeon report. "It tends to attract people who are rebellious."

7   For some people, though, sometimes a chair is just a chair. "I don't know—wherever there's an empty seat," said filmgoer Chris Marshall of Lake Hollywood, when asked where he likes to sit. "That works for me."

---

[1]Sheppard, Harrison. "At the Movies. You Are Where You Sit: Seating Choice Can Tell a Lot about a Person." Los Angeles Daily News 10 July 2001. N1.

Questions

About the Organization

1. What kind of introduction does this newspaper article have?
   a. It is a funnel introduction—it begins with a general statement and narrows down to the thesis statement.
   b. It begins with an example and ends with the thesis statement.
   c. It explains the reasons for the study and ends with the thesis statement.

2. What kind of conclusion does it have?
   a. It summarizes the four main personality types.
   b. It gives the writer's opinion on the study.
   c. It gives an example that contrasts with the main points.

3. What words in the thesis statement indicate that the article uses logical division of ideas as a pattern of organization?

   _____

About the Support

4. What two kinds of supporting details are used in this article?
   _____ and _____

5. The psychologist who made the study used one kind of support, and the writer of the article reporting the results of the study used another kind. Which person used which kind?
   a. The psychologist used _____.
   b. The writer used _____.

About the Content

6. How do we know if the psychologist is correct? Does the article mention the methods she used in her study to match seating preference and personality type, or does it report only the results?

Suggestions for Discussion or Writing

1. Do you agree or disagree with the author? Is there a connection between a person's choice of seats in a movie theater (or anywhere else) and his or her personality type? Think of other places where people choose a seat—a bus, a classroom, an airplane. Is there a connection between personality type and seat choice in these locations?

2. Brainstorm ideas and examples for an essay on one of the following topics.
   • You Are Where You Sit (in the classroom)
   • You Are What You Wear (fashion styles)
   • You Are What You Drive (automobiles)

Chronological Order: Process Essays

Ancient writing on Roman Forum, Italy

Chronos is a Greek word meaning time. **Chronological order** is a way of organizing ideas in the order of their occurrence in time. Chronological order has all sorts of uses. We use it to tell stories, to relate historical events, and to write biographies and autobiographies. We also use it to explain processes and procedures. For example, we would use chronological order to explain how to take a photograph, how to make a piece of pottery, how to perform a chemistry experiment, or how to set up an accounting system. Such essays are called "how to" essays, or **process essays**.

The model essay on pages 82–83 is a process essay. It explains two scientific processes involving nuclear energy. As you read the model, look for the two processes.

INTRODUCTORY
PARAGRAPH

Understanding Chernobyl

Clouds of radioactive steam shoot into the sky. Fires burn unstoppably, sending radioactive smoke and particles into the atmosphere. Men dressed in protective clothing work feverishly[1] to extinguish the fires and contain the contamination.[2] Hundreds of residents hastily grab their possessions and flee their homes. Roadblocks are erected to keep strangers away. This was the scene at the Chernobyl nuclear power plant in the former USSR in April 1986. The plant's nuclear reactor had exploded, spreading radioactive contamination over an area that stretched as far away as Norway and Sweden. This catastrophic[3] accident renewed fears about the safety of nuclear reactors around the world. Are such fears justified[4]? To understand how the accident at Chernobyl happened, it is necessary to understand how a nuclear power plant is constructed and how one operates.

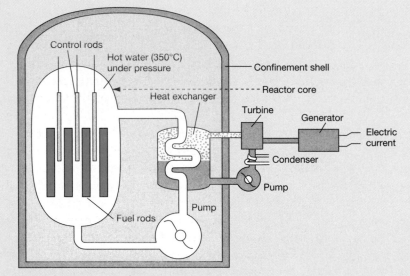

A nuclear power plant

BODY PARAGRAPH 1

A nuclear power plant contains a nuclear reactor that uses controlled nuclear fission[5] to produce electricity. The reactor consists of fuel rods alternating with control rods inside a very large container called the reactor core. The fuel rods contain radioactive fuel such as uranium-235, and the control rods contain neutron[6]-absorbing[7] substances such as boron and cadmium. By varying the depth of the control rods within the core, one can increase or decrease the absorption of neutrons, thereby speeding up or slowing down the fission process. If necessary, the rods can be dropped all the way into the core to stop the

---

[1]**feverishly:** very quickly
[2]**contamination:** pollution
[3]**catastrophic:** terrible, disastrous
[4]**justified:** appropriate, right
[5]**nuclear fission:** nuclear reaction resulting from splitting a nucleus
[6]**neutron:** electrically neutral particle inside an atom
[7]**absorbing:** taking inside itself, as a sponge absorbs water

reaction completely. A high-pressure water bath surrounds the rods. The water acts as a coolant by slowing down the neutrons. In some reactors, graphite[8] is added to the water because graphite also slows down neutrons. A confinement shell usually surrounds the parts containing radioactive material so that radioactivity cannot escape.

BODY PARAGRAPH 2

How do nuclear reactors produce electricity? First, a series of nuclear fissions are produced by bombarding the nuclei[9] of uranium-235 with neutrons. When a neutron strikes a nucleus, the nucleus splits, releasing energy. The released energy then heats the water surrounding the rods, whose outer shells are made of zirconium. The hot water is pumped to a heat exchanger, where steam is produced. Finally, the steam passes to a turbine that drives a generator to produce electricity.

BODY PARAGRAPH 3

How did the accident at Chernobyl happen? It happened because on the day of the accident, the safety system on the reactor had been disabled while operators performed an experimental test. During the test, the reactor cooled excessively and threatened to shut down. If this had happened, the operators would not have been able to restart the reactor for a long period of time. To avoid this situation, they removed most of the control rods, which was against all safety rules. Soon, the reactor began to overheat. When the reactor overheated, the fuel rods melted and spilled their radioactive contents into the superheated water, which then flashed into steam. Next, the increased pressure from the steam blew the top off the reactor, and because there was no confinement shell around the reactor, radioactive material shot into the sky. At the same time, hot steam reacted with the zirconium shells of the fuel rods and with the graphite in the coolant water to produce hydrogen gas, which then ignited.[10] The graphite burned for a long time, spreading even more radioactivity into the atmosphere.

CONCLUDING PARAGRAPH

In the end, the cost of the Chernobyl accident was enormous. Thirty-one people died, and several hundred were hospitalized. Thousands had to be evacuated and resettled. The soil around Chernobyl will remain contaminated for years. The lesson from Chernobyl is this: A well-designed nuclear power plant using normal fuel is not dangerous as long as proper safety procedures are followed. However, poor design and/or disregard for safety regulations can lead to catastrophe.

Writing Technique Questions

1. What is the thesis statement? How does it indicate that at least part of this essay will use chronological organization?
2. Which two paragraphs explain processes (how something works or how something happens)? What two processes are explained?
3. Which paragraph describes the design of a nuclear power plant?
4. What kind of introduction does this essay have—"funnel" or attention-getting?
5. What kind of conclusion does it have? Does it summarize the main points or paraphrase the thesis, or is it a different kind? Does it give a final comment? In your opinion, is this kind of conclusion appropriate for this essay?

---

[8]**graphite:** gray substance used in lead pencils
[9]**nuclei:** plural of *nucleus*, the central part of an atom
[10]**ignited:** began to burn

> *Three Keys*
>
> Here are three keys to organizing a process essay.
>
> 1. Discuss the steps in your process in the order in which they occur.
>   Divide the steps into separate paragraphs where natural breaks or
>   groups of steps occur. For example, to write about how to make
>   a ceramic vase, you might divide the body into four paragraphs:
>
>   I. Introductory paragraph
>   II. Body
>   A. Shaping the vase
>   B. First (bisque) firing
>   C. Glazing
>   D. Second firing
>   III. Concluding paragraph
>
> 2. Write a thesis statement that names the process and indicates
>   time order.
> 3. Use chronological order signal words and phrases to indicate the time
>   sequence.

Thesis Statements for a Process Essay

A thesis statement for a process essay in some way indicates the time order. Expressions such as *the process of, the procedure for, plan, develop, evolve, five stages*, and *several phases* indicate that time order will be used. Here are some examples:

Follow these steps to make a beautiful ceramic vase for your home.

The field of genetic engineering has developed rapidly in the past 10 years.

A child learns to share over a period of time.

Heating water by solar radiation is a simple process.

Sometimes the thesis statement tells the number of steps in the process.

The process of heating water by solar radiation involves three main steps.

The thesis statement may even name the steps.

The main steps in the process of heating water by solar radiation are (1) trapping the sun's energy, (2) heating and storing the hot water, and (3) distributing the hot water to its points of use.

PRACTICE 1

Thesis Statements for Chronological Order

A. Step 1 Check (✓) the thesis statements that suggest a chronological order. Put a double check (✓✓) next to the thesis statements that suggest the essay will describe a process or procedure.

Step 2 In the sentences you have checked, circle the word or words that indicate chronological order.

The first one has been done for you as an example.

✓✓   1. A child learns to handle responsibility in a series of small (steps.)

_____   2. A person's intelligence is the product of both heredity[1] and environment.

_____   3. There are two main reasons I believe women in the army should not be allowed in a war zone along with men.

_____   4. The procedure for submitting expense reports has recently changed.

_____   5. The tensions that led to last year's student riots had been developing for several years.

_____   6. North American directness often conflicts with Asian modesty.

_____   7. The two busiest travel days in the United States are the Wednesday before and the Sunday after Thanksgiving.

_____   8. Cultures celebrate the end of winter and the arrival of spring in different ways.

_____   9. The preparation of the poisonous puffer fish for eating is a delicate process that is not for amateur chefs.

_____ 10. The life cycle of the monarch butterfly is an interesting phenomenon.

B. Write a thesis statement for a process essay on five of the following topics. *Note*: You may want to use one of these topics for your own essay at the end of the chapter.

1. How to take a good photograph

    _____

2. How to research a topic for an essay

    _____

3. How diamonds are processed from a diamond mine to a diamond ring

    _____

4. How to perform a particular chemistry or physics experiment

    _____

5. How to transplant a tree

    _____

6. How a hybrid automobile works

    _____

---

[1]**heredity:** characteristics received from one's parents (hair color, height, and so on)

7. How to overcome a fear

_____

8. How GPS receivers work

_____

9. How to celebrate _____ (any special occasion, such as
   a favorite holiday, a special birthday, a wedding, an anniversary)

_____

10. How to detail a car[1]

_____

Topics on the Lighter Side
11. How to shop successfully on eBay

_____

12. How to flirt

_____

13. How to mend a broken heart

_____

14. How to get an A (or an F) in a class

_____

15. How to raise a spoiled (or a perfect) child

_____

Transition Signals for Chronological Order

Chronological order signal words are especially important in a process essay. You have to be very clear about the sequence of steps: Does one step happen before, after, or at the same time as another step? Chronological order signals include all time expressions.

---

[1]**detail a car:** clean a car thoroughly inside and out

Chronological Order Signal Words and Phrases	
first, first of all, second, third, etc. then, next, after that, soon, later, later on finally, last, last of all meanwhile, at the same time, now gradually, eventually	**First**, choose a destination for your camping trip. **Then** make a list of supplies and equipment. **Last of all**, have a good time. **Meanwhile**, have a supply of clean rags ready. **Gradually** increase your child's allowance.
Subordinators	
after since as until as soon as when before while	**After** you have chosen a destination, make a list of equipment and supplies that you will need. Praise your child **when** he or she does something well.
Others	
the first (second, last, final) step on the third day after leaving home later that morning for five minutes in 2004 several years ago a few weeks later in the next (past, last) 15 years	**The last step** is to decorate the cake. Continue stirring the soup **for five minutes**. **In 2004**, scientists announced a major discovery. **After leaving home**, I began to appreciate my parents. My parents emigrated to the United States **several years ago**. The court announced the decision **a few weeks later**.

Time subordinators such as *after, before*, and *as soon as* are useful as chronological order signals. To review them, turn to Time Clauses, pages 211–212.

PRACTICE 2

Transition Signals for Chronological Order

A. Reread the model essay on pages 82–83. Find and circle all chronological order signals, including time words, time phrases, and time clauses.

B. Fill in each blank with an appropriate chronological order signal from the list provided. Use each signal only once. Change small letters to capital letters and add commas where necessary.

as soon as the lesson begins	when you return	when he or she asks you to speak up
in conclusion	first	
in the next few minutes	finally	second
then	a third time	before you sit down
		next

How to Annoy a Teacher

It is quite easy to annoy a teacher—even the most patient, kind-hearted teacher in the world—if you follow these simple steps.

(1) _____ always come to class just a little late.

(2) _____ make as much noise as possible as you enter the room. (3) _____ greet all your friends with a cheerful wave— or even better, with a shouted greeting. (4) _____ slam your heavy backpack down on the floor next to your desk and do a few stretching exercises. (After all, you will be sitting still for the next 40 minutes or so!)
(5) _____ make a big, gaping[1] yawn and take your seat.

(6) _____ raise your hand and ask to be excused to go to the restroom. (7) _____ be sure to slam the door, and again, make as much noise as possible while taking your seat.

(8) _____ turn the pages of your book noisily, search in your backpack for a pencil, ask your neighbor if you can borrow an eraser, and announce in a loud voice that you cannot find your homework. (9) _____ raise your hand and ask to be excused to look for it in your locker.

If the teacher should happen to call on you during the class, mumble[2] an answer. (10) _____ mumble again—maybe a little louder this time, but still not loudly enough to be heard. If the teacher dares to ask you (11) _____ give a loud and clear answer to the previous question—the one your classmate answered a minute ago—and smile smugly[3] as you do so.

(12) _____ if these techniques do not achieve the desired results, you can always fold your arms across your desk, put your head down, and take a nap. Just do not forget to snore!

Review

These are the important points covered in this chapter.

1. Using chronological order to organize an essay means putting the ideas in order or sequence by occurrence in time.
2. Use chronological order for narrative essays (stories, history, biography, and autobiography) and for process essays (how to do or make something).
3. Following are the three keys to success in writing a chronological order essay:
   • Group the steps or events into paragraphs where natural breaks occur.
   • Write a thesis statement that indicates chronological order.
   • Use chronological order signal words and phrases to show the sequence of steps (in a process) or events (in a narration).

---

[1]**gaping:** wide open
[2]**mumble:** speak unclearly
[3]**smugly:** with a self-satisfied look

Writing Practice

PRACTICE 3

Writing an Essay in Chronological Order

Choose one of the process thesis statements from Practice 1B on pages 85–86 and write an essay using chronological order as a method of organization. Follow the steps in the writing process described in Appendix A. When you have finished, use the Self-Editing and Peer-Editing Worksheets on pages 323 and 324.

PRACTICE 4

Writing under Pressure

Note: These topics are intended to elicit a single paragraph, not an essay.

Choose one of the topics suggested and write a well-organized paragraph. Focus on using chronological order. Your instructor will give you a time limit.

- Spend 1 or 2 minutes at the beginning thinking of ideas and organizing them.
- Spend 1 minute at the end checking your work for errors.
- Spend the remaining time writing.

Topic Suggestions
What to do before, during, and after an earthquake
How to have a successful camping trip
How to build a good relationship with your boss
How to spend a perfect day in _____ (a city or town you know well)

Applying What You Have Learned

Chronological Order

In this magazine article, the author tells us how to keep our computers operating efficiently by performing regular maintenance chores. Even though his purpose is instructional, his tone is informal. By using humor (*Your PC is basically your backup brain*) and slang (*crud, guts, dust bunnies*), he makes the process entertaining to read.

Reading 1

Spring Cleaning, No Mops
The messiest place in your house may be your hard drive.
You don't do Windows? It's time to fix that.[4]

1　April is upon us, and it's time to do some serious spring cleaning. I'm not talking about the fridge, the attic and the shoe closet. If you're like me, your PC is basically your backup brain, and if you really want that warm feeling of renewal that comes but once a year, you've got to clean up your computer.

2　The most visible messes are the easiest to deal with. A moist paper towel will freshen up your monitor; a cotton swab can scrape the crud off the rollers in your mouse; a good burst from a can of compressed air will get the dust out of your keyboard. If your computer desktop is as messy as your real one, that's easily corrected, too. You just have to be merciless. Dump those obsolete documents.

---

[4]Pellegrini, Frank. "Spring Cleaning, No Mops." *Time* 8 Apr. 2002: 85

Delete old e-mails without looking back. Trash any program you haven't used since the last millennium.

3   Unfortunately, out of sight is not necessarily out of mind. Operating systems have a way of surreptitiously backing up everything you do, and some programs tend to grow roots. Just because you put something in the recycling bin or ran an uninstall program doesn't mean you got rid of it. On Windows machines there are several different files associated with each program, and to do a thorough cleaning job, you have to root out every one.

4   The problem is that deleting the wrong files can give your computer serious fits, so tread lightly. There are several popular utilities that will do the work safely for you. As a rule, you should stay out of the real guts of the machine—the files and settings that run your operating system—unless you really know your stuff.

5   You may still have to get rid of the temporary backup files that your computer made when you didn't hit Save often enough. Windows users can try to find and delete all files that end in .tmp. You'll be surprised how many hundreds have piled up; just don't delete any that the system says it still needs. After that, run your built-in mop-up programs—in Windows, look in System Tools for Disk Cleanup; with Macs, it's Disk First Aid in Utilities—and let the computer check itself for errors.

6   Now it's time to deal with everything your Internet browser brought home from its travels on the World Wide Web. Use Options or Preferences to get rid of unwanted cookies and clean out your cache files. Give your computer a blood test by going on the Web and downloading the latest in antivirus software. Then run a disk defragmenter to straighten out the tangle of files stored on your hard drive. This can speed up your computer's performance. But as with any major renovation, you should back up important documents beforehand, just to be safe.

7   The last step for desktop-computer owners is often the most satisfying. Grab your can of compressed air, unplug and open up your computer's box and behold—without touching anything—the dust bunnies that have been breeding in there ever since you brought it home. Eek!

Questions

About the Organization

1. Which sentence is true about the thesis statement of this magazine article?
   a. The thesis statement announces the topic and indicates that this is going to be a "how to" essay.
   b. The thesis statement announces the topic without indicating what pattern of organization it will use.
   c. There is no clear thesis statement.

2. Which sentence best describes the conclusion?
   a. The conclusion restates the thesis in different words.
   b. There is no formal conclusion; the conclusion is actually a final step.

3. What pattern of organization does the article use?
   a. Chronological order: process
   b. Logical division of ideas
   c. A combination of chronological process and logical division of ideas

About the Support

4. Which sentence would best serve as a topic sentence for paragraph 2?

   a. The first step is to clean the exterior of your computer.

   b. The first step is to clean up what you can easily see.

5. Paragraphs 3, 4, and 5 all discuss the same general topic, but only one paragraph has a topic sentence.

   a. Which paragraph has a topic sentence? _____
      Write the topic sentence here:

      _____

   b. Consider combining the other two paragraphs. Which of the following sentences best serves as a topic sentence for the combined paragraph?

      (1) Next, delete your old files safely by using a built-in program.

      (2) The next step, getting rid of old files and programs, is more difficult.

      (3) Next, empty your recycle bin.

About Coherence

6. Look for chronological order signal words and phrases.

   a. Which paragraphs begin with chronological order signals? _____ and _____
      Write the signals here:

      _____

      _____

   b. What other chronological order signals can you find in paragraphs 5 and 6? List them here:

      _____

      _____

Suggestions for Discussion or Writing

1. Explain another procedure or process that involves recent technology. For example, explain how to e-mail photos that you have taken with a digital camera, or how to program a TiVo.

2. Would you like to live in a "smart" house of the future? Describe what a typical day in such a house might be like.

3. Does technology simplify or complicate our lives? Studies have shown that despite having vacuum cleaners, washing machines, microwave ovens, and dishwashers, women spend as much time on household tasks as their grandmothers did without these time-saving machines.

The next reading is from Senator Daniel Inouye's autobiography, *Journey to Washington*. Senator Inouye is a United States Senator from the State of Hawaii. He is of Japanese ancestry and served in the U.S. Army's 442nd Regimental Combat Team during World War II. This group of soldiers was composed of *nisei* (second-generation Japanese Americans) from Hawaii and were famous for their extreme courage. Senator Inouye lost an arm in battle and returned to Hawaii a hero.

In this passage, Inouye describes what he did after he returned home to Hawaii and how he became engaged to his wife.

Reading 2

A Japanese Betrothal[1]

1   For a while there was a great, wild spree of homecoming celebrations. Two 442nd vets meeting on the street was reason enough for a party. But finally it was time to get back to normal living. The first thing I did was to register at the university. Doctoring was out, but I didn't care. I wanted now to become a lawyer, in the hope of entering public life. The prelaw courses required a lot of work, and they were harnessed to my extracurricular activities in student government and veterans' organizations. Then one unforgettable autumn day I met Margaret Awamura. Marriage had never occurred to me before that moment, but afterward, it never left my mind. I proposed on our second date. It was December 6, 1947. I know because we have celebrated the occasion together ever since.

2   Of course, because we were *nisei*, it wasn't as simple as all that. As soon as I informed my parents, they began to arrange things in the Japanese way. Tradition calls for a ceremonial event involving *nakoudos*—go-betweens—who represent the families of the prospective bride and groom and settle the terms of the marriage. By prearrangement the Inouye team (my parents, our *nakoudos,* and I) arrived at the Awamuras' one evening bearing gifts of rice, sake, and fish and took places on the floor. Our *nakoudos* faced their *nakoudos* across a low table. Behind them sat the respective families, the parents first and, farthest away from the action, Maggie and me, as though we were only incidental onlookers. Now and then I caught her eye and we smiled secretly. Only the *nakoudos* spoke.

3   First, gifts were exchanged. Then one of our representatives began to extol the virtues of Daniel Ken Inouye, a fine upstanding man, a war hero, and so forth. Next, our side listened to a recitation of Maggie's qualities: she had earned a master's degree, she was an accomplished seamstress, and her family's reputation for honor was unimpeachable. (I would have liked to add that she was beautiful, too.)

4   The *nakoudos* consulted briefly with their clients and recommended that the marriage be approved. Then at last glasses were filled, and a toast was drunk. Maggie and I were engaged—officially!

Questions

About the Organization

1. This reading could be divided into two parts.
   a. What is the topic of the first part?
   b. What is the topic of the second part?
   c. Which sentence serves as a transition between the two parts?
   d. Which part explains a process?

2. Circle all the chronological order signals in the excerpt.

---

[1]Inouye, Daniel. "A Japanese Betrothal." Go for Broke: Condensed from Journey to Washington. 25 Aug. 2003 <http://inouye.senate.gov/gfb/text.html#betrothal>.

About the Supporting Details

3. This reading tells about courtship customs in two different cultures.

   a. Which sentence tells about courtship customs in U.S. culture? Write the opening words of this sentence.

   _____

   b. Write the opening words of the part that tells about Japanese customs.

   _____

About Unity

4. In the first paragraph, look for one sentence that breaks the unity of the paragraph. Write the opening words of this sentence.

   _____

Suggestions for Discussion or Writing

1. Senator Inouye describes the process of a traditional Japanese betrothal. Describe a betrothal process that you are familiar with.

2. In some cultures, marriages are arranged by parents or other relatives or with the help of a matchmaker. In the United States, most people marry for love. What are the advantages of each system? What are the disadvantages?

3. The Inouyes were both of Japanese ancestry, so they shared a common culture. However, there are many intercultural marriages in Hawaii and in other parts of the world. If someone marries a person from a different culture, how should they learn to share each other's customs? Recommend a process.

4. Have you ever had the experience of getting used to new customs? If so, explain the process by which you began to share others' customs.

6 Cause/Effect Essays

Athenian silver tetra drachma, 4th century B.C.E.

Another common pattern of essay organization is called cause and effect. In a **cause/effect essay**, you discuss the causes (reasons) for something, the effects (results), or both causes and effects. You might use cause/effect organization to answer typical test questions such as these:

EDUCATION   Explain the decline in reading ability among schoolchildren.

ENVIRONMENTAL STUDIES   Discuss the effects of global warming on the environment.

BUSINESS, ECONOMICS   Discuss NAFTA[1] and its effects on the U.S. economy.

HISTORY   Discuss the causes of the U.S. Civil War.

PSYCHOLOGY   Explain the causes and effects of the "Stockholm syndrome."

---

[1]**NAFTA:** North American Free Trade Agreement, a trade agreement among Canada, Mexico, and the United States

Organization for Cause/Effect Order

You can organize a cause/effect essay in two main ways: "block" organization and "chain" organization. In block organization, you first discuss all the causes as a block (in one, two, three, or more paragraphs, depending on the number of causes). Then you discuss all the effects together as a block. You can discuss either causes or effects first. Of course, you can also discuss *only* causes or *only* effects.

Block Organization

In block organization, a short paragraph often separates one major section from another major section. This paragraph is called a transition paragraph. Its purpose is to conclude one section and introduce another section. You do not always have to write a transition paragraph, but it is helpful when your topic is long and complex. For example, an essay about global warming might include several paragraphs about the causes and several paragraphs about the effects, with a transition paragraph between the two blocks.

Essays that discuss mainly (or only) causes or mainly (or only) effects might have a transition paragraph between blocks of different kinds of causes or between blocks of different kinds of effects. For example, you might use a transition paragraph to separate the personal effects of our increased life expectancy from its many effects on the economy.

In short, a block-style cause/effect essay could have many different patterns. Some possibilities are shown below.

Block Organization

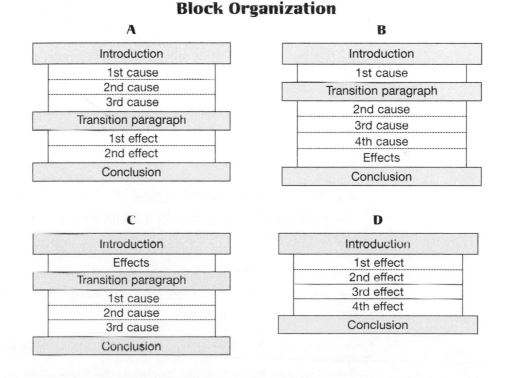

As you read the following model essay, try to determine which of the patterns the model essay follows: A, B, C, or D.

MODEL

Cause/Effect Essay (Block Organization)

Shyness

1   If you suffer from shyness, you are not alone, for shyness is a universal phenomenon.[1] According to recent research, "close to 50 percent of the general population report that they currently experience some degree of shyness in their lives. In addition, close to 80 percent of people report having felt shy at some point in their lives" (Payne, par. 3).[2] As shyness is so prevalent in the world, it is not surprising that social scientists are learning more about its causes. They have found that shyness in an individual can result from both biological and environmental factors.

2   Recent research reveals that some individuals are genetically predisposed to[3] shyness. In other words, some people are born shy. Researchers say that between 15 and 20 percent of newborn babies show signs of shyness: they are quieter and more vigilant. Researchers have identified physiological differences between sociable and shy babies that show up as early as two months. In one study, two-month-olds who were later identified as shy children reacted with signs of stress to stimuli such as moving mobiles[4] and tape recordings of human voices: increased heart rates, jerky movements of arms and legs, and excessive crying. Further evidence of the genetic basis of shyness is the fact that parents and grandparents of shy children more often say that they were shy as children than parents and grandparents of non-shy children (Henderson and Zimbardo 6).[5]

3   However, environment can, at least in some cases, triumph over biology. A shy child may lose much of his or her shyness. On the other hand, many people who were not shy as children become shy as adults, a fact that points to environmental or experiential causes.

4   The first environmental cause of shyness may be a child's home and family life. Children who grew up with a difficult relationship with parents or a dominating older sibling are more likely to be inhibited[6] in social interactions. Another factor is the fact that today's children are growing up in smaller and smaller families, with fewer and fewer relatives living nearby. Growing up in single-parent homes or in homes in which both parents work full time, children may not have the socializing experience of frequent visits by neighbors and friends. Because of their lack of social skills, they may begin to feel socially inhibited, or shy, when they start school (7).

5   A second environmental cause of shyness in an individual may be one's culture. In a large study conducted in several nations, 40 percent of participants in the United States rated themselves as shy, compared to 57 percent in Japan and 55 percent in Taiwan. Of the countries participating in the study, the lowest percentage of shyness was found in Israel, where the rate was 31 percent.

---

[1]**phenomenon:** occurrence or fact (plural: *phenomena*)
[2]Payne, Karen S. "Understanding and Overcoming Shyness." California Institute of Technology Counseling Center. 7 Nov. 2004 <http://www.counseling.caltech.edu/articles/shyness.html>.
[3]**predisposed to:** likely to get
[4]**mobiles:** a toy that hangs over a baby's bed with moving shapes
[5]Henderson, Lynne, and Philip Zimbardo. "Shyness." Encyclopedia of Mental Health. 8 Oct. 2004 <http://www.shyness.com/encyclopedia.html>.
[6]**inhibited:** self-conscious, shy

Researchers Henderson and Zimbardo say, "One explanation of the cultural difference between Japanese and Israelis lies in the way each culture deals with attributing credit for success and blame for failure. In Japan, an individual's performance success is credited externally to parents, grandparents, teachers, coaches, and others, while failure is entirely blamed on the person." Therefore, Japanese learn not to take risks in public and rely instead on group-shared decisions. "In Israel, the situation is entirely reversed," according to Henderson and Zimbardo. "Failure is externally attributed to parents, teachers, coaches, friends, anti-Semitism, and other sources, while all performance success is credited to the individual's enterprise." The consequence is that Israelis are free to take risks since there is nothing to lose by trying and everything to gain (10).

6   In addition to family and culture, technology may play a role as well. In the United States, the number of young people who report being shy has risen from 40 percent to 50 percent in recent years (10). The rising numbers of shy young people may be "due in part to the growing dependence on non-human forms of communication, coming about as a result of our huge advances in technology" (Payne, par. 4). Watching television, playing video games, and surfing the Web have displaced recreational activities that involve social interaction for many young people. Adults, too, are becoming more isolated as a result of technology. Face-to-face interactions with bank tellers, gas station attendants, and store clerks are no longer necessary because people can use machines to do their banking, fill their gas tanks, and order merchandise. College students take online telecourses. Telecommuters work at home, giving up daily contact with coworkers. Everyone texts, e-mails, and converses anonymously[7] in online chat rooms. As a result, people have less opportunity to socialize in person, become increasingly awkward at it, and eventually start avoiding it altogether. In short, they become shy.

7   While being shy has some negative consequences, it has positive aspects, too. For one thing, it has been mentioned that shy people are good listeners ("Shyness").[8] Furthermore, a university professor writing about his own shyness says, "Because of their tendency toward self-criticism, shy people are often high achievers, and not just in solitary activities like research and writing. Perhaps even more than the drive toward independent achievement, shy people long to make connections to others, often through altruistic[9] behavior" (Benton).[10]

8   To sum up, shyness has both genetic and environmental causes. Some people come into the world shy, while others become shy as a result of their experiences in life. It appears that most people have experienced shyness at some time in their lives, and recent research indicates that the number of shy people is increasing. Therefore, if you are shy, you have lots of company.

---

[7]**anonymously:** without telling one's name
[8]"Shyness." Wikipedia, the Free Encyclopedia. 7 Nov. 2004 <http://en.wikipedia.org/wiki/Shyness>.
[9]**altruistic:** unselfish, benevolent
[10]Benton, Thomas H. "Shyness and Academe." San Francisco Chronicle: Chronicle of Higher Education Careers Section 24 May 2004. 7 Nov. 2004 <http://chronicle.com/jobs/2004/05/2004052401c.htm>.

Writing Technique Questions
1. Is the topic of this essay primarily the causes or the effects of shyness?
2. Which paragraph(s) discuss(es) the causes?
3. Which paragraph(s) discuss(es) the effects?
4. What two subtopics are named in the thesis statement?
5. Which paragraph(s) discuss(es) the first subtopic?
6. Which paragraph(s) discuss(es) the second subtopic?
7. What is the function of paragraph 3?
8. Which pattern (A, B, C, or D) does the model follow?

PRACTICE 1

*Block
Organization*

Fill in the boxes to show the block organizational pattern of the essay. Write in the topic of each paragraph and tell whether it is a cause or an effect. The first two boxes have been filled in for you.

INTRODUCTION

Thesis statement: They have found that shyness in an individual can result from both biological and environmental factors.

1st cause: genetics

CONCLUSION

Chain Organization

The other organizational pattern you can use to write about causes and effects is chain organization. In this pattern, causes and effects are linked to each other in a chain. One event causes a second event, which in turn causes a third event, which in turn causes a fourth event, and so on. Each new cause and its effect are links in a chain. Depending on the complexity of the ideas in each link, you can devote an entire paragraph to one link, or you may include several links in one paragraph, or you may describe the entire chain in one paragraph. Chain organization usually works better than block organization when the causes and effects are too closely linked to be separated. Notice the chain pattern in the following diagram.

Introduction	How Fertile Land Becomes Desert
Cause ↓	People move into new areas and clear land for agriculture by cutting down trees.
Effect ↓	The tree roots no longer hold the soil in place.
Cause ↓	The tree roots do not hold the soil in place.
Effect ↓	The topsoil washes away during heavy rains.
Cause ↓	The topsoil washes away during heavy rains.
Effect ↓	There is no good soil to grow crops in.
Cause ↓	There is no good soil to grow crops in.
Effect	People move to new areas and clear land for agriculture by cutting down trees.
Conclusion	

The following short essay describes a simple chain reaction.

MODEL

Cause/Effect Essay (Chain Organization)

SAD

1   Years ago, medical researchers identified a psychological disorder that they appropriately named **S**easonal **A**ffective **D**isorder, or SAD. People who suffer from SAD become very depressed during the winter months. Doctors now understand the causes of this condition, which affects millions of people, particularly in areas of the far north where winter nights are long and the hours of daylight are few.

2   SAD results from a decrease in the amount of sunlight sufferers receive. Doctors know that decreased sunlight increases the production of melatonin, a sleep-related hormone that is produced at increased levels in the dark. Therefore, when the days are shorter and darker, the production of this hormone increases. Shorter, darker days also decrease production of seratonin, a chemical that helps transmit nerve impulses. Lack of seratonin is known to be a cause of depression ("Seasonal" HH, par. 1).[1] Depression may result from the resulting imbalance of these two substances in the body. Also, doctors believe that a decrease in the amount of sunlight the body receives may cause a disturbance in the body's natural clock ("Seasonal" NMHA, par. 2).[2] Doctors believe that the combination of chemical imbalance and biological clock disturbance results in symptoms such as lethargy,[3] oversleeping, weight gain, anxiety, and irritability—all signs of depression.

3   Since absence of light seems to be the cause of this disorder, a daily dose of light appears to be the cure. Doctors advise patients to sit in front

---

[1]"Seasonal Affective Disorder." The Healthy House Ltd. 30 Nov. 2004 <http://www.healthy-house.co.uk/allergy/information.php?allergy_id=11>.

[2]"Seasonal Affective Disorder." National Mental Health Association. 30 Nov. 2004 <http://www.nmha.org/infoctr/factsheets/27.cfm>.

[3]**lethargy:** inactivity; tiredness

of a special light box that simulates[1] natural light for a few hours every day. An hour's walk outside in winter sunlight may also help (par. 4).

4   In conclusion, the depressive effect of low sunlight levels may help explain the high suicide rate in the Scandinavian countries; more important, it may suggest a remedy: When the days grow short, turn on the lights.

Writing Technique Questions
1. Which paragraph contains the chain of causes and effects?
2. What is the effect of decreased sunlight in winter?
3. What other change results from a decrease in the amount of sunlight?
4. What is the final result?

PRACTICE 2

Chain Organization

Fill in the boxes to complete the flowchart, which illustrates the cause/effect chain described in the model essay "SAD."

```
                    ┌─────────────────────┐
                    │    Less sunlight     │
                    └─────────────────────┘
                              ↓
┌──────────────────────────────────────────────────────────────────┐
│ Body produces                                                       │
│ more _____ and          +          _____     │
│ less _____                                                   │
└──────────────────────────────────────────────────────────────────┘
                              ↓
┌──────────────────────────────────────────────────────────────────┐
│   Lethargy, oversleeping, weight gain, anxiety, irritability        │
└──────────────────────────────────────────────────────────────────┘
```

The type of cause/effect organization you choose depends on your topic.

- A chain pattern is usually easier if the causes and effects are very closely interrelated. You might use a chain pattern to write about the causes of a particular disease or phenomenon in nature such as a thunderstorm or a rainbow.
- The block pattern is usually easier with larger, complex topics such as global warming or homelessness.
- Sometimes you will want to use a combination of block and chain organization. The model essay on pages 96–97 uses block organization, but in paragraphs 4, 5, and 6, you will find chain organization.

_____

[1]**simulates:** imitates

Cause/Effect Signal Words and Phrases

Just as certain transition signals show time order and logical division, certain words and phrases signal cause/effect relationships. You probably know many of them already.

Cause Signal Words

Coordinators	
for	Bison were indispensable to the Native American tribes, **for** this one animal provided them with nearly everything they needed for survival: meat, clothing, shelter, tools, and weapons.
	Note: When used in this way, *for* has the same meaning as *because*. However, you MUST use a comma in front of *for*, and you MUST NOT use a comma in front of *because*.

Subordinators	
because since as	Bison were indispensable to the Native American tribes **because/since/as** this one animal provided them with nearly everything they needed for survival: meat, clothing, shelter, tools, and weapons.

Others	
to result from to be the result of	The bison's near extinction **resulted from/was the result of** loss of habitat and overhunting.
due to because of	Bison nearly became extinct **due to/because of** loss of habitat and overhunting.
the effect of the consequence of	One **effect of/consequence of** westward expansion was the destruction of habitat for the bison.
as a result of as a consequence of	The areas in which bison could roam freely shrank **as a result of/as a consequence of** the westward expansion of the 1800s.

PRACTICE 3

Recognizing Cause Signal Words

Step 1 Underline the part of the sentence that states a cause.
Step 2 Circle the word or words that introduce the cause.
Step 3 Be able to discuss the use of each word or phrase you have circled. What kind of grammatical structure follows each one? Notice especially the difference between the use of *because* and *because of*.

The first one has been done for you as an example.

1. The computer is a learning tool (since) it helps children to master math and language skills. (After *since*, we must use a clause with a subject and a verb.)
2. Due to the ability of computers to keep records of sales and inventory, many big department stores rely on them.
3. A medical computer system is an aid to physicians because of its ability to interpret data from a patient's history and provide a diagnosis. (How would you rewrite this sentence using *because* instead of *because of*?)
4. War, famine, and ethnic violence have caused a flood of refugees in the past 50 years.

5. Hollywood movies are known for their special effects because U.S. audiences seem to demand them.
6. Since European audiences seem to prefer movies that explore psychological or philosophical issues, European movies are generally quieter and more thought-provoking.
7. Smog results from chemical air pollutants being trapped under a layer of warm air.
8. John's promotion is the result of his brilliant management skills and company loyalty.
9. Little is known about life on the ocean floor, for scientists have only recently developed the technology to explore it.
10. Holes are created in the protective ozone layer of the stratosphere as a result of the burning of fossil fuels.

Effect Signal Words

Transition Words and Phrases	
as a result as a consequence therefore thus consequently hence	Workers building the new transcontinental railroad needed meat; **as a result/as a consequence/therefore/thus/consequently/hence**, hunters killed bison by the thousands. *Note:* Notice the difference between *as a result* and *as a result of*. *As a result* is followed by a full sentence (independent clause) and introduces an effect. *As a result of* is followed by a noun phrase and introduces a clause.
Coordinators	
so	Native Americans began trading bison skins to the settlers for steel knives and guns, **so** they began killing bison in larger numbers.
Others	
to result in **to cause**	Loss of habitat and overhunting **resulted in/caused** the near extinction of bison.
to have an effect on **to affect**	The reduced numbers of bison **had a terrible effect on/affected** the lives of the Native Americans who had depended on them for survival.
the cause of **the reason for**	The rescue of the bison from near extinction is **a cause of/a reason for** celebration.
thereby	The 85 bison that survived were given refuge in Yellowstone National Park in 1892, **thereby** saving this species from total extinction. *Note: Thereby* is most frequently used in front of *-ing* phrases.

PRACTICE 4

Recognizing Effect Signal Words

Step 1 Underline the part of the sentence that states an effect.
Step 2 Circle the word or words that introduce the effect.
Step 3 Be able to discuss the use of each word or phrase that you have circled. What kind of grammatical structure follows each one? How is the sentence punctuated?

1. The performance of electric cars is inferior to the performance of cars with conventional internal combustion engines; consequently, some improvements must be made in them if they are to become popular.
2. However, electric cars are reliable, economical, and nonpolluting; therefore, the government is spending millions of dollars to improve their technology.
3. Electric cars use relatively inexpensive electricity for power; thus, they cost less to operate than cars that use gasoline.
4. The cost of gasoline is rising; as a result, some automobile manufacturers have begun to produce electric models.
5. His patient diplomacy resulted in the successful negotiation of a peace treaty.
6. It has been documented that lack of sleep affects a person's ability to think clearly.
7. Cold water is denser than warm water and will therefore sink.
8. Freshwater is less dense than salt water, so it tends to float on the surface of a body of salt water.
9. Air pollution creates holes in the protective ozone layer of the stratosphere, thereby allowing harmful ultraviolet radiation to reach Earth's surface.
10. The cause of the patient's rapid recovery was the excellent care he received from his doctor.

PRACTICE 5

Using Cause/Effect Signal Words

Step 1 Decide which sentence in each item is a cause and which is an effect. Write *C* for cause or *E* for effect next to each sentence.

Step 2 Combine the sentences in each item into a new sentence that shows a cause/effect relationship. Use the cause or effect signal word or phrase given to form your new sentence, and circle the word. You will have to add, delete, or change words in most sentences.

The first one has been done for you as an example.

1. __E__ There are fewer hours of daylight.
   __C__ In winter, the sun is lower in the sky.
   (thus) _In winter, the sun is lower in the sky; (thus) there are fewer hours of_ _daylight._

2. _____ Some breeds of dogs have a stronger desire to perform a service than other breeds.
   _____ They are more suitable as search-and-rescue animals.
   (since) _____

3. _____ Seals and other aquatic mammals can see when they are hunting for food in the dark ocean depths at night.
   _____ They have very large eyes.
   (due to) _____

4. _____ Metals have many free-moving electrons.
   _____ Metals are good conductors of heat.
   (consequently) _____
   _____

5. _____ My company began offering employees flexible working hours.
   _____ Productivity has increased.
   _____ Absenteeism has declined.
   (as a result) _____
   _____

6. _____ Radiation could escape into the atmosphere.
   _____ The Chernobyl nuclear power plant had no confinement shell.
   (hence) _____
   _____

7. _____ Operators had disregarded safety rules.
   _____ The nuclear reactor at Chernobyl underwent a meltdown.
   (because of) _____
   _____

8. _____ During a weather phenomenon known as El Niño, a mass of warm
   water flows eastward across the Pacific Ocean toward South
   America.
   _____ The temperature of the water off the coast of Peru rises as much
   as 10°F.
   (thereby) *Note*: You must change the verb *rise* to *raise*. _____
   _____

9. _____ Weather around the world changes.
   _____ During an El Niño, the jet stream blows in a different pattern.
   (therefore) _____
   _____

10. _____ In some areas of the world, heavy rains fall.
    _____ Devastating floods and mudslides happen.
    (cause—*verb*) _____
    _____

11. _____ In other parts of the world thousands of people suffer starvation.
    _____ Drought happens.
    (as a result of) _____
    _____

Review

These are the important points you should have learned from this chapter.

1. Cause/effect organization is a common pattern in academic writing to write about causes (or reasons) and effects (or results).
2. There are two common cause/effect patterns of organization.
   - In block organization, the causes (or reasons) are grouped together in one block, and the effects (or results) are grouped together in another block. There may be a transition paragraph between blocks.
   - In chain organization, the causes and effects are too closely linked to be separated. One cause leads to an effect, which is the cause of the next effect.
3. Use a variety of cause/effect signal words to help your reader follow your ideas.

Writing Practice

PRACTICE 6

Writing a Cause-and-Effect Essay

Choose one of the suggested topics and write an essay that discusses it in terms of cause and effect. Use either block or chain organization or a combination of both.

Choose a topic that interests you or that is related to your major field of study. For example, if you plan to study medicine or nursing, write on a topic related to those subjects. If you are interested in the environment, write about El Niño or global warming. Follow the steps in the writing process described in Appendix A. When you have finished, use the Self-Editing and Peer-Editing Worksheets on pages 325 and 326.

Topic Suggestions
Education
    Effects of reducing class size
    Head Start programs
    Tutoring programs for college students
    Falling reading scores among schoolchildren
    High school dropouts
Environmental issues
    El Niño *or* La Niña
    Global warming
    Benefits of recycling
    Neighborhood cleanup days
Health sciences
    Increased life expectancy
    Eradication of a particular disease or health problem (*Examples*: polio, malnutrition)
    Eating disorders
    Benefits of health education programs (*Examples*: dental hygiene, nutrition, infectious disease immunization)

Social issues
    Homelessness
    Rising divorce rate
    Americans with Disabilities Act
    Family and Medical Leave Act
Political/economic issues
    Globalization
    Refugees
    Inflation

Topics on the Lighter Side

- What if your school decided not to give any more quizzes, tests, or grades to students? What could be the reasons for such a decision? What would be the effects?
- What would be the effects if children and parents in a family reversed roles, that is, if the children took on the role of parents, and the parents took on the role of children?

PRACTICE 7

Writing under Pressure

Note: These topics are intended to elicit a single paragraph, not an essay.

Choose one of the topics suggested and write a well-organized paragraph. Your instructor will give you a time limit.

- Spend 1 or 2 minutes at the beginning brainstorming and organizing your ideas.
- Spend 1 minute at the end checking your work.
- Spend the remaining time writing.

Causes of stress	Effects of an unreasonable fear (for example, fear of flying)
Effects of stress	
Effects of cell phones on society	Benefits of daily exercise
Reasons for the popularity of television game shows/reality shows/soap operas	Consequences of eating an unbalanced diet

Applying What You Have Learned

Cause/Effect Order

Background: Wolves are predators. They kill cattle, sheep, chickens, and other animals that are farmers' and ranchers' source of income. In 1914, the United States Congress provided money to eradicate wolves. The government paid hunters to help ranchers protect their livestock by killing the wolves. Sixty years later, wolves had disappeared from the western United States. Then in 1973, Congress enacted the Endangered Species Act, and the Wolf Recovery Program was started to reintroduce wolves in some areas. Currently about 160 wolves have been reintroduced to central Idaho and Yellowstone National Park. Farmers and ranchers are strongly opposed to this program and have filed lawsuits to stop it.

The author of the following essay favors the program. As you read, look for the reasons she gives for supporting the wolves' return. The model essay at the beginning of this chapter focused on causes, but this essay focuses on effects: What were the effects of the wolves' absence? What are the effects of the wolves' return?

Welcoming Back the Top Dog[1]

1   In our homes, on our beds, and deep within our hearts lie creatures for whom the wild is more than a whisper—domesticated versions of animals long reviled by humankind. Forebears of our beloved dogs and cats, wolves and mountain lions have shared a fate far removed from that of their tamer cousins. Feared for their intelligence and physical prowess, wolves and mountain lions were nearly eradicated. It is only recently that we have begun to understand the vital role these predators play in keeping nature in balance. Only recently have we stopped persecuting and started appreciating the wonders of these wild beings.

2   Just in the nick of time. Luckily, when given political protection from trigger-happy humans and habitat with sufficient prey, wolves and mountain lions thrive and their populations quickly revive. While mountain lions have always eked out an existence in California, wolves were exterminated decades ago. But now, the potential exists for wolves to move naturally into the far reaches of northern California and Oregon from the northern Rockies.

3   Wolves were extinct in the lower 48 states for more than half a century. Their restoration to the wildlands of Montana, Idaho, and Yellowstone National Park in the mid-1990s created virtual laboratories for wildlife biologists—and people like you and me—to observe the species in its natural element. We began to see almost immediately that wolves generate a ripple effect throughout the ecosystem for which many other species, some endangered themselves, benefit.

4   Making a living in the wild is hard. As a top predator, wolves make life easier by putting food on the ground for scavengers. Grizzly bears, bald eagles, gold eagles, ravens, coyotes, mountain lions, magpies, wolverines, and beetles all enjoy feasting on wolf kills. Thanks to the wolves, the endangered grizzly bear is enjoying a renaissance and its numbers have taken a turn for the better in parts of the West. In Yellowstone, individual grizzly bears are taking advantage of a good thing: They've been seen following wolf packs, waiting for them to make a kill and then stealing the carcass before the hard-working wolves have had a chance to take even a bite! Ninety-pound wolves are no match for one-thousand-pound grizzlies.

5   The dance of life and death between predator and prey makes many of us uncomfortable, yet prey species are also benefiting from the return of the wolf. Unlike human hunters, who target healthy adult animals, wolves cull the sick and elderly from elk, deer, moose, and bison herds, reducing the spread of disease and keeping the prey population healthier.

6   "It's important to remember that predators and prey evolved in lockstep together over millions of years," says Amaroq Weiss, BS, MS, JD, western director of species conservation for Defenders of Wildlife. "They make each other work."

---

[1]Cardo, Sheri "Welcoming Back the Top Dog." Animal Chronicles 15.1 (Spring 2004): 1+. A Marin Humane Society Publication.

7   "As an example of how a keystone predator like the wolf keeps a prey population healthier, we have only to look at what's happening in Wisconsin," says Weiss. "Chronic wasting disease (CWD) in deer is an enormous problem in the southern part of the state, where there are no wolves. However, in northern Wisconsin, to which wolves have returned in recent years, CWD in deer is unknown. While no studies have been completed to confirm this relationship, the evidence on the ground is extremely compelling.

8   Plant life also gains where this high-ranking carnivore is around. Prior to wolves being reintroduced into Yellowstone, the ungulates (hooved mammals) had it easy. With no hunters or predators around, they could do as they pleased—and what pleased them was hanging out on river banks, browsing on the young willow and aspen. But with wolves back in the picture, the elk and moose have had to move around a lot more; as a result, the compromised vegetation is flourishing once again.

9   The beneficial impacts of this change are numerous. The willow and aspen can now mature, thereby creating habitat for migratory songbirds. The increased vegetation reduces erosion and cools the rivers and ponds, thus making them more hospitable to fish. Beavers are back building dams.

10   Environmentalism is all about relationships, and the trickle-down effects . . . that wolves have on other species, and the ecosystem in general, is significant. It is easy to see why wolves are called an umbrella species: An entire web of life is protected by the existence of this top carnivore. Imagine what the ecological impact would be if wolves were allowed to return to more of their historical homeland.

Questions

About the Introduction and Conclusion

1. The thesis statement for this essay is the last sentence of paragraph
   a. 1.
   b. 2.
   c. 3.
   d. There is no thesis statement.
   Hint: Rereading the conclusion will help you answer this question.

2. The conclusion of this essay
   a. summarizes the main ideas.
   b. repeats the thesis statement in different words.

About the Organization

3. This essay is a cause/effect essay that discusses mainly
   a. the causes of the wolves' return to certain areas of the United States.
   b. effects of the return of wolves to certain areas of the United States.
   c. both the causes and the effects.

4. This essay uses block organization to make three main points about the return of wolves.
   (1) _____
   (2) _____
   (3) _____

5. Two paragraphs, when added together, use the chain pattern. These two paragraphs are
   a. 5 and 6.
   b. 8 and 9.

About the Support

6. The topic sentence for paragraph 4 is the
   a. first sentence.
   b. second sentence.
   c. There is no topic sentence.

7. The topic sentence for paragraph 5 is the
   a. first half of the first sentence (up to the word *yet*).
   b. second half of the first sentence (after the word *yet*).

8. Which two paragraphs do not have topic sentences?
   a. 4 and 5
   b. 6 and 7
   c. 7 and 8
   d. 8 and 9
   e. 9 and 10

9. Paragraph 7 supports the point made in paragraph
   a. 4.
   b. 5.

About Coherence

10. What cause/effect signal word is used in the
    a. last sentence of paragraph 3? _____
    b. last sentence of paragraph 8? _____
    c. second sentence of paragraph 9? _____
    d. third sentence of paragraph 9? _____

11. What key noun appears in every paragraph except paragraphs 6 and 9? _____

12. What two synonyms in the first paragraph substitute for the key noun? _____ and _____

13. What transition signal in the topic sentence of paragraph 8 tells the reader that an additional main point will be discussed? _____

Suggestions for Discussion or Writing

1. The author says that wolves are necessary to keep nature in balance. Why are they necessary? In other words, what positive effects do wolves have on the ecosystem?

2. Take the side of the farmers and ranchers. Why should wolves not be reintroduced into the environment? What effects will their reintroduction have?

3. As a class, choose another endangered species or a different environmental issue. Form groups to research your chosen topic. Gather the following information:

   three interesting facts about the species
   two statistics
   two quotations

   Share your information in a group or class discussion.

Topic Suggestions

California condors	blue whales
American bald eagles	American bison
manatees	African elephants
giant pandas	tigers

Comparison/Contrast Essays

Pre-Columbian hieroglyphs, Mexico

In a **comparison/contrast essay**, you explain the similarities and the differences between two items. Comparison and contrast is a very common pattern in most academic fields. It is also a common type of essay test question. You might encounter questions such as these:

POLITICAL SCIENCE   Compare the forms of government of Great Britain and the United States.

AMERICAN LITERATURE   Compare the characters of Uncle Melik and his nephew in William Saroyan's short story "The Pomegranate Trees."

BUSINESS   Compare and contrast methods for promoting a new business, product, or service.

As you read the following model essay, study its organization.

MODEL

*Comparison/
Contrast Essay*

Japan and the United States: Different but Alike[1]

1   The culture of a place is an integral[2] part of its society whether that place is a remote Indian village in Brazil or a highly industrialized city in Western Europe. The culture of Japan fascinates people in the United States because, at first glance, it seems so different. Everything that characterizes the United States—newness, racial heterogeneity,[3] vast territory, informality, and an ethic of individualism[4]—is absent in Japan. There, one finds an ancient and homogeneous[5] society, an ethic that emphasizes the importance of groups, and a tradition of formal behavior governing every aspect of daily living, from drinking tea to saying hello. On the surface at least, U.S. and Japanese societies seem totally opposite.

2   One obvious difference is the people. Japan is a homogenous society of one nationality and a few underrepresented minority groups, such as the ethnic Chinese and Koreans. All areas of government and society are controlled by the Japanese majority. In contrast, although the United States is a country with originally European roots, its liberal immigration policies have resulted in its becoming a heterogeneous society of many ethnicities—Europeans, Africans, Asians, and Latinos. All are represented in all areas of U.S. society, including business, education, and politics.

3   Other areas of difference between Japan and the United States involve issues of group interaction and sense of space. Whereas people in the United States pride themselves on individualism and informality, Japanese value groups and formality. People in the United States admire and reward a person who rises above the crowd; in contrast, a Japanese proverb says, "The nail that sticks up gets hammered down." In addition, while North Americans' sense of size and scale developed out of the vastness of the continent, Japanese genius lies in the diminutive and miniature.[6] For example, the United States builds airplanes, while Japan produces transistors.

4   In spite of these differences, these two apparently opposite cultures share several important experiences.

5   Both, for example, have transplanted cultures. Each nation has a "mother" society—China for Japan and Great Britain for the United States—that has influenced the daughter in countless ways: in language, religion, art, literature, social customs, and ways of thinking. Japan, of course, has had more time than the United States to work out its unique interpretation of the older Chinese culture, but both countries reflect their cultural ancestry.

---

[1]Adapted from Harris, Neil. "We're Different but Alike." Japan Salutes America on Its Bicentennial. Tokyo: America-Japan Society, 1976.
[2]**integral:** necessary for completeness
[3]**heterogeneity:** variety
[4]**ethic of individualism:** belief in the value of the individual person over the group
[5]**homogeneous:** characterized by sameness, consistency
[6]**diminutive and miniature:** very small

6 Both societies, moreover, have developed the art of business and commerce, of buying and selling, of advertising and mass producing, to the highest levels. Few sights are more reassuring to people from the United States than the tens of thousands of busy stores in Japan, especially the beautiful, well-stocked department stores. To U.S. eyes, they seem just like Macy's or Neiman Marcus at home. In addition, both Japan and the United States are consumer societies. The people of both countries love to shop and are enthusiastic consumers of convenience products and fast foods. Vending machines selling everything from fresh flowers to hot coffee are as popular in Japan as they are in the United States, and fast-food noodle shops are as common in Japan as McDonald's restaurants are in the United States.

7 A final similarity is that both Japanese and people in the United States have always emphasized the importance of work, and both are paying penalties for their commitment to it: increasing stress and weakening family bonds. People in the United States, especially those in business and in the professions, regularly put in twelve or more hours a day at their jobs, just as many Japanese executives do. Also, while the normal Japanese workweek is six days, many people in the United States who want to get ahead voluntarily work on Saturday and/or Sunday in addition to their normal five-day workweek.

8 Japan and the United States: different, yet alike. Although the two societies differ in many areas such as racial heterogeneity versus racial homogeneity, individualism versus group cooperation, and informal versus formal forms of behavior, they share more than one common experience. Furthermore, their differences probably contribute as much as their similarities toward the mutual interest the two countries have in each other. It will be interesting to see where this reciprocal fascination leads in the future.

Writing Technique Questions

1. In which paragraph(s) are the similarities discussed? In which paragraph(s) are the differences discussed?
2. What is the function of paragraph 4?

Organization of Comparison/Contrast Essays

The first key to writing a successful comparison/contrast essay is to organize it carefully.

Point-by-Point Organization

One way to organize a comparison/contrast essay is to use point-by-point organization, which is similar to the logical division pattern studied in Chapter 4.

Suppose, for example, that you want to compare two jobs. First, make a list of factors that are important to you: salary, benefits, opportunities for advancement, workplace atmosphere, commuting distance from your home, and so on. Each factor, or point of comparison, is like a subtopic in a logical division essay.

Point of Comparison	Job X	Job Y	Same or Different?
Salary frequency of raises	$30/hour annual evaluation	$25/hour semi-annual evaluation	different
Benefits[1] vacation health insurance pension plan sick leave	good	good	same
Advancement opportunities	not good	good	different
Workplace atmosphere	high pressure, competitive	friendly, supportive	different
Commuting distance	30 minutes	32 minutes	same

In your essay, each point of comparison becomes the topic of a paragraph. You can put the paragraphs in any order you wish—perhaps in the order of their importance to you personally.

MODEL

Point-by-Point Organization

I. **Introduction**
   Thesis statement: One way to decide between two job offers is to compare them on important points.
II. **Body**
   A. Salary
   B. Benefits
   C. Opportunities for advancement
   D. Workplace atmosphere
   E. Commuting distance from home
III. **Conclusion**

Block Organization

The other way to organize a comparison/contrast essay is to arrange all the similarities together in a block and all the differences together in a block. You could discuss either the similarities first or the differences first. You often insert a transition paragraph or transition sentence between the two blocks. The model essay comparing Japan and the United States uses block organization.

---

[1]You should evaluate each benefit item separately. They are grouped together here for convenience.

MODEL

Block Organization

> **I. Introduction**
> **Thesis statement:** One way to decide between two job offers is to compare them on important points.
> **II. Body**
>   **A.** Similarities
>   1. Benefits
>   2. Commute distance from home
>   **B.** Differences
>   1. Salary
>   2. Opportunities for advancement
>   3. Workplace atmosphere
> **III. Conclusion**

    The number of paragraphs in each block depends on the topic. For some topics, you may write about all the similarities in a single paragraph; for other topics, you may need to discuss each similarity in a separate paragraph. The same is true for differences. Of course, some topics may have one paragraph of similarities and several paragraphs of differences, or vice versa.

PRACTICE 1

Outlining a Comparison/ Contrast Essay

Complete the outline of the model essay "Japan and the United States: Different but Alike."

  I. Introduction
    Thesis statement: On the surface at least, U.S. and Japanese societies seem totally opposite.
  II. Body
    A. _____
      1. Japan is a homogeneous society.
      2. _____
    B. _____
      1. Individualism versus groups
      2. _____
      3. Rising above the crowd, admired, and rewarded versus

         _____
      4. _____
        a. The United States builds airplanes.
        b. _____

In spite of these differences, these two apparently opposite cultures share several important experiences.

    C. Both have transplanted cultures.
      1. _____
      2. _____

D. _____
   1. Department stores
   2. _____
      a. _____
      b. Fast foods
         (1) _____
         (2) McDonald's restaurants
E. _____
   _____
   _____
   1. _____
   2. _____

III. Conclusion

Comparison and Contrast Signal Words

The second key to writing successful comparison/contrast essays is the appropriate use of comparison and contrast signal words. These are words that introduce points of comparison and points of contrast. It is not sufficient simply to describe each item that you are comparing. You must refer back and forth to, for example, Job X and Job Y and use comparison and contrast signal words to show what is the same and what is different about them. Of course, you should also use transition signals such as *first, second, one . . . , another . . . , the final . . . , for example*, and *in conclusion* in addition to these special ones.

The following chart lists some of the words and phrases used to discuss similarities.

Comparison Signal Words

Transition Words and Phrases	
similarly likewise	Human workers can detect malfunctions in machinery; **similarly/likewise**, a robot can be programmed to detect equipment malfunctions.
also	Human workers can detect malfunctions in machinery; a robot can **also**.
too	Human workers can detect malfunctions in machinery; a robot can **too**.
Subordinators	
as just as	Robots can detect malfunctions in machinery, **as/just as** human workers can. *Note:* Use a comma when *as* and *just as* show comparison even when the dependent clause follows the independent clause as in the above example.

Comparison Signal Words (continued)

Coordinators	
and	Robots **and** human workers can detect malfunctions in machinery.
both . . . and	**Both** robots **and** human workers can detect malfunctions in machinery.
not only . . . but also	**Not only** robots **but also** human workers can detect malfunctions in machinery.
neither . . . nor	**Neither** robots **nor** human workers are infallible.[1]
Others	
like (+ noun) just like (+ noun) similar to (+ noun)	Robots, **like/just like/similar to** human workers, can detect malfunctions in machinery.
(be) like (be) similar (to) (be) the same as	Robots **are like/are similar to/are the same as** human workers in their ability to detect malfunctions in machinery.
(be) the same	In their ability to detect malfunctions in machinery, robots and human workers **are the same**.
(be) alike (be) similar	Robots and human workers **are alike/are similar** in their ability to detect malfunctions in machinery.
to compare (to/with)	Robots can **be compared to/be compared with** human workers in their ability to detect malfunctions in machinery.

PRACTICE 2

Using Comparison Signal Words

A. Add comparison signal words to connect the following comparisons. The items contain both sentences and short phrases. You should write one complete new sentence for each item and use different comparison signal words in each. The first one has been done for you as an example.

1. The United States has a democratic form of government. Great Britain has a democratic form of government.

   The United States has a democratic form of government, just as Great Britain does.

2. The United States operates under a two-party system. Great Britain operates under a two-party system.

3. The British Parliament has two separate houses, the House of Commons and the House of Lords. The United States Congress has two separate houses, the Senate and the House of Representatives.

---

[1] **infallible:** perfect, without errors

4. The U.S. House of Representatives = the British House of Commons. The U.S. Senate = the British House of Lords.

_____

_____

5. The members of the U.S. House of Representatives are elected by district. The members of the British House of Commons are elected by district.

_____

_____

6. The method of choosing cabinet members in the United States. The method of choosing cabinet members in Great Britain. (Use the comparison signal _the same_.)

_____

_____

7. In Great Britain, the prime minister appoints the cabinet. The U.S. president appoints the cabinet.

_____

_____

8. The British monarch has the right to veto[1] any law passed by Parliament. The U.S. president has the right to veto any law passed by Congress.

_____

_____

B. Write five sentences of your own, comparing two things with which you are familiar. Use a different comparison signal in each sentence. _Note_: You may want to use one of the topics given at the top of page 119 for your essay at the end of the chapter.

1. _____

_____

2. _____

_____

3. _____

_____

4. _____

_____

5. _____

_____

---

[1]**veto:** cancel

Topic Suggestions

Two cities	Two sports stars
Two siblings	Two diets
Two friends	Two types of teachers or bosses
Two restaurants	Two classes
Two cars	Two airlines
Two sports	Two movies

Contrast Signal Words

Contrast signal words fall into two main groups according to their meaning. The words in the first group show a relationship that is called *concession*. The words in the second group show an opposition relationship.

Contrast Signal Words: Concession (Unexpected Result)

Concession signal words indicate that the information in one clause is not the result you expect from the information given in the other clause.

UNEXPECTED RESULT
Although I studied all night, <u>I failed the exam</u>.

My failing the exam is not the result you might expect from the information in the first clause: *I studied all night.*

Look at both Contrast Clauses and Concession Clauses on pages 222–223 for additional examples of contrast subordinators.

Transition Words and Phrases	
however nevertheless nonetheless still	Millions of people go on diets every year; **however/nevertheless/ nonetheless/still,** very few succeed in losing weight.
Subordinators	
although even though though	**Although/Even though/Though** most dieters initially lose a few pounds, most gain them back again within a few weeks.
Coordinators	
but yet	Doctors say that "fad" diets do not work, **but/yet** many people still try them.
Others	
despite (+ noun) in spite of (+ noun)	**Despite/In spite of** 10 years of dieting, I am still fat.

Contrast Signal Words: Direct Opposition

The second group of contrast signal words shows that two things are direct opposites. With direct opposites, the signal word can introduce either piece of information.

I am short, whereas my brother is tall. OR My brother is tall, whereas I am short.

Transition Words and Phrases	
however in contrast in (by) comparison on the other hand	Rock music is primarily the music of white performers; **however/ in contrast/in comparison/by comparison/on the other hand**, jazz is performed by both white and black musicians.
on the contrary	Jazz is not just one style of music; **on the contrary**, jazz has many styles such as Chicago jazz, Dixieland, ragtime, swing, bebop, and cool jazz, to name just a few. *Note: On the contrary* contrasts a truth and an untruth.
Subordinators	
while whereas	New Orleans-style jazz features brass marching-band instruments, **while/whereas** ragtime is played on a piano. *Note*: Use a comma with *while* and *whereas* even when the dependent clause follows the independent clause.
Coordinators	
but	Jazz music was born in the southern part of the United States, **but** it now enjoys a worldwide audience.
Others	
differ (from)	Present-day rock music **differs from** early rock music in several ways.
compared (to/with)	Present-day rock music has a harder sound **compared to/compared with** early rock.
(be) different (from) (be) dissimilar to	The punk, rap, grunge, and techno styles of today are very **different from/ dissimilar to/unlike** the rock music performed by Elvis Presley 50 years ago, but they have the same roots.
(be) unlike	**Unlike** rock, a music style started by white musicians, rhythm-and-blues styles were influenced primarily by black musicians.

PRACTICE 3

Using Contrast Signal Words

A. Add contrast signal words to connect the following items. The items contain both complete sentences and short phrases. You should write one complete new sentence for each item, and use a different contrast signal in each. The first one has been done for you as an example.

1. The government of the United States/the government of Great Britain/ dissimilar in several aspects

   The governments of the United States and Great Britain are dissimilar in *several aspects.*

2. The chief executive in Great Britain is called the prime minister. The chief executive in the United States is called the president.

   _____

   _____

3. In the United States, the president fulfills the functions of both political leader and head of state. These two functions are separate in Great Britain.

   _____

   _____

4. In other words, Great Britain has both a monarch and a prime minister. The United States has only a president.

   _____

   _____

5. The president of the United States may be of a different political party than the majority of Congress. The British prime minister is the head of the political party that has the most seats in Parliament.

   _____

   _____

6. The United States has a written constitution. Great Britain has no written constitution.

   _____

   _____

7. In the United States, elections are held on a regular schedule, no matter how popular or unpopular the government is. In Great Britain, elections are held whenever the prime minister loses a vote of confidence.

   _____

   _____

8. The members of the U.S. Senate are elected. The members of the British House of Lords are appointed or inherit their positions.

   _____

   _____

9. As you can see, the two systems of government differ in several major aspects. They are both democracies.

   _____

   _____

B. Write five sentences of your own, contrasting two things with which you are familiar. Use a different contrast signal in each sentence.

1. _____
   _____
2. _____
   _____
3. _____
   _____
4. _____
   _____
5. _____
   _____

Topic Suggestions

Digital cameras/film cameras
Computers/humans
City life/country life
The cost of living in two
    places
Family life in two cultures

Living in a small town/living
    in a large city
Taking public transportation/
    driving your own car
Any topic from Practice 2B
    on pages 118–119

Review

These are the important points covered in this chapter.

1. Comparison/contrast is a common pattern for writing about similarities and differences. It is used in all academic fields.
2. There are two common ways to organize a comparison/contrast essay.
   * In point-by-point organization, you discuss each similarity and each difference in some other order—usually order of their importance—without grouping them into blocks. In this type of organization, you may discuss a similarity and then a difference, and then a similarity and then a difference.
   * In block organization, you first discuss all the similarities in a block and then all the differences in another block. (You may, of course, begin with the block of differences.)
3. Use comparison and contrast signal words to help your reader understand your points of comparison and contrast.

Writing Practice

PRACTICE 4

Writing an Essay Using Comparison/ Contrast Organization

Choose one of the suggested topics and write an essay using comparison/contrast organization. Use either point-by-point or block organization.

Follow the steps in the writing process described in Appendix A. When you have finished, use the Self-Editing and Peer-Editing Worksheets on pages 327 and 328.

Topic Suggestions

Two cultures or one aspect of two cultures, such as family life, schools, child-raising practices, courtship and marriage customs.

Living at home and living away from home

High school and college or university

Two authors whose books you have read

Two products (for example, digital/film cameras, gasoline-powered/hybrid automobiles, Apple computers/PCs)

Topics on the Lighter Side

Any of the topics from Practice 2B on pages 118–119

Morning people/night people

Optimists/pessimists

Spenders/savers

PRACTICE 5

Writing under Pressure

Note: These topics are intended to elicit a single paragraph, not an essay.

Choose one of the topics suggested and write a well-organized paragraph. Focus on using the techniques of comparison/contrast.

- Spend 1 or 2 minutes at the beginning thinking of ideas and organizing them.
- Spend 1 minute at the end checking your work for errors.
- Spend the remaining time writing.

Topic Suggestions

Shopping at two kinds of stores (for example, small family-owned stores and megastores)

Two jobs you have had

"A" students and "F" students, or "A" students and "C" students

Two pets you have owned

Two times of day (for example, early morning and late at night, or early morning and early evening)

Applying What You Have Learned

Comparison/ Contrast

The following reading is from a chapter of a college textbook in cultural anthropology. It discusses cultural differences in the custom of exchanging gifts at a marriage.

Marital Exchanges[1]

1   In most cultures, the marriage of a man and a woman is accompanied by some kind of transfer of goods or services. These marital exchanges are used to create in-law relationships, compensate a family for the loss of one of its members, provide for the new couple's support, or provide a daughter with an inheritance that helps attract a desirable husband.

2   Marital exchanges take numerous forms, including the North American custom of wedding showers and wedding gifts. In these, the presents given by relatives and friends supposedly help the newlyweds establish an independent household. We give things that are useful to the couple jointly, with food-preparation and other household utensils easily the most common type of gift. Many couples even register at stores so that their relatives and friends will provide the items they want.

3   From a cross-cultural perspective, the most unusual feature of North American marital exchange is that nothing is transferred between the relatives of the groom and bride: The couple treat the gifts as their private property. Like most of our other customs, this seems natural to us. Of course the gifts go to the couple—what else could happen to them?

4   Plenty else, as we shall see in a moment. For now, notice that the fact that the couple receives the gifts fits with several other features of Euro-American marriage.

5   First, in addition to creating new nuclear families, marriage is the bond through which new independent households are started. So the husband and wife "need their own stuff." If, in contrast, the newlyweds moved in with one of their relatives, they would not have as great a need for their own pots and pans, wine glasses, silver candlesticks, and other "stuff."

6   Second, our marriage-gift customs fit with the value our culture places on the privacy of the marital relationship: It is a personal matter between the husband and wife, and their relatives should keep their noses out. If the in-laws get along and socialize, that's great, but our marriages generally do not create strong bonds between families of the bride and groom. (In fact, the two families often compete for the visits and attention of the couple and their offspring.) . . . The fact that the in-laws do not exchange gifts with each other is a manifestation of the absence of a necessary relation between them after the wedding. If, in contrast, the marriage created an alliance between the two sets of relatives, some kind of an exchange would probably occur between them to symbolize and cement their new relations.

7   Third, gifts are presented to the couple, not to the husband or wife as individuals, and are considered to belong equally and jointly to both partners. But there are marriage systems in which the property of the wife is separate from that of her husband; if divorce should occur, there is no squabbling over who gets what and no need for prenuptials.

---

[1]Peoples, James, and Garrick Bailey. "Marriage, Family, and Residence." <u>Humanity: An Introduction to Cultural Anthropology</u>, 6th ed. Belmont, CA: Wadsworth, 2003: 177–178.

8   With this background in mind, what kinds of martial exchanges occur in other cultures?

9   **Bridewealth**   *Bridewealth* is the widespread custom that requires a man and his relatives to transfer wealth to the relatives of his bride. It is easily the most common of all marital exchanges, found in more than half the world's cultures. The term *bridewealth* is well chosen because the goods transferred usually are among the most valuable symbols of wealth in the local culture. In sub-Saharan Africa, cattle and sometimes other livestock are the most common goods used for bridewealth. Peoples of the Pacific Islands and Southeast Asia usually give their bridewealth in pigs or shell money and ornaments. . . .

10   **Brideservice**   As the term implies, *brideservice* is the custom whereby a husband is required to spend a period of time working for the family of his bride. A Yanomamo [a native tribe living in the rain forests of the Amazon] son-in-law is expected to live with his wife's parents, hunting and gardening for them until they finally release control over their daughter. Among some !Kung [a tribe living in the Kalahari desert of Africa] bands, a man proves his ability as a provider by living with and hunting for his wife's parents for three to ten years, after which the couple is free to camp elsewhere.

11   Brideservice is the second most common form of marital exchange; it is the usual compensation given to the family of a bride in roughly one-eighth of the world's cultures. However, sometimes it occurs alongside other forms of marital exchange and occasionally is used to reduce the amount of bridewealth owed.

12   **Dowry**   A marital exchange is called *dowry* when the family of a woman transfers a portion of their own wealth or other property to their daughter and her husband. The main thing to understand about dowry is that it is *not* simply the opposite of bridewealth; that is, it is not "groomwealth." It is, rather, ordinarily the share of a woman's inheritance that she is allowed to take into her marriage for the use of her new family, although her parents are still alive. The woman and her family do not acquire marital rights over her husband when they provide a dowry, as they would if dowry were the opposite of bridewealth; rather, the bride and her husband receive property when they marry, rather than when the bride's parents die. By doing so, parents give their female children extra years of use of the property and also publicly demonstrate their wealth.

13   . . . Dowry is a relatively rare form of marital exchange, occurring in only about 5 percent of the societies recorded by anthropology. Dowry today is common in parts of India, where it includes jewelry, household utensils, women's clothing, and money. Much of the dowry is presented to the bride on her wedding day, but her parents and maternal uncle often provide gifts periodically throughout the marriage. Dowry, then, is not always a one-time expense for a family but may represent a continual drain on their resources.

14   There are other forms of exchanges that occur at marriages, including some in which both sets of relatives exchange gifts as a material symbol of the new basis of their relationship. And the three forms discussed above are not mutually exclusive. For example, in most of traditional China, both bridewealth and dowry occurred at most marriages. The groom's family would make a payment to the bride's family and the bride's family would purchase some furniture and other household goods for their daughter to take with her when she moved into her husband's household. For wealthier families dowry was usually displayed by being transported ostentatiously over the streets between the households of the bride and groom. Dowry thus became a Chinese "status symbol." Sometimes, if the bride's family

was substantially poorer than the groom's, part of the bridewealth payment would be spent on purchasing goods for the woman's dowry. This was legal and common until after the Communist Revolution in 1949, when the leaders outlawed both bridewealth and dowry, though both continue in some places to this day.

Questions

About the Organization

1. In which paragraphs do the authors describe the North American form of marital exchange?
   a. 1–7
   b. 2–7
   c. 1–4
   d. 2–4

2. Excluding the North American form of marital transfer, what other forms do the authors discuss? List them in order:
   a. _____
   b. _____
   c. _____
   Why are they discussed in this particular order? In other words, what pattern did the authors use to organize this part of the reading?

   _____

3. Which two paragraphs contain the phrase *in contrast*?
   Paragraphs _____ and _____
   a. In the first paragraph containing the phrase *in contrast*, what is contrasted?

      _____

   b. What is contrasted in the second paragraph containing *in contrast*?

      _____

4. What is contrasted in paragraph 7?

   _____

   Is there a contrast signal word in this paragraph? If so, what is it?

   _____

5. In which paragraphs do the authors contrast the customs of *bridewealth* and *dowry*?
   a. 9, 10, 12, 14
   b. 9 and 12
   c. 12 only

Suggestions for Discussion or Writing

1. Which type of marital exchange is followed in the culture you are the most familiar with?
2. Tell about other wedding customs (besides gift-giving) that may differ from North American customs.
3. At North American weddings, most of the attention is focused on the bride. It is her "big day." The groom plays an almost secondary role. Why do you think this is so? Is this the case in other cultures?

Paraphrase and Summary

Sumerian cuneiform

Academic writing normally requires that you support your ideas and opinions with facts, statistics, quotations, and similar kinds of information. There are four ways to use information from outside sources. You can quote it directly or indirectly, skills that you practiced in Chapter 3. You can also **paraphrase** or **summarize** it, skills that you will practice in this chapter. Writing paraphrases and summaries are important tools in academic writing.

Paraphrasing

When you paraphrase, you rewrite information from an outside source in your own words without changing the meaning. Because you include in your rewriting all or nearly all of the content of the original passage, a paraphrase is almost as long as the original. (A summary, by contrast, is much shorter than the original.)

MODEL

Paraphrase

Original Passage

Language is the main means of communication between peoples. But so many different languages have developed that language has often been a barrier rather than an aid to understanding among peoples. For many years, people have dreamed of setting up an international universal language which all people could speak and understand. The arguments in favor of a universal language are simple and obvious. If all peoples spoke the same tongue, cultural and economic ties might be much closer, and good will might increase between countries (Kispert).[1]

Paraphrase

Humans communicate through language. Because there are so many different languages, however, people around the world have a difficult time understanding one another. Some people have wished for a universal international language that speakers all over the world could understand. Their reasons are straightforward and clear. A universal language would build cultural and economic bonds. It would also create better feelings among countries (Kispert).

Writing Technique Questions

1. How many sentences are there in the original passage? In the paraphrase?
2. Compare the original passage and the paraphrase sentence by sentence. Analyze how the sentence structure and words differ by answering the following questions.
   a. What is the first word of the first sentence in the original passage? Where does this word appear in first sentence of the paraphrase?
   b. What is the first word of the second sentence in the original passage? What word replaces it in the second sentence of the paraphrase?
   c. What words replace *have dreamed of* in the third sentence? What word replaces *arguments in favor of* in the fourth sentence?
   d. Which sentence in the original becomes two sentences in the paraphrase?

Plagiarism

It is important to learn how to use information from outside sources without committing plagiarism. *Plagiarism* is wrongly using someone else's words or ideas, and it is a serious offense. Students who plagiarize may fail a class or even be expelled from school.

There are two kinds of plagiarism.

1. When you use information from an outside source *without citing the source* (telling where you got the information), you are guilty of plagiarism.
2. Even when you cite your source, *if your paraphrase is too similar to the original*, you are guilty of plagiarism.

---

[1]Kispert, Robert J. "Universal language." World Book Online Reference Center. 2004. World Book, Inc. 13 Nov. 2004 <http://www.worldbookonline.com/wb/Article?id=ar576960>.

Read the following paraphrases and decide which kind of plagiarism each example is guilty of.

MODEL

Plagiarism

Unacceptable Paraphrase 1

Humans communicate through language. However, because there are so many languages in the world, language acts as an obstacle instead of as an aid to understanding. People have long wished for a universal international language that speakers all over the world could understand. A universal language would certainly build cultural and economic bonds. It would also create better feelings among countries.

Unacceptable Paraphrase 2

Language is the principal means of communication between peoples. However, because there are numerous languages, language itself has frequently been a barrier rather than an aid to understanding among the world population. For many years, people have envisioned a common universal language that everyone in the world could communicate in. The reasons for having a universal language are clearly understandable. If the same tongue were spoken by all countries, they would undoubtedly become closer culturally and economically. It would probably also create good will among nations (Kispert).

Paraphrase 1 is plagiarism because the source is not cited. Paraphrase 2 is plagiarism because it is too similar to the original passage. For example, in the first sentence, only one word has been changed: *main* replaces *principal*. In the second sentence, only a few words have been changed. You can avoid the first kind of plagiarism by always citing your sources. You can avoid the second kind of plagiarism by learning to paraphrase correctly.

See Appendix E: Research and Documentation of Sources, pages 303–311, for information on how to cite sources.

How to Write a Good Paraphrase

There are three keys to writing a good paraphrase:

1. Use your own words and your own sentence structure.
2. Make your paraphrase approximately the same length as the original.
3. Do not change the meaning of the original.

You can write a good paraphrase if you follow these steps.

Step 1 Read the original passage several times until you understand it fully. Look up unfamiliar words, and find synonyms for them. It may not be possible to find synonyms for every word, especially technical vocabulary. In this case, use the original word.

Step 2 It helps to take notes. Write down only a few words for each idea—not complete sentences. Here are one writer's notes on the original passage about universal language:

> language—people use to communicate—but so many—difficult
> to understand one another—people wish—universal international
> language—reasons: cultural, economic bonds, better feelings
> between countries

It may be helpful to make a brief outline such as the following:

A. Language—people use to communicate
 1. So many languages make it difficult to understand one another.
 2. People wish for one universal international language.

B. Reasons
 1. Cultural, economic bonds
 2. Better feelings between countries

Step 3 Write your paraphrase from your notes. Don't look at the original while you are writing.

Step 4 Check your paraphrase against the original to make sure you have not copied vocabulary or the sentence structure too closely. Above all, make sure that you have not changed the meaning of the original or given any wrong information.

Step 5 Add an in-text citation at the end.

PRACTICE 1

Choosing the Best Paraphrase

Step 1 Read the original passages.
Step 2 Choose the best paraphrase from the choices given and mark it "Best."
Step 3 Mark the others "Too sim." for too similar, "No cit." if there is no in-text citation, or "Inc./Inacc." for incomplete and/or inaccurate information.

The first one has been done for you as an example.

Original Passage 1
Source: Page 16 of a three-page article in the October 15, 2003, issue of *Space Science* magazine. The title of the article is "Manned Mars Flight: Impossible Dream?" The author is Patrick Clinton, a NASA (National Aeronautics and Space Administration) physician.

Living aboard a space station in orbit around Earth for months at a time poses problems for astronauts' bodies as well as for their minds.

Best   **A.** An article in *Space Science* magazine reports that lengthy space station duty may lead to physical and mental problems for astronauts (Clinton 16).

No cit.   **B.** An article in *Space Science* magazine reports that astronauts who live aboard space stations for long periods of time may experience physical as well as mental problems.

Too sim.   **C.** An article in *Space Science* reports that living in a space station orbiting Earth for a long time can cause difficulties for astronauts' bodies and minds (Clinton 16).

Inc./Inacc.   **D.** An article in *Space Science* reports that astronauts will become physically sick and have mental problems if they visit a space station (Clinton 16).

Original Passage 2
Source: Page 16 of the same article in passage 1.

One major problem is maintaining astronauts' physical health. Medical treatment may be days or even weeks away, as there may not be a doctor on board. Illnesses such as appendicitis or ulcers, routinely treated on Earth, could be fatal in space because of the delay in getting to a doctor.

   A. NASA physician Patrick Clinton states that one problem is astronauts' physical health. With no doctor on board, common illnesses like appendicitis and ulcers could be fatal to astronauts because it would take too long to get them back to Earth.

   B. NASA physician Patrick Clinton states that keeping the astronauts physically healthy is one problem. If the crew does not include a doctor, the delay in getting treatment for an ordinary illness, such as appendicitis or ulcers, could mean death (16).

   C. NASA physician Patrick Clinton states that the physical health of astronauts is a huge problem. Spaceships do not usually have medical doctors among the crew, so astronauts who get appendicitis on a long space journey will die (16).

   D. NASA physician Patrick Clinton states that one big problem is keeping astronauts in good physical health. Medical treatment might take days or weeks to get because there may not be a doctor on the spaceship. Ordinary illnesses such as appendicitis and ulcers could be deadly because it would take too long to get to a doctor (16).

Original Passage 3

Source: Page 17 of the same article as in passages 1 and 2.

Another health problem is the potential for bone deterioration. In a weightless environment, the body produces less calcium. Astronauts must exercise at least three hours a day to prevent bone loss.

_____ **A.** Another problem is the possibility of bone loss, according to NASA physician Patrick Clinton. In weightless space, the body makes less calcium. Astronauts have to exercise a minimum of three hours a day to avoid losing bone (17).

_____ **B.** According to NASA physician Patrick Clinton, weight can be a problem. Astronauts must take extra calcium and exercise at least three hours a day to keep from gaining weight and to prevent bone damage (17).

_____ **C.** According to NASA physician Patrick Clinton, astronauts could suffer bone loss. Being weightless causes the body to lose calcium, which is important for strength, so exercising at least three hours daily is necessary to keep their bones strong.

_____ **D.** According to NASA physician Patrick Clinton, astronauts also face possible bone loss. Because weightlessness causes the body to lose calcium, exercising at least three hours daily is necessary to keep their bones strong (17).

PRACTICE 2

Writing Paraphrases

Write a paraphrase of each of the passages that follow.

Step 1 Read the original passage several times until you understand it well. You may find it helpful to underline the main points.

Step 2 Make notes in the space provided, changing vocabulary words wherever possible.

Step 3 Write your paraphrase in your own words. Remember to change both vocabulary and sentence structure.

Step 4 Check your paraphrase to make sure you have not changed the meaning of the original passage.

Step 5 Add an in-text citation in the proper form at the end of each paraphrase.

Step 6 If your instructor requests, prepare an entry for a works-cited list for each source.

Original Passage 1

Source: Page 18 of a three-page article in the October 15, 2003, issue of _Space Science_ magazine. The title of the article is "Manned Mars Flight: Impossible Dream?" The author is Patrick Clinton, a NASA physician.

A second major problem is maintaining astronauts' mental health. Being confined for long periods of time in dark and hostile space undoubtedly produces anxiety. Loneliness and boredom are other psychological concerns.

Notes

Your Paraphrase

_____

_____

_____

_____

_____

Original Passage 2

Source: Page 18 of the same article as in passage 1.

Finally, how can astronauts "let off steam" when interpersonal conflicts develop? Even best friends can irritate each other when forced to spend weeks together in isolation. Space stations are small, cramped, busy workplaces, and there is little privacy. Also, space exploration is dangerous, which adds to the stress aboard a spaceship.

Notes

Your Paraphrase

_____

_____

_____

_____

_____

Original Passage 3

Source: A Letter to the Editor written by Cory Brunish, which appeared on page 9 of the February 16, 2004, issue of *Time* magazine.

Why should we spend vast amounts to reach Mars when there is a very high chance of its not providing anything that would improve our lot here on Earth? Why not allocate those billions for "home improvement"? Think of the progress that could be made in curing cancer, AIDS, and other diseases; in cleaning our water, air, and soil; and in feeding hungry nations. Why confront the hazards of outer space when we should be fighting homelessness, poverty, and unemployment on Earth?

Notes

Your Paraphrase

_____

_____

_____

_____

_____

_____

Original Passage 4

Source: Page 48 of a nine-page magazine article written by Jeffrey Kluger. The article appeared on pages 42–50 in the January 26, 2004, issue of *Time* magazine. The title of the article is "Mission to Mars: First the Rover Lands, and Now Bush Wants to Send People. We Can Do It Even Faster Than Planned, but Here Is What It Will Take."

Speed is everything on the way to Mars and not only because a seven-month trip in a confined space can be torturous. The bigger problem is that it can be lethal because of radiation exposure in deep space, where the absence of Earth's magnetic field leaves astronauts far more exposed to deadly cosmic energy than they are in orbit or on the way to the moon.

Notes

Your Paraphrase

_____

_____

_____

_____

_____

Using Paraphrases as Support

The purpose of learning to paraphrase is to be able to use paraphrases as supporting material in your writing. As you read the following model, notice how a student in a media studies class used a paraphrase of a passage from on online news article to support her idea.

MODEL

Using Paraphrases as Support

Original Passage

Source: Paragraph 2 of an article written by Kivi Leroux in the online magazine *E Magazine* titled "Subliminal Messages: Primetime TV Programs Educate Viewers on the Environment." It appeared in the "Currents" section of the July–August 1999 edition.

For 10 years, the Environmental Media Association (EMA) has been working to weave the environment into prime-time television programming. Created by and for professionals in the entertainment industry, EMA works with the stars in front of the cameras as well as the creative staff behind them to include environmental themes in scripts, show environmental products on sets, and make environmentally sound decisions in the studios.

Paraphrase

According to an article in *E Magazine*, environmental messages have been deliberately put into prime-time television shows for the past decade. Environmental Media Association, an organization of professionals in the entertainment business, encourages television actors, writers, directors, and producers to promote environmentalism in three ways: by using environmental issues in scripts, by using environmental products as props, and by making environmentally conscious choices in studios (Leroux, par. 2).

Writing Topic

Television programming in the United States is often criticized for promoting the wrong values. Do you agree or disagree with this criticism?

Completed Paragraph

Although it is sometimes true that television programming in the United States promotes the wrong values, I do not entirely agree. Many educational television channels promote good values. For example, the Discovery Channel, the History Channel, National Geographic, and other similar channels educate the public about science, history, nature, and the environment. Also, even prime-time television programming often provides a public service by spreading public service messages. In fact, environmental messages have been deliberately put into prime-time television shows for the past decade. Environmental Media Association, an organization of professionals in the entertainment business, encourages television actors, writers, directors, and producers to promote environmentalism in three ways: by using environmental issues in scripts, by using environmental products as props, and by making environmentally conscious choices in studios (Leroux, par. 2). Seeing the star of a prime-time television show recycling plastic bottles or using an environmentally friendly product is more persuasive than almost any other type of public service message. In short, television programs promote positive values in both direct and indirect ways.

PRACTICE 3

*Using
Paraphrases
as Support*

Some people feel that we should not send a manned spacecraft to Mars. Write a paragraph in which you agree with this statement.

Step 1 Write a topic sentence that states your opinion.
Step 2 Write several supporting sentences, using paraphrases that you wrote in Practice 2 (pages 132–134) to support your points. Include some additional supporting sentences and transition signals to connect the ideas and make your paragraph flow smoothly.
Step 3 Add an in-text citation at the end of each paraphrase you use.

Summarizing

Another way to use borrowed information from an outside source is to summarize it. What is the difference between a paraphrase and a summary? When you retell a story that someone has told you, you repeat the story in your own words. If your retelling is about the same length as the original, it is a paraphrase. If you shorten the story—retelling only the most important points and leaving out the details—it is a summary.

MODEL

*Paraphrase and
Summary*

Original Passage (85 words)

Language is the main means of communication between peoples. But so many different languages have developed that language has often been a barrier rather than an aid to understanding among peoples. For many years, people have dreamed of setting up an international universal language which all people could speak and understand. The arguments in favor of a universal language are simple and obvious. If all peoples spoke the same tongue, cultural and economic ties might be much closer, and good will might increase between countries (Kispert).

Paraphrase (63 words, about the same length as the original)

Humans communicate through language. Because there are so many different languages, however, people around the world have a difficult time understanding one another. Some people have wished for a universal international language that speakers all over the world could understand. Their reasons are straightforward and clear. A universal language would build cultural and economic bonds. It would also create better feelings among countries (Kispert).

Summary (28 words, much shorter)

People communicate through language; however, having different languages creates communication barriers. A universal language could bring countries together culturally and economically as well as increase good feelings among them (Kispert).

Writing Technique Questions
1. How many sentences are there in the original passage? In the paraphrase? In the summary?
2. Compare the paraphrase and the summary. What two details were left out of the summary?

How to Write a Good Summary

There are three keys to writing a good summary:

1. Use your own words and your own sentence structure.
2. Remember that a summary is much shorter than a paraphrase. Include only the main points and main supporting points, leaving out most details.
3. Do not change the meaning of the original.

PRACTICE 4

Choosing the Best Summary

Read the original passage and the two summaries that follow it. Then answer these questions.

1. Which of the two is the better summary? Why?
2. Which summary contains an idea that was not in the original? Which sentence expresses this added idea?

Original Passage

Source: The following passage is excerpted from a newspaper article written by Marc Lacey. It appeared on page A3 of the *New York Times* on November 12, 2004. The title of the article is "Using a New Language in Africa to Save Dying Ones."

Swahili speakers wishing to use a "compyuta"—as *computer* is rendered in Swahili—have been out of luck when it comes to communicating in their tongue. Computers, no matter how bulky their hard drives or sophisticated their software packages, have not yet mastered Swahili or hundreds of other indigenous African languages.

But that may soon change. Across the continent, linguists are working with experts in information technology to make computers more accessible to Africans who happen not to know English, French, or the other major languages that have been programmed into the world's desktops.

There are economic reasons for the outreach. Microsoft, which is working to incorporate Swahili into Microsoft Windows, Microsoft Office, and other popular programs, sees a market for its software among the roughly 100 million Swahili speakers in East Africa. The same goes for Google, which last month launched www.google.co.ke, offering a Kenyan version in Swahili of the popular search engine.

But the campaign to Africanize cyberspace is not all about the bottom line. There are hundreds of languages in Africa—some spoken only by a few dozen elders—and they are dying out at an alarming rate. The continent's linguists see the computers as one important way of saving them. UNESCO estimates that 90 percent of the world's 6,000 languages are not represented on the Internet and that one language disappears somewhere around the world every two weeks.

Summary A

People who speak Swahili who want to communicate using a "compyuta," which is the Swahili word for computer, are unable to do so in their own language. It makes no difference that computers have huge hard drives and sophisticated software. They cannot operate in Swahili or other African languages, of which there are hundreds. Soon, however, they may be able to. Linguists in Africa are working with information technology specialists to make computers operable to Africans who do not know any of the languages currently used on the Internet. Economics is bringing about this change. Microsoft sees a market for its software among Swahili speakers in East Africa. Google now has a search engine for speakers of Swahili in Kenya. Other software companies will probably soon develop products for African consumers. In addition to economics, there is another reason for making the computer accessible to Africans. Hundreds of African languages are dying out, and linguists view the computer as a way to save them. According to UNESCO estimates, 90 percent of the world's 6,000 languages are not on the Internet, and one language becomes extinct every day somewhere in the world. The hope is that computers can help save them (Lacey).

Summary B

Many Africans who do not speak any of the major languages on the Internet have been unable to use computers in their native languages. Computers cannot yet accommodate languages such as Swahili. However, that situation may soon change. Linguists and computer experts are working to develop computers that work in Swahili and other African languages. Economics is one reason for doing so. Computer companies such as Microsoft and Google see a potentially huge market for its products in Africa. Another important reason is to save languages that are in danger of becoming extinct (Lacey).

The steps for writing a summary are similar to those for writing a paraphrase.

Step 1 Read the original passage several times until you understand it fully. Look up any words that you don't understand.

Step 2 Decide what the important ideas are. It helps to underline important ideas. It also helps to take notes. Write down only a few words for each idea—not complete sentences.

Step 3 Write your summary from your notes. Don't look at the original while you are writing.

Step 4 Check your summary against the original to make sure you have not changed the meaning.

Step 5 Add an in-text citation at the end of the summary.

PRACTICE 5

Writing Summaries

Write a one-paragraph summary of each of the following passages.

Step 1 Read the original passage several times until you understand it well. You may find it helpful to underline the main points.

Step 2 Make notes in the space provided, changing vocabulary words wherever possible.

Step 3 Write a summary of each passage in your own words.

Step 4 Add an in-text citation at the end of each summary.

Original Passage 1

Source: Various paragraphs of a news article written by Randolph E. Schmid. It was published online by the Associated Press on February 26, 2004. The title of the article is "Share of people who are native English speakers declining." The article is 25 paragraphs long. The Web site address is <http://pqasb.pqarchiver.com/ap/571281251.html?did=571281251&FMT=ABS&FMTS=FT&date=Feb+26%2C+2004&author=RANDOLPH+E.+SCHMID&desc=Share+of+people+who+are+native+English+speakers+declining.

The world faces a future of people speaking more than one language, with English no longer seen as likely to become dominant, a British language expert says in a new analysis. "English is likely to remain one of the world's most important languages for the foreseeable future, but its future is more problematic—and complex—than most people appreciate," said language researcher David Graddol (Schmid, pars. 1–2).

He sees English as likely to become the "first among equals" rather than having the global field to itself (par. 3). . . . The share of the world's population that speaks English as a native language is falling, Graddol reports in a paper in Friday's issue of the journal *Science* (par. 5).

"There is a distinct consciousness in many countries, both developed and developing, about this dominance of English. There is some evidence of resistance to it, a desire to change it" said [Scott] Montgomery [the author of another article published in the same issue of *Science*]. For example, he said, in the early years of the Internet it was dominated by sites in English, but in recent years there has been a proliferation of non-English sites, especially Spanish, German, French, Japanese, and others (pars. 19–20).

Nonetheless, English is strong as a second language, and teaching it has become a growth industry, said Montgomery, a Seattle-based geologist and energy consultant (par. 21).

Graddol noted, though, that employers in parts of Asia are already looking beyond English. "In the next decade the new 'must learn' language is likely to be Mandarin" (par. 22).

Notes

Summary

_____

_____

_____

_____

_____

_____

_____

_____

Original Passage 2
Source: Paragraphs 1 and 2 from a December 20, 2001, online article entitled "A world empire by other means." The author's name is not given. It was published on Economist.com, the Web site of a British magazine. The Web site address is <http://www.economist.com/displaystory.cfm?story_id=S%26% 2BXL%2FRA%5F%24%0A>

It [English] is everywhere. Some 380 million people speak it as their first language and perhaps two-thirds as many again as their second. A billion are learning it, about a third of the world's population are in some sense exposed to it, and by 2050, it is predicted, half the world will be more or less proficient in it. It is the language of globalization—of international business, politics, and diplomacy. It is the language of computers and the Internet. You'll see it on posters in Côte d'Ivoire, you'll hear it in pop songs in Tokyo, you'll read it in official documents in Phnom Penh. Deutsche Welle broadcasts in it. Bjork, an Icelander, sings in it. French business schools teach in it. It is the medium of expression in cabinet meetings in Bolivia. Truly, the tongue spoken back in the 1300s only by the "low people" of England, as Robert of Gloucester put it at the time, has come a long way. It is now the global language.

How come? Not because English is easy. True, genders are simple, since English relies on "it" as the pronoun for all inanimate nouns, reserving masculine for bona fide males and feminine for females (and countries and ships). But the verbs tend to be irregular, the grammar bizarre, and the match between spelling and pronunciation a nightmare. English is now so widely spoken in so many places that umpteen versions have evolved, some so peculiar that even "native" speakers may have trouble understanding each other. But if only one version existed, that would present difficulties enough. Even everyday English is a language of subtlety, nuance, and complexity. John Simmons, a language consultant for Interbrand, likes to cite the word "set," an apparently simple word that takes on different meanings in a sporting, cooking, social, or mathematical context—and that is before any little words are combined with it. Then, as a verb, it becomes "set aside," "set up," "set down," "set in," "set on," "set about," "set against," and so on, terms that "leave even native speakers bewildered about [its] core meaning."

Notes

Summary

_____
_____
_____
_____
_____
_____
_____
_____
_____

PRACTICE 6

Using Summaries as Support

Some people say that English is easy to learn, but difficult to master. Write a paragraph in which you agree with this statement.

Step 1 Begin with a clear topic sentence.

Step 2 Support your topic sentence with a summary—or a part of a summary—that you wrote in Practice 5. If you wish, include examples from your own knowledge and experience.

Step 3 Add an in-text citation at the end of each piece of summarized information you use.

Review

These are the important points you should have learned from this chapter.

1. In academic writing, you are expected to use information from outside sources to support your ideas. In addition to using quotations, you may also use paraphrases and summaries.
   - Paraphrase: Rewrite the author's meaning in your own words. Include all or almost all of the ideas that are in the original. Change the sentence structure and substitute synonyms where possible to avoid plagiarizing.
   - Summary: Condense a writer's words and summarize the main ideas in as few of your own words as possible.
2. Keep in mind that the U.S. system of education values students' original thinking and writing. Use outside sources *to support your own ideas*. Don't write a paper that contains only the ideas of others.
3. Don't just drop a paraphrase or summary into your paper. Make the connection between the borrowed information and your idea clear.
4. Document your sources to avoid plagiarizing and to help the reader find the sources of your information.

Argumentative Essays

Mani stones, Nepal

An **argumentative essay** is an essay in which you agree or disagree with an issue, using reasons to support your opinion. Your goal is to convince your reader that your opinion is right. Argumentation is a popular kind of essay question because it forces students to think on their own: They have to take a stand on an issue, support their stand with solid reasons, and support their reasons with solid evidence.

In a general writing test such as the TOEFL exam, you might encounter questions such as these:

The U.S. Declaration of Independence states that "all men are created equal." Agree or disagree with this statement. Support your opinion with reasons and examples.

The most important element in a friendship is trust. Agree or disagree with this statement. Support your opinion with reasons and examples.

In an academic class, your instructor might ask questions such as these:

CRIMINAL JUSTICE

Some cities in the United States and the United Kingdom have passed laws establishing curfews for young people. Young people (usually age 17 and younger) may not be out on the streets after 9 or 10 P.M. Do you agree or disagree with such curfews?

HEALTH SCIENCES

Stem cell research offers a potential cure for many fatal diseases. Many people oppose stem cell research because it involves using cells from human embryos. Do you agree or disagree that stem cell research should be prohibited?

BUSINESS ETHICS

Companies that do business abroad sometimes find that local business practices include activities considered unethical at home—offering gifts of money or awarding contracts to family members, for example. Should companies go along with local business practices in order to become successful, or should they refuse to do so and risk failure as a result?

What is unique about an argumentative essay is that you do not just give reasons to support your point of view. You must also discuss the other side's reasons and then rebut them. (*Rebut* means to point out problems with the other side's reasons to prove that they are not good reasons.) We do this because we want readers to know that we have considered all sides of the issue. When we show that we are reasonable and open-minded, readers are more likely to listen to our point of view.

Organization of Argumentative Essays

There are several ways to organize an argumentative essay. You can use a block pattern or a point-by-point pattern. The outlines in the following chart show these two possible patterns.

Block Pattern	Point-by-Point Pattern

I. Introduction
Explanation of the issue
Thesis statement
	I. Introduction
	Explanation of the issue, including
	    a summary of the other side's
	    arguments
	Thesis statement

II. Body
Block 1
A. Summary of other side's arguments
B. Rebuttal to the first argument
C. Rebuttal to the second argument
D. Rebuttal to the third argument
 	
Block 2
E. Your first argument
F. Your second argument
G. Your third argument
	II. Body
	
	A. Statement of the other side's first
	    argument and rebuttal with your
	    own counterargument
	B. Statement of the other side's second
	    argument and rebuttal with your own
	    counterargument
	C. Statement of the other side's third
	    argument and rebuttal with your own
	    counterargument

III. Conclusion	**III.** Conclusion—may include a summary of your point of view

There are many variations on these two patterns. Which pattern you use will depend on your topic. With some topics, one pattern works better than others. The important thing is to present your side and rebut the other side in a logical and organized way.

As you read the following model essay, study its organization.

MODEL

Argumentation

Separating the Sexes, Just for the Tough Years

1   The middle school years (grades 7 and 8) are known to be the "tough years." These are the years when the uneven pace of girls' and boys' physical, emotional, and cognitive development is most noticeable. Girls are ahead of boys on all counts, and both suffer. Educators debate whether separating boys and girls during these difficult years might improve students' academic performance. Separate classes are now prohibited in public schools that receive federal funds, but a change in the federal law that prohibits them is under consideration. Although some parents and educators oppose same-sex classes, there is some evidence that separating boys and girls in middle school yields positive results.

2   Opponents of single-sex education claim that test scores of students in all-girl or all-boy classes are no higher than those of students in mixed classes ("Study").[1] However, the research is inconclusive. Despite the fact that some research shows no improvement in test scores, other research shows exactly opposite results (Blum).[2] More important, many psychologists believe that test scores are the wrong measuring sticks. They believe that self-confidence and self-esteem issues are more important than test scores. In same-sex classes, girls report increased confidence and improved attitudes toward math and science, for example ("Study"). These are results that cannot be calculated by a test but that will help adolescents become successful adults long after the difficult years of middle school are past. New York University professor Carol Gilligan is certain that girls are more likely to be "creative thinkers and risk-takers as adults if educated apart from boys in middle school" (Gross).[3] Boys, too, gain confidence when they do not have to compete with girls. Boys at this age become angry and fight back in middle school because they feel inferior when compared to girls, who literally "out-think" them. With no girls in the classroom, they are more at ease with themselves and more receptive to learning (Gross).

3   Opponents also maintain that separate classes (or separate schools) send the message that males and females cannot work together. They say that when students go into the work force, they will have to work side-by-side with the opposite sex, and attending all-girl or all-boy schools denies them the opportunity to learn how to do so ("North").[4] However, such an argument completely ignores the fact that children constantly interact with members of the

---

[1]"Study: All-Girls Schools Don't Improve Test Scores." CNNinteractive 12 Mar. 1998. 2 June 2004 <http://www.cnn.com/US/9803/same.sex.classes/>.

[2]Blum, Justin. "Scores Soar at D.C. School with Same-Sex Classes." washingtonpost.com 27 June 2002. 2 June 2004 <http://www.washingtonpost.com/ac2/wp-dyn/A52023–2002Jun26?/language=printer>.

[3]Gross, Jane. "Splitting Up Boys and Girls, Just for the Tough Years." The New York Times 31 May 2004: A16.

[4]"North Carolina School Stops Same-Sex Classes." American Civil Liberties Union News 5 Apr. 2000. 2 June 2004 <http://archive.aclu.org/news/2000/w040500d.html>.

opposite sex outside school. From playing and squabbling with siblings to negotiating allowances, chores, and privileges with their opposite-sex parent, children learn and practice on a daily basis the skills they will need in their future workplaces.

4   The final argument advanced by opponents of same-sex education is that it is discriminatory and, therefore, unconstitutional. However, research supports exactly the opposite conclusion: that discrimination is widespread in mixed classes. Several studies have shown that boys dominate discussions and receive more attention than girls and that teachers call on boys more often than they call on girls, even when girls raise their hands ("North"). Clearly, this is discriminatory.

5   It should be evident that the arguments against same-sex classes are not valid. On the contrary, many people involved in middle-school education say that same-sex classes provide a better learning environment. Boys and girls pay less attention to each other and more attention to their schoolwork (Marquez).[5] As one teacher noted, "Girls are more relaxed and ask more questions; boys are less disruptive and more focused" ("North"). Girls are less fearful of making mistakes and asking questions in math and science; boys are less inhibited about sharing their ideas in language and literature. Furthermore, schoolchildren are not disadvantaged by lack of contact with the opposite sex because they have many opportunities outside the school setting to interact with one another. Finally, discrimination occurs in mixed classes, so discrimination is not a valid argument. Therefore, in my opinion, the law prohibiting same-sex classes in public schools should be changed.

Writing Technique Questions

1. In which paragraph does the writer give background information to help readers understand the issue?
2. Does the thesis statement mention both sides of the issue, or does it give the writer's point of view only?
3. How many opposing arguments are given? Where are they given?
4. Where does the writer rebut the opposing arguments—in one paragraph or in separate paragraphs?
5. What is the function of the last paragraph?
6. Which type of organization does this essay use—block or point-by-point?

---

[5]Marquez, Laura. "No Distractions? Proposed Title IX Changes Would Allow Separate Classrooms for Girls and Boys." <u>ABC News</u> 13 May 2004. 2 June 2004 <http://abcnews.go.com/sections/WNT/US/same_sex_classrooms_040513.html>.

PRACTICE 1   Complete the outline of the model essay.

Outlining

Separating the Sexes, Just for the Tough Years

I. Introduction (explanation of the issue)

Thesis statement: _____

_____

II. Body

  A. Opposing argument 1

   Opponents of single-sex education claim that test scores show that there is no advantage to all-girl or all-boy classes.

   Rebuttal to argument 1

   1. Research is inconclusive—show opposite results
   2. Other results that cannot be calculated
      a. Girls _____
      b. Boys _____

  B. Opposing argument 2

   _____

   Rebuttal to argument 2

   _____

      a. Settling squabbles with siblings
      b. Negotiating with opposite-sex parent

  C. Opposing argument 3

   _____

   Rebuttal to argument 3

   _____

      a. _____
      b. Teachers call on boys more often

  D. Own point of view

   1. Same-sex classes provide a better learning environment
   2. Reasons
      a. Boys and girls _____
      b. Girls _____
      c. Boys _____

III. Conclusion

Five Keys

An argumentative essay contains these five key elements:

1. An explanation of the issue
2. A clear thesis statement
3. A summary of the opposing arguments
4. Rebuttals to the opposing arguments
5. Your own arguments

The Introductory Paragraph

The introductory paragraph of the model contains an explanation of the issue, which is a necessary part of an argumentative essay. However, you may also begin an argumentative essay with a more engaging introduction—with surprising statistics, for example, or with a dramatic story. For instance, the writer of the model essay could have opened with a dramatization of typical boys' and girls' behavior in a mixed middle school class.

If you write an attention-getting introduction, you may need to explain the issue in a second introductory paragraph and write your thesis statement at the end of this (the second) paragraph.

> In an eighth-grade English class at Kent Middle School, the students are discussing *The Diary of Anne Frank*, written by a 13-year-old Jewish girl while she hid with her family in an Amsterdam attic for more than two years during the Holocaust. The girls in the class identify easily with Anne and freely share their feelings about the book. The boys, by contrast, snicker[1] or snooze[2]—anything to avoid revealing any tender feelings. In the next class, math, the dynamic is reversed: The girls sit quietly, while the boys shout out answers and race each other to the blackboard to solve algebra equations. These scenes are typical in most middle school classes in the United States.
> The middle school years (grades 7 and 8) are known . . .

Thesis Statement

The thesis statement in an argumentative essay states clearly which side you are for:

> Curfew laws are unfair and should be abolished.

> In my opinion, stem cell research should receive the full support of our government.

A thesis statement often mentions the opposing point of view. Notice that the writer's opinion is expressed in the main (independent) clause, and the opposing point of view is normally put into a subordinate structure.

> SUBORDINATE STRUCTURE
> Despite the claims that curfew laws are necessary to control juvenile gangs,
> MAIN (INDEPENDENT) CLAUSE
> **curfew laws are clearly unconstitutional.**

> SUBORDINATE STRUCTURE
> Although there are certainly reasons to be cautious with stem cell research
> MAIN (INDEPENDENT) CLAUSE
> or any new technology, **I believe that its potential benefits far outweigh its dangers.**

---

[1]**snicker:** laugh quietly in a way that is not nice
[2]**snooze:** sleep

Use expressions such as the following to introduce opposing points of view.

> **Some people feel that** the United States should have a national health care plan like Canada's.
>
> **Many think that** genetically engineered crops are a grave danger to the environment.
>
> **Smokers say that** they have a right to smoke.
>
> **It may be true that** the U.S. Constitution gives citizens the right to own weapons.

Then connect the opposing point of view to your own with transition signals of contrast.

> Some people feel that the United States should have a national health care plan like Canada's**; however,** others feel that government should stay out of the health care business.
>
> **Although/Even though** many think that genetically engineered crops are a grave danger to the environment, such crops can alleviate world hunger and malnutrition.
>
> Smokers say that they have a right to smoke **in spite of the fact that/despite the fact that** smoking will kill them.
>
> **While/Whereas** it may be true that the U.S. Constitution gives citizens the right to own weapons, the men who wrote the Constitution lived in a different time.

PRACTICE 2

Thesis Statements

Add an opposing point of view to each of the following thesis statements. If necessary, rewrite the part of the sentence that is given to you. The first one has been done for you as an example.

1. Doctors or family members should never be allowed to "pull the plug."[1]
   <u>Although some people believe that doctors and family members should never be allowed to "pull the plug," I believe that it is sometimes more humane to do so.</u>

2. The sale of CDs with songs containing lyrics that degrade women should be prohibited.

   _____

   _____

3. Television is the worst invention of modern times.

   _____

   _____

4. Environmental protection laws go too far.

   _____

   _____

---

[1]**pull the plug:** let a person who is in an irreversible coma die by disconnecting him or her from life-sustaining machines

5. The advertising industry performs many public services.

_____

_____

6. Choose your own topic. Then write a thesis statement that expresses both sides of the issue.

_____

_____

PRACTICE 3

Supporting Arguments

Think of two or three supporting arguments for each thesis statement. Notice that two of the thesis statements state only the writer's point of view, and two state both sides of the argument. The first one has been done for you as an example.

1. Censorship of the arts is always wrong.
   a. <u>Freedom to express oneself is a fundamental right stated in the U.S. Bill of Rights.</u>
   b. <u>Public morality is relative—what is objectionable in some cultures is acceptable in others.</u>
   c. <u>Many masterpieces—books, sculptures, and paintings—would be banned.</u>

2. Violence in video games, movies, and television programs should be censored.
   a. _____
   b. _____
   c. _____

3. Despite the fact that education's primary responsibility is to train minds, not bodies, I believe that schools should require students to practice a sport at least one hour each day.
   a. _____
   b. _____
   c. _____

4. Although some people think that curfew laws will help control teenage gangs, they are wrong for several reasons.
   a. _____
   b. _____
   c. _____

5. Engaged couples should be required to take marriage preparation classes for one full year before their wedding.
   a. _____
   b. _____
   c. _____

6. Your own topic: _____
   a. _____
   b. _____
   c. _____

Review

These are the important points covered in this chapter.

1. An argumentative essay is a kind of essay in which you try to persuade your reader to agree with your opinion about a controversial topic.
2. An argumentative essay contains these five elements:
   - An explanation of the issue
   - A clear thesis statement
   - A summary of the opposing arguments
   - Rebuttals to the opposing arguments
   - Your own arguments
3. Use either a block pattern or a point-by-point pattern. Be sure to include the opposite point of view as well as your own.
4. Use contrast transition signals to connect opposing arguments and your counter-arguments.

Writing Practice

Choose topic 1 or 2 and write an argumentative essay.

1. Agree or disagree with the following statement:
   It is worth the expense and risk to make a manned flight to Mars.

2. Agree or disagree with the following statement:
   The future status of English as the global language is assured.

Writing an argumentative essay requires especially careful planning.

Step 1 Clarify in your mind what the two sides of the argument are. Decide which side you agree with.

Step 2 Write a thesis statement. Your thesis statement can state either just your point of view or both points of view.

Step 3 Research the topic to get ideas and supporting reasons for both sides of the argument. The readings for this chapter on pages 151–152 and 154–155 provide material for your essay. Read the articles and do the exercises for your topic before you begin this writing assignment. You should use quotations, summaries, or paraphrases from the appropriate parts of the readings to support your arguments. You may also use material from Practices 1, 2, and 5 in Chapter 8 in your essay.

Step 4 Decide whether you will use block or point-by-point organization. Then develop an outline similar to one of the outlines on page 143.

Step 5 Write your first draft. Write an explanatory or an attention-getting introduction, as you prefer.

Step 6 Use the Self-Editing Worksheet on page 329 and revise your essay if necessary.

Step 7 Exchange papers with a classmate. Review each other's essays and complete the Peer-Editing Worksheet on page 330.

Step 8 Make changes if necessary and write a final copy to hand in to your instructor. Your instructor may ask you to hand in your outline, drafts, and editing worksheets along with your final copy.

Step 9 If your instructor asks you to use formal documentation of your sources, prepare a Works Cited list. Learn how in Appendix E, pages 308–311.

Applying What You Have Learned

Argumentative Essays

Topic 1

It is/is not worth the expense and risk to make a manned flight to Mars.

Reading 1
This reading presents several arguments in favor of sending a manned flight to Mars.

Why We Should Send a Manned Mission to Mars[1]

1   Mars has fascinated Earth-bound humans since prehistoric times, due to its captivating red hue and proximity and similarity to Earth. The romance of space travel and the exploration of new worlds is a major argument in favor of a manned mission to Mars. Supporters claim that exploring and colonizing the moon and Mars will give us a better understanding of our own home planet, Earth. Other supporters are motivated by feelings of national pride, saying the prestige of the United States is at stake. Still others believe that the research required by such a complex mission will help the United States retain its position as a leader in science and technology.

2   The success of the Apollo program in the 1960s and 1970s created a generation of astronaut heroes that inspired the nation. "In 1969, America sent men to the moon, not machines," Ben Wattenberg said on PBS's *Think Tank*. "[H]uman beings are exploratory creatures . . . mankind needs big ideas and big projects to ennoble and inspire society. Don't our little boys and girls need heroes and heroines to say, 'Look at him, look at her, she's there'?" President George W. Bush once said in an address to the nation, "Mankind is drawn to the heavens for the same reason we were once drawn to unknown lands and across the open sea. We choose to explore space because doing so improves our lives and lifts our national spirit."

3   Many supporters of manned travel to Mars argue that because of its similarity to Earth, Mars offers opportunities to discover the origins of life and ways to protect the environment on Earth.

4   "We cling to the hope of a neighboring planet that harbors . . . at least some primitive forms of life. If Mars contains even nanobacteria—or indisputable evidence of past life of the simplest forms—this will profoundly change our conception of our place in the universe," wrote Thomas Gangale. "If Mars is dead now, but was once alive, understanding how Mars died may give us a crucial understanding of how close we are coming to killing the Earth."

---

[1] Adapted from Joulwan, Melissa. "You Decide: Manned Mission to Mars." 13 May 2004 KQED 13 May 2004. 10 June 2004 <http://www.kqed.org/topics/news/perspectives/youdecide/pop/mars/index.jsp?flash=true>.

5   The Mars Society [a group that supports Mars exploration] shares that opinion. In its Founding Declaration, the society wrote, "As we begin the twenty-first century, we have evidence that we are changing the Earth's atmosphere and environment in significant ways. . . . Mars, the planet most like Earth, will have even more to teach us about our home world. The knowledge we gain could be key to our survival."

6   And many scientists assert that the best way to attain that knowledge is with human scientists. "Robots can do a lot," Chris Welch, a lecturer in space technology at Kingston University, told the BBC. "But having multiple trained human beings there would tell us so much more." Dava Newman, associate professor of aeronautics at the Massachusetts Institute of Technology, agreed. "It's risky and it's also very costly, but there's just so much humans can do as explorers that we don't have any other way to accomplish."

7   China, Russia, and the European Union have all announced plans to boost their space programs in coming years, including sojourns to the moon and Mars. Some people believe it's essential to U.S. international status that the United States lead the way in space exploration. "Republican officials said conservative lawmakers who might balk at the cost [of a manned mission to Mars] are likely to be lured by the chance to extend the U.S. military supremacy in space when China is pursuing lunar probes and Russia is considering a Mars mission," Mike Allen and Eric Pianin wrote in *The Washington Post*.

8   The European Space Agency (ESA) has developed a long-term plan—known as Aurora—that will use robotics to first explore low-Earth orbit and then move farther out into planetary excursions, including Mars. The ESA intends to send a rover to Mars by 2009 and a manned mission to the moon by 2024 that will "demonstrate key life support and habitation technologies as well as aspects of crew performance and adaptation." The final step in the Aurora program is a human mission to Mars in the 2030s.

9   Regaining the top position in science and technology is another reason to support a Mars mission. According to *The New York Times*, the dominance the United States once had in science and innovation has declined in recent years as the number of international prizes and journal publications awarded to European and Asian researchers has increased. Jennifer Bond, vice president for international affairs for the Council on Competitiveness said, "Many other countries have realized that science and technology are key to economic growth and prosperity. They're catching up to us." She warned that people in the United States should not "rest on their laurels." A poll by the Associated Press seems to indicate that many people in the United States agree with her. Seventy-two percent of respondents in the poll deemed it important for the United States to be the "leading country in the world in the exploration of space."

10   "America is not going to remain at peace, and we're not going to remain the most prosperous nation, and we're not going to remain a free nation unless we remain the technological leader of the world," said Representative Dana Rohrabacher, chairman of the House Subcommittee on Space and Aeronautics. "And we will not remain the technological leader of the world unless we are the leaders in space."

Questions

1. Paragraph 1 summarizes four reasons why the United States should send a manned mission to Mars. List them here.

   a. _____

   b. _____

   c. _____

   d. _____

2. Which paragraph discusses the first reason? _____
   In your opinion, which sentence in the paragraph expresses this reason most clearly and concisely? Copy the sentence here. _____
   _____

3. Which paragraph(s) discuss(es) the second reason? _____
   Summarize the reason here. _____
   _____
   _____
   _____
   _____
   _____
   _____
   _____
   _____

4. Which paragraph(s) discuss(es) the third reason? _____
   Summarize the reason here. _____
   _____
   _____
   _____
   _____
   _____
   _____
   _____

5. Which paragraph(s) discuss(es) the fourth reason? _____
   Summarize the reason here. _____
   _____
   _____
   _____
   _____
   _____
   _____

Reading 2

This article from a popular weekly news magazine argues against sending a manned spacecraft to explore Mars.

Why We Shouldn't Go to Mars: Someday people may walk on the planet, but not until it makes technological sense[1]

1   "Two centuries ago, Meriwether Lewis and William Clark left St. Louis to explore the new lands acquired in the Louisiana Purchase," George W. Bush said, announcing his desire for a program to send men and women to Mars.[2] "They made that journey in the spirit of discovery. . . . America has ventured forth into space for the same reasons."

2   Yet there are vital differences between Lewis and Clark's expedition and a Mars mission. First, Lewis and Clark were headed to a place amenable to life; hundreds of thousands of people were already living there. Second, Lewis and Clark were certain to discover places and things of immediate value to the new nation. Third, the Lewis and Clark venture cost next to nothing by today's standards. In 1989 NASA estimated that a people-to-Mars program would cost $400 billion, which inflates to $600 billion today. The Hoover Dam cost $700 million in today's money, meaning that sending people to Mars might cost as much as building about 800 new Hoover Dams. A Mars mission may be the single most expensive non-wartime undertaking in U.S. history.

3   The thought of travel to Mars is exhilarating. Surely men and women will someday walk upon that planet, and surely they will make wondrous discoveries about geology and the history of the solar system, perhaps even about the very origin of life. Many times I have stared up at Mars in the evening sky—in the mountains, away from cities, you can almost see the red tint—and wondered what is there or was there.

4   But the fact that a destination is tantalizing does not mean the journey makes sense, even considering the human calling to explore. And Mars as a destination for people makes absolutely no sense with current technology.

5   Present systems for getting from Earth's surface to low-Earth orbit are so fantastically expensive that merely launching the 1,000 tons or so of spacecraft and equipment a Mars mission would require could be accomplished only by cutting health-care benefits, education spending, or other important programs— or by raising taxes. Absent some remarkable discovery, astronauts, geologists, and biologists once on Mars could do little more than analyze rocks and feel awestruck beholding the sky of another world. Yet rocks can be analyzed by automated probes without risk to human life, and at a tiny fraction of the cost of sending people.

6   It is interesting to note that when President Bush unveiled his proposal, he listed these recent major achievements of space exploration: pictures of the rings of Saturn and the outer planets, evidence of water on Mars and the moons of Jupiter, discovery of more than 100 planets outside our solar system, and study of the soil of Mars. All these accomplishments came from automated probes or

---

[1]Easterbrook, Greg. "Why We Shouldn't Go to Mars: Someday people may walk on the planet, but not until it makes technological sense." Time 26 Jan. 2004: 51.

[2]The Louisiana Purchase was a very large area of land that was bought by the United States from France in 1803. Two men, Lewis and Clark, spent more than two years exploring and mapping the area.

automated space telescopes. Bush's proposal, which calls for "reprogramming" some of NASA's present budget into the Mars effort, might actually lead to a reduction in such unmanned science—the one aspect of space exploration that's working really well.

7   Rather than spend hundreds of billions of dollars to hurl tons toward Mars using current technology, why not take a decade—or two decades, or however much time is required—researching new launch systems and advanced propulsion? If new launch systems could put weight into orbit affordably, and if advanced propulsion could speed up that long, slow transit to Mars, then the dream of stepping onto the red planet might become reality. Mars will still be there when the technology is ready.

8   Space exploration proponents deride as lack of vision the mention of technical barriers or the insistence that needs on Earth come first. Not so. The former is rationality, the latter the setting of priorities. If Mars proponents want to raise $600 billion privately and stage their own expedition, more power to them; many of the great expeditions of the past were privately mounted. If Mars proponents expect taxpayers to foot their bill, then they must make their case against the many other competing needs for money. And against the needs for health care, education, poverty reduction, reinforcement of the military, and reduction of the federal deficit, the case for vast expenditures to go to Mars using current technology is very weak.

9   The drive to explore is part of what makes us human, and exploration of the past has led to unexpected glories. Dreams must be tempered by realism, however. For the moment, going to Mars is hopelessly unrealistic.

Questions

1. Most of paragraph 1 is a quotation by George W. Bush. Rewrite the direct quotation as an indirect quotation. Be sure to include a reporting phrase.

   _____

   _____

   _____

2. Paragraph 2 begins with a transition signal that signals contrast.
   a. What two things are contrasted? _____ and

      _____

   b. On what three points are they contrasted?
      (1) _____
      (2) _____
      (3) _____

3. Paragraph 4 contains the thesis statement for the essay. Copy it here. _____

   _____

   _____

4. Paragraphs 5, 6, 7, and 8 mention several reasons for not sending a manned spacecraft to Mars. Summarize the reasons here. _____

_____

_____

_____

_____

_____

_____

_____

_____

_____

_____

5. What kind of conclusion does this essay have?
   a. It summarizes arguments against a manned Mars mission.
   b. It paraphrases the thesis statement.

Topic 2

The future status of English as the global language is/is not assured.

Reading 1

This article, from a British weekly news magazine, discusses the reasons that English has become the dominant language around the world.

The World Language[1]

1   India has about a billion people and a dozen major languages of its own. One language, and only one, is understood—by an elite—across the country: that of the foreigners who ruled it for less than 200 years and left 52 years ago. After 1947, English had to share its official status with north India's Hindi and was due to lose it in 1965. It did not happen: Southern India said no.

2   Today, India. Tomorrow, unofficially, the world. [The spread of English] is well under way; at first, because the British not only built a global empire but settled America, and now because the world (and notably America) has acquired its first truly global—and interactive—medium, the Internet.

3   David Crystal, a British expert, estimates that some 350 million people speak English as their first language. Maybe 250–350 million do or can use it as a second language; in ex-colonial countries, notably, or in English-majority ones, like 30 million recent immigrants to the United States or Canada's 6 million francophone Quebeckers. And elsewhere? That is a heroic guess: 100 million to 1 billion is Mr. Crystal's, depending how you define "can." Let us be bold: In all, 20–25 percent of Earth's 6 billion people can use English; not the English of England, let alone of Dr. Johnson, but English.

---

[1]"The World Language." <u>The Economist. Millennium Issue</u> 31 Dec. 1999: 85.

4   That number is soaring as each year brings new pupils to school and carries off monolingual oldies—and now as the Internet spreads. And the process is self-reinforcing. As business spreads across frontiers, the company that wants to move its executives around and to promote the best of them, regardless of nationality, encourages the use of English. So the executive who wants to be in the frame or to move to another employer learns to use it. English has long dominated learned journals: German, Russian or French (depending on the field) may be useful to their expert readers, but English is essential. So, if you want your own work published—and widely read by your peers—then English is the language of choice.

5   The growth of the cinema, and still more so of television, has spread the dominant language. Foreign movies or sitcoms may be dubbed into major languages, but for smaller audiences they are usually subtitled. Result: A Dutch or Danish or even Arab family has an audiovisual learning aid in its living room, and usually the language spoken on screen is English.

6   The birth of the computer and its American operating systems gave English a nudge ahead; that of the Internet has given it a huge push. Any Web-linked household today has a library of information available at the click of a mouse. And, unlike the books on its own shelves or in the public library, maybe four-fifths is written in English. That proportion may lessen, as more non-English sites spring up. But English will surely dominate.

7   The Web of course works both ways. An American has far better access today than ever before to texts in German or Polish or Gaelic. But the average American has no great incentive to profit from it. That is not true the other way round. The Web may even save some minilanguages. But the big winner will be English.

Questions

1. Paraphrase paragraph 3, which gives several statistics about the number of people who use English. _____

   _____

   _____

   _____

   _____

   _____

   _____

   _____

2. How many reasons are given in paragraphs 4 and 5 for the spread of English throughout the world? _____ List them here. _____

   _____

   _____

3. Copy a sentence from paragraph 4 that best expresses the idea that business helps spread the use of English. Include a reporting phrase that names the source of the quoted sentence. _____

_____

_____.

4. Summarize paragraphs 5 and 6 in two or three sentences. _____

_____

_____

_____

_____

_____

Reading 2

This newspaper article contains support for the view that English is not destined to become the world language. It tells about a law that was considered in Brazil to prohibit the use of English in some areas of Brazilian life. The original article was divided into many short paragraphs, which is the style used in newspapers because newspaper columns are narrow. Here, paragraphs have been combined to improve the coherence.

Brazil Considers Linguistic Barricade[1]

1   In Brazil's shopping malls, the massive consumerist shrines formerly known here as *centros comerciais*, windows that used to advertise a *promoção* now trumpet "Sale." *Descontos* has become "50 percent off," and the upcoming collections that were once billed as *primavera/verão* are now touted as "spring/summer." A hairdressing salon calls itself Exuberant; a watch store is named Overtime; a restaurant goes by the name New Garden.

2   In Brazil, the largest Portuguese-speaking nation in the world, English is taking over. And Deputy Aldo Rebelo says "Basta!" "It is time to fight this disrespect of our language," says Mr. Rebelo, the author of a new bill designed to "promote and defend" the Lusitanian [Portuguese] language. "People feel humiliated and offended by having to pronounce words in a language that is not theirs. But they are obliged to, because shop owners or other people want to exhibit a false knowledge," Rebelo says. "This is the public domain; people need to buy things, to go into shopping centers, but people cannot communicate fluently because of the abuse of foreign expressions in our language."

3   Rebelo's tongue-lashing against linguistic invasion is a reaction to globalization's march. He is not alone in the defense of mother tongues. Poland recently passed a law to enforce language purity by banning foreign words from everyday transactions unless Polish translations are provided alongside. A Polish language council will catch violators, who could face stiff fines. Poland's campaign has been compared to the notorious French effort to stamp out "franglais."

4   With 178 million native speakers worldwide, Portuguese ranks seventh among most-spoken native languages after Mandarin, Hindi, Spanish, English, Arabic, and Bengali.

---

[1]Downie, Andrew. "Brazil Considers Linguistic Barricade." <u>Christian Science Monitor</u> 6 Sep. 2000: 26 pars. 13 Sep. 2004 <http://csmonitor.com/cgi-bin/durableRedirect.pl?/durable/2000/09/06/fp7s2-csm.shtml>.

5   Rebelo's bill . . . rejects the increasing influx of English expressions and requires that Brazil's native tongue be used in business, formal, and social situations. While those strictures are laughed off by many as unenforceable—one envisions "language police" monitoring cafe chatter and the like—Rebelo's bill thunders that those not respecting Portuguese are "damaging Brazil's cultural patrimony." The linguistic outlaws would face as yet undecided punishment—perhaps classes in Portuguese, Rebelo has suggested.

6   One goal of the bill is linguistic purity among government officials, Rebelo says, citing the offenses of President Fernando Henrique Cardoso, who recently used the English expression "fast track" in a speech.

7   The bill would particularly affect the worlds of finance and commerce, where throwing up a sign in English is seen as a trendy way of grabbing potential customers' attention. According to a recent study, 93 of the 252 stores in São Paulo's Morumbi shopping center featured English words in their names. That would change under Rebelo's law. The owners of Laundromat would have to wash their hands of the name. Hot dogs would be off the menu, and personal trainers would have to find a new way to describe their services. The Banco do Brasil's "Personal Banking" would need to translate itself, and the Rock in Rio music festival would have to dance to a different tune. Children's clothing store Kid Smart would lose its exotic appeal in a country where most people do not speak English.

8   Although Rebelo recognizes that in today's fast-paced and shrinking world, words like "e-mail," "mouse," and "delete" have entered Portuguese almost overnight, he says the rush to use English words ignores the fact that in many cases perfectly good Portuguese ones already exist. "We can say *entrega a domicílio* because everyone knows what it means, so why use the word 'delivery'?" Rebelo asks, highlighting one recent fad. "Restaurants use 'valet parking,' but why not use *maniobrista*? This law will prohibit these abuses."

9   Linguistic experts agree and point to the richness of Portuguese. Used as an official language in seven countries outside of Portugal, Portuguese boasts 24 vowel sounds, compared with five in English, and includes more than 350,000 words derived primarily from Latin, Arabic, and Iberian tribal languages.

10   Antonio Olinto, an author and member of the Brazilian Academy of Letters, says that, although it is impossible to legislate how people talk, the proposal has value because it has created a debate about the use of foreign words in Brazil. While stopping the trend is impossible, he says, Brazil can counter the linguistic invasion by adapting its language, just as it did with the word "football" (soccer), which over time became *futebol*. "Globalization exists, and I don't think there is any way of escaping it," says Mr. Olinto. "But in time, words will be adapted into Portuguese, and things will get better." Rebelo acknowledges that the desire to speak English may eventually ebb, but he called on Brazilians meanwhile to use their mother tongue whenever possible.

11   The legislator advises those tempted to utter or write foreign words to consult the style book of *O Estado de São Paulo*, one of the nation's biggest newspapers, which offers the following wordy wisdom: "(1) You have a language, Portuguese, that is just as good and as functional as any other. (2) It is your language."

12   But it's the cash register, not linguistic pride, that inspires lingerie store manager Silvana Cannone when she's looking for just the right word. "We cut the letters out ourselves, and 'Sale' is shorter than *Promoção*, so it's easier," she explains, "Nowadays, everyone knows what 'sale' means. And besides, it sounds more chic."

Questions

1. The introductory paragraph to this essay is
   a. a funnel introduction.
   b. a historical introduction.
   c. a series of examples

2. The main topic of this essay is
   a. a proposed law in Brazil banning the use of English in certain situations.
   b. the prevalence of English in Brazil.
   c. the reasons English is popular among shopkeepers and other businesses in Brazil.

3. Find the sentence that, in your opinion, best expresses the main topic and paraphrase it here. _____
   _____
   _____
   _____
   _____

4. Summarize Mr. Rebolo's reasons. _____
   _____
   _____
   _____
   _____
   _____
   _____
   _____

5. Find a paragraph that discusses other countries' opposition to English. Write a one-sentence summary of that paragraph here. _____
   _____
   _____
   _____

Sentence Structure

Types of Sentences

Page from the Gutenberg Bible, 15th century

Clauses

Clauses are the building blocks of sentences. A clause is a group of words that contains (at least) a subject and a verb.

Clauses	Not clauses
SUBJECT VERB ecology is a science	to protect the environment
SUBJECT VERB because pollution causes cancer	after working all day

There are two kinds of clauses: independent and dependent.

Independent Clauses

An **independent clause** contains a subject and a verb and expresses a complete thought. It can stand alone as a sentence by itself. An independent clause is formed with a subject and a verb and often a complement.

Subject	Verb	(Complement)
The sun	rose.	
Water	evaporates	rapidly in warm climate zones.

Dependent Clauses

A **dependent clause** begins with a subordinator such as *when, while, if, that*, or *who*. A dependent clause does not express a complete thought, so it is not a sentence by itself. A dependent clause is also called a *sentence fragment*. By itself, it is an incomplete sentence, and it is an error. A dependent clause is formed with a subordinator, a subject, and a verb.

Subordinator	Subject	Verb	(Complement)
. . . when	the sun	rose . . .	
. . . because	water	evaporates	rapidly in warm climate zones . . .
. . . whom	the voters	elected . . .	
. . . if	the drought	continues	for another year . . .

A few of the most common subordinators follow. For a complete list, turn to Appendix C, pages 292–295.

Subordinators

after	before	that	when	which
although	even though	though	whenever	while
as, just as	how	unless	where	who
as if	if	until	wherever	whom
as soon as	since	what	whether	whose
because	so that			

PRACTICE 1

Independent and Dependent Clauses

Remember that an independent clause by itself is a complete sentence, but a dependent clause by itself is an incomplete sentence. Write *Indep.* next to the complete sentences and put a period (.) after them. Write *Dep.* next to the incomplete sentences. The first two have been done for you as examples.

    Indep.   1. Globalization means more travel for businessmen and women.

    Dep.   2. As business executives fly around the globe to sell their companies' products and services

    _____ 3. Jet lag affects most long-distance travelers

    _____ 4. Which is simply the urge to sleep at inappropriate times

    _____ 5. During long journeys through several time zones, the body's inner clock is disrupted

    _____ 6. For some reason, travel from west to east causes greater jet lag than travel from east to west

_____ 7. Also, changes in work schedules can cause jet lag

_____ 8. When hospital nurses change from a day shift to a night shift, for example

_____ 9. Although there is no sure way to prevent jet lag

_____ 10. There are some ways to minimize it

_____ 11. Because jet lag is caused at least partially by loss of sleep, not just a change in the time of sleep

_____ 12. A traveler should plan to arrive at his or her destination as late as possible

_____ 13. Upon arriving, he or she should immediately go to bed

_____ 14. Then the traveler should start to live in the new time zone immediately

_____ 15. Even when the traveler arrives early in the morning and cannot go to bed immediately

Kinds of Sentences

A sentence is a group of words that you use to communicate your ideas. Every sentence is formed from one or more clauses and expresses a complete thought.

The four basic kinds of sentences in English are simple, compound, complex, and compound-complex. The kind of sentence is determined by the kind of clauses used to form it.

Simple Sentences

A **simple sentence** is one independent clause.

Freshwater boils at 100 degrees Celsius at sea level.

Freshwater boils at 100 degrees and freezes at 0 degrees Celsius.

Freshwater and salt water do not boil and do not freeze at the same temperatures.

Notice that the second sentence has two verbs, *boils* and *freezes*. This is called a compound verb. The third sentence has both a compound subject and a compound verb. All three examples are simple sentences because they have only one clause.

PRACTICE 2

Simple Sentences

Use a separate sheet of paper for this exercise.

1. Write two simple sentences with one subject and one verb.
2. Write two simple sentences with one subject and two verbs.
3. Write two simple sentences with two subjects and one verb.
4. Write two simple sentences with two subjects and two verbs.

Compound Sentences

A **compound sentence** is two or more independent clauses joined together. There are three ways to join the clauses:

1. With a coordinator

   Salt water boils at a higher temperature than freshwater, **so** food cooks faster in salt water.

2. With a conjunctive adverb

   Salt water boils at a higher temperature than freshwater; **therefore,** food cooks faster in salt water.

3. With a semicolon

   Salt water boils at a higher temperature than freshwater; food cooks faster in salt water.

Let's study each type of compound sentence in more detail.

Compound Sentences with Coordinators

A compound sentence can be formed as follows:

Independent clause, + coordinator + independent clause

Salt water boils at a lower temperature than freshwater, **so** food cooks faster in salt water.

There are seven coordinators, which are also called coordinating conjunctions. You can remember them by the phrase FAN BOYS (For, And, Nor, But, Or, Yet, So). The following sentences illustrate the meanings of the seven FAN BOYS coordinators. (*Punctuation note*: There is a comma after the first independent clause.)

Coordinators (Coordinating Conjunctions)

To add a reason	
for	Japanese people live longer than most other nationalities, **for** they eat healthful diets.

To add a similar, equal idea	
and	They eat a lot of fish and vegetables, **and** they eat lightly.

To add a negative equal idea	
nor	They do not eat a lot of red meat, **nor** do they eat many dairy products. *Note: Nor* means "and not." It joins two negative independent clauses. Notice that question word order is used after *nor*.

To add an opposite idea	
but	Diet is one factor in how long people live, **but** it is not the only factor.

To add an alternative possibility	
or	However, people should limit the amount of animal fat in their diets, **or** they risk getting heart disease.

To add an unexpected or surprising continuation	
yet	Cigarette smoking is a factor in longevity, **yet** Japanese and other long-lived Asians have a very high rate of tobacco use.

To add an expected result	
so	Doctors say that stress is another longevity factor, **so** try to avoid stress if you wish to live a longer life.

But and *yet* have similar meanings: They both signal that an opposite idea is coming. *But* is preferred when the two clauses are direct opposites. When the second clause is an unexpected or surprising continuation because of information given in the first clause, *yet* is preferred. (*But* is acceptable for both meanings; *yet* for only one meaning.) Compare:

I want to study art, **but** my parents want me to study engineering. (direct opposite)

I am very bad at math, **yet** my parents want me to study engineering. (surprising continuation after "I am very bad a math")

PRACTICE 3

But versus Yet

Which coordinator would you use to connect the two clauses in these sentences? Write either *but* or *yet* in the blank space.

1a. Too much sun damages the skin, _____ many people still do not use sunscreen.

b. Too much sun damages the skin, _____ too little sun also causes health problems.

2a. The company's sales increased last year, _____ its profits declined.

b. The company moved its marketing division to Phoenix, _____ the operations division stayed in Boston.

3a. Population growth has slowed in most developing countries, _____ it has not slowed enough to avoid serious problems.

b. The fertility rate in India has decreased from 6 to 3 births per female, _____ India's population is expanding at the rate of 18 million per year.

PRACTICE 4

Compound Sentences with Coordinators

A. Form compound sentences by adding another independent clause to the following independent clauses. Be sure to write a complete clause containing a subject and a verb. Circle the coordinator and add punctuation. The first one has been done for you as an example.

1. The college campus is located in the center of the city, ⓢⓞ it is very easy to get there by public transportation.

2. According to the Big Bang Theory, the universe began expanding about 13.7 billion years ago and _____

3. Does the universe have an outer edge or _____
_____?

4. Scientists predict that intelligent life exists somewhere in the universe but _____

5. Mars probes have photographed rocks with water markings on them yet _____

6. We may not be able to communicate with other life forms for _____
_____

7. Instead of taking the psychology final exam, we can write a 10-page research paper or _____

8. I want to write a research paper yet _____

9. Three weeks before the end of the term, I had not started my paper nor _____
_____

10. I needed help choosing a topic so _____
_____

B. For each pair of the following sentences form a compound sentence by joining the two independent clauses with a coordinator that best fits the meaning. Use each FAN BOYS coordinator once. Write your new sentences on a separate sheet of paper, and punctuate them correctly. The first one has been done for you as an example.

1. Nuclear accidents can happen. Nuclear power plants must have strict safety controls.

   Nuclear accidents can happen, so nuclear power plants must have strict safety controls.

2. The accident at the nuclear power plant at Three Mile Island in the United States created fears about the safety of this energy source. The disaster at Chernobyl in the former Soviet Union confirmed them.

3. Solar heating systems are economical to operate. The cost of installation is very high.

4. Energy needs are not going to decrease. Energy sources are not going to increase. (Use *nor* and question word order in the second clause, deleting the word *not*).

5. Burning fossil fuels causes serious damage to our planet. We need to develop other sources of energy.

6. Ecologists know that burning fossil fuels causes holes in the ozone layer. People continue to do it.

7. Developing nations especially will continue this harmful practice. They do not have the money to develop "clean" energy sources.

8. All nations of the world must take action. Our children and grandchildren will suffer the consequences.

C. Write seven compound sentences of your own, using each coordinator once.

Compound Sentences with Conjunctive Adverbs

A second way to form a compound sentence is as follows:

Independent clause; + conjunctive adverb, + independent clause

Salt water boils at a higher temperature than freshwater; **therefore,** food cooks faster in salt water.

Punctuation note: Put a semicolon before and a comma after the conjunctive adverb.

Several transition signals, such as *on the other hand, as a result*, and *for example*, act like conjunctive adverbs; they can also connect independent clauses with a semicolon and a comma. The following chart lists common conjunctive adverbs and a few transition signals that can be used in this way.

Conjunctive Adverbs

To add a similar, equal idea	
also besides furthermore in addition moreover	Community colleges offer preparation for many occupations; **also/besides/furthermore/ in addition/moreover,** they prepare students to transfer to a four-year college or university.
as well	Community colleges offer preparation for many occupations; they prepare students to transfer to a four-year college or university **as well**.
too	Community colleges offer preparation for many occupations; they prepare students to transfer to a four-year college or university, **too.**

To add an unexpected or surprising continuation	
however nevertheless nonetheless still	The cost of attending a community college is low; **however/nevertheless/nonetheless/still,** many students need financial aid.

To add a complete contrast	
on the other hand in contrast	Tuition at a community college is low; **on the other hand/in contrast,** tuition at private schools is high.

To give an alternative possibility	
otherwise	Students must take final exams; **otherwise,** they will receive a grade of Incomplete.

To add an expected result	
accordingly as a result consequently hence therefore thus	Native and nonnative English speakers have different needs; **accordingly/as a result/ consequently/hence/therefore/thus,** most schools provide separate English classes for each group.

To add an example	
for example for instance	Most colleges now have a writing requirement for graduation; **for example/for instance,** students at my college must pass a writing test before they register for their final semester.

PRACTICE 5

*Compound
Sentences with
Conjunctive
Adverbs*

A. Form compound sentences by adding a second independent clause to each independent clause. Be sure to add a complete clause containing a subject and a verb. Circle the conjunctive adverb and add punctuation. Some of these sentences are from Practice 4A on page 167. The first one has been done for you as an example.

1. The college campus is located in the center of the city; (therefore), *it is very easy to get there by public transportation.*

2. According to the Big Bang Theory, the universe began expanding about 13.7 billion years ago moreover _____

   _____

3. Students must pay their tuition and fees before they register for classes otherwise _____

   _____

4. Scientists predict that intelligent life exists somewhere in the universe however _____

   _____

5. Mars probes have photographed rocks with water markings on them nevertheless _____

   _____

6. My roommate scored high on the English placement test as a result _____

   _____

7. Tuition and fees increase every year for example _____

   _____

8. The class thought the teacher would give a test last Friday instead _____

   _____

B. On a separate sheet of paper, combine the pairs of sentences in items 3, 5, 6, and 8 from Practice 4B on page 168, using conjunctive adverbs instead of coordinators. Punctuate your new sentences correctly. The first one has been done for you as an example.

1. Nuclear accidents can happen. Nuclear power plants must have strict safety controls.

   Nuclear accidents can happen; therefore, nuclear power plants must have strict safety controls.

C. Write five compound sentences, using each of these conjunctive adverbs once: *in addition, nevertheless, on the other hand, therefore,* and *for instance.*

Compound Sentences with Semicolons

A third way to form a compound sentence is to connect the two independent clauses with a semicolon alone:

┌─────────────────── INDEPENDENT CLAUSE ───────────────────┐
Poland was the first Eastern European country to turn away from communism;

┌── INDEPENDENT CLAUSE ──┐
others soon followed.

This kind of compound sentence is possible only when the two independent clauses are closely related in meaning. If they are not closely related, they should be written as two simple sentences, each ending with a period.

PRACTICE 6

Compound Sentences with Semicolons

PRACTICE 7

Editing Practice

A. Place a semicolon between the two independent clauses in the following compound sentences.

1. The practice of yoga strengthens the body and promotes flexibility it also strengthens the mind and refreshes the soul.
2. Motherhood causes some women to quit their jobs others continue working despite having young children to care for.
3. Three hundred guests attended his wedding two attended his funeral.

B. On a separate sheet of paper, write three compound sentences of your own, using a semicolon to join the independent clauses.

Use what you have learned about forming compound sentences to improve the following mini-essay, which contains many short, simple sentences. Combine sentences wherever possible. Try to use each of the three methods at least once. There are many possible ways to combine sentences.

Robots

[1]A robot is a mechanical device that can perform boring, dangerous, and difficult tasks. [2]First of all, robots can perform repetitive tasks without becoming tired or bored. [3]They are used in automobile factories to weld and paint. [4]Robots can also function in hostile environments. [5]They are useful for exploring the ocean bottom as well as deep outer space. [6]Finally, robots can perform tasks requiring pinpoint accuracy. [7]In the operating room, robotic equipment can assist the surgeon. [8]For instance, a robot can kill a brain tumor. [9]It can operate on a fetus with great precision.

[10]The field of artificial intelligence is giving robots a limited ability to think and to make decisions. [11]However, robots cannot think conceptually. [12]Robots cannot function independently. [13]Humans have to program them. [14]They are useless. [Use *otherwise* to combine sentences 13 and 14.] [15]Therefore, humans should not worry that robots will take over the world—at least not yet.

Complex Sentences

A **complex sentence** contains one independent clause and one (or more) dependent clause(s). In a complex sentence, one idea is generally more important than the other. We place the more important idea in the independent clause and the less important idea in the dependent clause.

There are three kinds of dependent clauses: adverb, adjective, and noun. You will study all of these kinds of clauses in greater detail in Chapters 12, 13, and 14.

Complex Sentences with Adverb Clauses

An adverb clause acts like an adverb; that is, it tells where, when, why, and how. An adverb clause begins with a subordinator, such as *when, while, because, although, if, so,* or *that.* It can come before or after an independent clause.

┌──────────────── DEPENDENT ADVERB CLAUSE ────────────────┐ ┌──── INDEPENDENT CLAUSE ────┐
Although women in the United States could own property, they could not vote until 1920.

┌──────────── INDEPENDENT CLAUSE ────────────┐ ┌──── DEPENDENT ADVERB CLAUSE ────┐
A citizen can vote in the United States when he or she is 18 years old.

Complex Sentences with Adjective Clauses

An adjective clause acts like an adjective; that is, it describes a noun or pronoun. An adjective clause begins with a relative pronoun, such as *who, whom, which, whose,* or *that,* or with a relative adverb, such as *where* or *when.* It follows the noun or pronoun it describes.

┌──── DEPENDENT ────┐
│ ADJECTIVE CLAUSE │
Men who are not married are called bachelors.

┌──── DEPENDENT ADJECTIVE CLAUSE ────┐
Last year we vacationed in Cozumel, which features excellent scuba diving.

Complex Sentences with Noun Clauses

A noun clause begins with a *wh-* question word, *that, whether,* and sometimes *if.* A noun clause acts like a noun; it can be either the subject or an object of the independent clause.

┌──────────────── DEPENDENT NOUN CLAUSE ────────────────┐
That there is a hole in the ozone layer of Earth's atmosphere is well known.

┌──── DEPENDENT ────┐
│   NOUN CLAUSE   │
Scientists know what caused it.

In the first example, *That there is a hole in the ozone layer of Earth's atmosphere* is the subject of the verb *is.* In the second example, *what caused it* is the object of the verb *know.*

PRACTICE 8

Complex Sentences

A. **Step 1** Underline the independent clause of each sentence with a solid line.
   Step 2 Underline the dependent clause with a broken line. One sentence has two dependent clauses.
   Step 3 Write *Sub.* above the subordinator. Refer to the list of subordinators on page 163.

The first one has been done for you as an example.

Sub.
1. <u>Because the cost of education is rising,</u> <u>many students must work part-time.</u>
2. When students from other countries come to the United States, they often suffer from culture shock.
3. Because financial aid is difficult to obtain, many students have to work part-time.
4. Please tell me where the student union is.
5. Engineers, who have an aptitude for drafting and mechanics, must also be artistic and imaginative.
6. While the contractor follows the blueprint, the engineer checks the construction in progress.
7. Since the blueprint presents the details of the engineer's plans, it must be interpreted accurately by the contractor.
8. Students should declare a major by their junior year unless they have not made up their minds.
9. Even though students declare a major now, they can change it later.
10. The government says that inflation is holding steady.
11. Economists are concerned that the rate of inflation will double if the government does not take immediate steps to control it.

B. **Step 1** Add a logical independent clause to each of the dependent clauses.
Step 2 Punctuate each sentence correctly.

The first one has been done for you as an example.

1. *I cannot register for classes* _____ until I pay my tuition.
2. Unless I take 12 units each term _____.
3. _____ that computer engineering is a popular major.
4. _____ who taught this course last term?
5. Because I had to look for a part-time job _____ _____.
6. _____ if I want to get to school on time.
7. _____ whether I should take advanced calculus.
8. _____ whom I met at the math club meeting last week.
9. When I left my country _____.
10. _____ that my college adviser recommends.

Compound-Complex Sentences

A Compound-complex sentence has at least three clauses, at least two of which are independent. You can use almost any combination of dependent and independent clauses. Just be sure that there is at least one independent clause. In the following examples, independent clauses are underlined with a solid line and dependent clauses with a dotted line.

1. I wanted to travel after I graduated from college; however, I had to go to work immediately.

2. After I graduated from college, I wanted to travel, but I had to go to work immediately.

3. I wanted to travel after I graduated from college, but I had to go to work immediately because I had to support my family.

4. I could not decide where I should work or what I should do, so at first I did nothing.

Punctuate the compound part of a compound-complex sentence like a compound sentence; that is, use a semicolon/comma combination (sentence 1), or put a comma before a coordinator joining two independent clauses (sentences 2, 3, and 4).

Punctuate the complex part like a complex sentence. With adverb clauses, put a comma after a dependent adverb clause (sentence 2) but not before it (sentence 3). With noun clauses (sentence 4), use no commas.

Punctuate the following sentences.

PRACTICE 9

Punctuation

Step 1 Underline the independent clauses with a solid line and the dependent clauses with a broken line.

Step 2 Add commas and/or semicolons as necessary.

1. Information and communication technology is reaching out to help people in the poorest countries improve their lives for example fishermen on the Bay of Bengal can now receive online weather reports that tell them when it is safe to go out.

2. Furthermore, when the fishermen bring in a boatload of fish they can find out the current market prices for their fish, which will help them bargain with the middlemen to whom they sell their catch.

3. The cost of the cheapest computer is at least $200 and since this is more than an individual fisherman can afford several fishing villages together can pool their money and buy one to share.

4. The worldwide reach of the Internet is also providing employment opportunities in developing countries and as greater numbers of people learn the technology these opportunities will expand.

5. When you call your U.S. bank you may find yourself speaking to a customer service representative who is sitting in the Philippines or Puerto Rico and when you need technical support for your home computer you will probably get help from a programmer in New Delhi.

Sentence Types and Writing Style

Now that you know the basic kinds of sentences in English, you can develop a good writing style. Writing that uses only one kind of sentence is boring and may not convey the message that you intend.

As you read the model essay, notice the kinds of sentences.

- Paragraphs 1 and 4 have too many compound sentences. This style is boring because so many sentences use *and* as the connector.
- Paragraph 2 has too many simple sentences. This style sounds choppy.
- Paragraph 3 uses a good mixture of sentence types.

MODEL

Problems with Style

Rosa Parks

1   Rosa Parks is a famous African-American woman, **and** she is often called "the mother of the civil rights movement." She was born into a poor but hardworking African-American family in Alabama, **and** no one suspected that she would become the spark that ignited the civil rights movement in the United States. This movement changed U.S. society forever, **and** it helped African-Americans attain equal rights under the law.

2   Parks became famous quite by accident. One day in 1955, she was on her way home from her job in a Montgomery, Alabama, department store. She boarded a city bus with three other African-Americans. They sat in the fifth row. The fifth row was the first row African-Americans were allowed to sit in. A few stops later, the front four rows filled up. A white man was left standing.

3   According to the laws of that time, African-Americans had to give up their seats to whites, so the bus driver asked Parks and the three other African-Americans to get up and move. Although the others complied, Parks refused. She later said she was not tired from work, but tired of being treated like a second-class citizen. The bus driver called the police, who arrested Parks and took her away in handcuffs.

4   Over the weekend, a protest was organized, **and** on the following Monday, African-American people in Montgomery began a boycott of the public buses, **and** the boycott was tremendously successful, **and** it lasted more than a year. The Supreme Court of the United States finally ruled that segregation on public transportation was unconstitutional. African-Americans had won a huge victory, **and** they realized their power to change the system.

Now read the same essay with the sentence structure revised.

MODEL

Revised Essay

Rosa Parks

1   Rosa Parks is a famous American African-American woman who is often called "the mother of the civil rights movement." When she was born into a poor but hardworking African-American family in Alabama, no one suspected that she would become the spark that ignited the civil rights movement in the United States. This movement changed U.S. society forever by helping African-American people attain equal rights under the law.

2   Parks became famous quite by accident. One day in 1955, on her way home from her job in a Montgomery, Alabama, department store, she boarded a city bus with three other African-Americans. They sat in the fifth row, which was the first row African-Americans were allowed to sit in. A few stops later, the front four rows filled up, and a white man was left standing.

3   According to the laws of that time, African-Americans had to give up their seats to whites, so the bus driver asked Parks and the three other African-Americans to get up and move. Although the others complied, Parks refused. She later said she was not tired from work, but tired of being treated like a second-class citizen. The bus driver called the police, who arrested Parks and took her away in handcuffs.

4   Over the weekend, a protest was organized, and on the following Monday, African-American people in Montgomery began a boycott of the public buses. The boycott was tremendously successful, lasting for more than a year. The Supreme Court of the United States finally ruled that segregation on public transportation was unconstitutional. Because they had won a huge victory, African-Americans realized their power to change the system.

PRACTICE 10

Combining Sentences in Different Ways

A. Improve this paragraph, which contains too many compound sentences. Change compound sentences into complex sentences, using one of the subordinators listed. Use each subordinator once. Rewrite the paragraph on a separate sheet of paper.

| because | although | when | after | as soon as | since |

Equal Rights for Women

Russian women started to gain equality earlier than women in the United States. In the former Soviet Union, men and women had access to equal education and job opportunities, and that reflected the Soviet philosophy. The 1937 Soviet constitution declared that women and men had equal rights and responsibilities, and women joined the workforce. Also, millions of Russian men were away in the military during World War II, so Russian women filled their places at work. Soviet women worked full time at their jobs, but they also had the primary responsibility for taking care of the family. They finished their work, and they had to shop, cook the evening meal, and perhaps wash, iron, or mend the family's clothes. U.S. women started to demonstrate that they could do the work of men during World War II.

B. Use what you know about the different kinds of sentences to improve this short essay, which contains too many simple sentences. Use different methods of combining the sentences. Rewrite the essay on a separate sheet of paper.

Nonverbal Communication

1   Nonverbal communication, or body language, is used everywhere in the world. It is a very powerful means of communication. It communicates much more than spoken words.

2   One example of nonverbal communication is what occurs between parents and child. Parents smile at their child. They communicate love, acceptance, and reassurance. The child feels comfortable and safe. The smile signifies approval. The child is happy and well adjusted.

3   Another example of nonverbal communication is the image a person shows in public. A woman is walking alone on an unfamiliar and possibly dangerous street. She wants to appear confident. She walks quickly. She may be tired. She walks with her shoulders straight and her head held high. Her eyes are focused straight ahead. Someone is looking at her. She returns the glance without hesitation. In contrast, a nervous woman appears afraid. She walks slowly with her shoulders and eyes down.

4   Indeed, body language can express more than spoken language. Merely by raising an eyebrow, clenching a jaw, or softening the eyes, a person can express disapproval, anger, or love. It is a very strong method of communication.

Review

These are the important points covered in this chapter.

1. **Clauses** are the main building blocks of sentences. There are two kinds of clauses: independent and dependent.

   a. An **independent clause**
      - expresses a complete thought.
      - can be a sentence by itself.

      English grammar is easy.

   b. A **dependent clause**
      - begins with a subordinator.
      - cannot be a sentence by itself.
      - is one of three types: adverb, adjective, or noun.

      ADVERB
      . . . because grammar is easy . . .

      ADJECTIVE
      . . . which is in Spanish . . .

      NOUN
      . . . that grammar is easy . . .

2. We build **different kinds of sentences** in English by combining clauses in different patterns.

a. A **simple sentence** is one independent clause.

English grammar is easy.

b. A **compound sentence** is two independent clauses joined by
 • a coordinator,
 • a conjunctive adverb, or
 • a semicolon.

Grammar is easy, so I learned it quickly.

Grammar is easy; therefore, I learned it quickly.

Grammar is easy; I learned it quickly.

c. A **complex sentence** is one independent and one (or more) dependent clauses.

WITH AN ADVERB CLAUSE
Because grammar is easy, I learned it quickly. I learned grammar quickly because it is easy.

WITH AN ADJECTIVE CLAUSE
One of my favorite films is *Like Water for Chocolate*, which is in Spanish.

WITH A NOUN CLAUSE
She does not agree that grammar is easy.

d. A **compound-complex sentence** has two independent clauses and one (or more) dependent clauses.

Because grammar is easy, I learned it quickly, but it took me several years to master writing.

3. The type of sentence you write depends on your message. When you want to show that ideas are equal, use more coordinated structures, such as compound sentences. When ideas are not equal, use more subordinated structures, such as complex sentences. Develop a good writing style by mixing sentence types.

CHAPTER 11

Using Parallel Structures and Fixing Sentence Problems

Bread seal of Gaza, Israel

In this chapter, you will learn to use parallel structure to add symmetry and style to your sentences. You will also learn to recognize and repair common sentence problems: fragments, run-ons, comma splices, choppy, and stringy sentences.

Parallelism

Parallelism is an important element in English writing, especially when you are listing and comparing and contrasting items or ideas. Parallelism means that each item in a list or comparison follows the same grammatical pattern. If you are writing a list and the first item in your list is a noun, write all the following items as nouns also. If the first item is an *-ing* word, make all the others *-ing* words; if it is an adverb clause, make all the others adverb clauses.

In the examples that follow, the sentences in the column on the right follow the rule of parallelism.

Not Parallel	Parallel
My English conversation class is made up of Chinese, Spaniards, and some are from Bosnia.	My English conversation class is made up of **Chinese, Spaniards,** and **Bosnians.** *(The items are all nouns.)*
The students who do well attend class, they do their homework, and practice speaking in English.	The students who do well **attend class, do their homework,** and **practice speaking in English.** *(The items are all verbs + complements.)*
The teacher wanted to know which country we came from and our future goals.	The teacher wanted to know **which country we came from** and **what our future goals were.** *(The items are both noun clauses.)*
The language skills of the students in the evening classes are the same as the day classes.	**The language skills of the students in the evening classes** are the same as **the language skills of the students in the day classes.** *(The items are both noun phrases.)*

Notes

1. You may substitute a pronoun for the second "the language skills" in the last example:

   The language skills of the students in the evening classes are the same as **those** of the students in the day classes.

2. All the words in the first item do not always have to be repeated in the second. You may repeat all or some of the words, depending on what you wish to emphasize. The following sentences are both correct:

   Before you write a paper or **before you take a test,** you must organize your thoughts.

   Before you **write a paper** or **take a test,** you must organize your thoughts.

Parallelism with Coordinators: *And, Or, But*

Words, phrases, and clauses that are joined by *and, or,* and *but* are written in parallel form. Notice the parallel structures joined by coordinators in the following sentences.

The Federal Air Pollution Control Administration regulates automobile exhausts, **and** the Federal Aviation Administration makes similar regulations for aircraft.

The states regulate the noise created by motor vehicles **but** not by commercial aircraft.

Pesticides cannot be sold if they have a harmful effect on humans, on animal life, **or** on the environment.

Parallelism with Correlative (Paired) Conjunctions

Use parallel forms with the paired conjunctions *both . . . and, either . . . or, neither . . . nor,* and *not only . . . but also.*

Paired conjunctions are placed directly *before* the elements they join in the sentence. Notice the parallel structures in these clauses joined by paired conjunctions:

A new law provides the means for **both** <u>regulating pesticides</u> **and** <u>ordering their removal</u> if they are dangerous.

Air pollutants may come **either** <u>from the ocean as natural contaminants given off by sea life</u> **or** <u>from the internal combustion engines of automobiles</u>.

If **neither** <u>industry</u> **nor** <u>the public</u> works toward reducing pollution problems, future generations will suffer.

Many people are **neither** <u>concerned about pollutants</u> **nor** <u>worried about their future impact</u>.

At the present time, air pollution is controlled through laws passed **not only** <u>to reduce the pollutants at their sources</u> **but also** <u>to set up acceptable standards of air quality</u>.

PRACTICE 1

Parallelism

A. Two or more items in each of the following sentences are written in parallel grammatical form. Underline the items or ideas that are parallel, and circle the word or words that connect the parallel structures. The first one has been done for you as an example.

1. An ideal environment for studying includes <u>good lighting, a spacious desk,</u> (and) <u>a comfortable chair</u>.
2. You know you are truly fluent in another language when you can calculate in it and when you begin to dream in it.
3. People often spend as much time worrying about the future as planning for it.
4. You can learn a second language in the classroom, at home, or in a country where the language is spoken.
5. My new personal computer is both fast and reliable.
6. My old typewriter is neither fast nor reliable.
7. Ann is growing older but unfortunately not wiser.
8. Young people buy computers not only to do schoolwork but also to play games.
9. If industrial nations continue to burn fossil fuels and if developing nations continue to burn their rain forests, the level of CO_2 in the atmosphere will continue to increase.
10. Before the judge announced the punishment, he asked the murderer if he wanted to speak either to the victim's family or to the jury.
11. The criminal neither admitted guilt nor asked for forgiveness before he was sent to prison.

B. Rewrite the following sentences in parallel form. Underline the part of the sentence that is not parallel and correct it. Remember that you do not have to repeat all the words in the second item. The first one has been done for you as an example.

1. The disadvantages of using a credit card are overspending and <u>you pay</u> high interest rates.

   The disadvantages of using a credit card are overspending and paying high interest rates.

2. Credit cards are accepted by department stores, airlines, and they can be used in some gas stations.

   _____

   _____

3. You do not need to risk carrying cash or to risk to miss a sale.

   _____

   _____

4. With credit cards, you can either pay your bill with one check, or you can stretch out your payments.

   _____

   _____

5. You can charge both at restaurants and when you stay at hotels.

   _____

   _____

6. Many people carry not only credit cards but they also carry cash.

   _____

   _____

7. Many people want neither to pay off their balance monthly nor do they like paying interest.

   _____

   _____

8. Not making any payment or to send in only the minimum payment every month is poor money management.

   _____

   _____

C. On a separate sheet of paper, write seven original sentences in parallel form, using the following conjunctions one time each. Write sentences on the topics suggested, or choose topics of your own.

and	two weekend activities you enjoy
or	two foods you would not eat/give to a baby
but	one school subject that you excel at and one that you struggle with
both . . . and	two advantages of being bilingual
either . . . or	two places you might spend a month's vacation or a honeymoon
neither . . . nor	two places you would never spend a month's vacation or a honeymoon
not only . . . but also	two reasons to get a college degree

Sentence Problems

In this section, you will learn to recognize and correct some common errors in sentence structure: sentence fragments and choppy, run-on, and "stringy" sentences.

Sentence Fragments

Sentence fragments are incomplete sentences or parts of sentences. Remember that a complete sentence must contain at least one main or independent clause.

Study the following examples of sentence fragments and the suggested methods for correcting them.

1. Because some students work part-time while taking a full load of classes.

PROBLEM This is a dependent clause. It begins with a subordinator (*because*). It does not express a complete thought because there is no independent clause.

TO CORRECT (1) Add an independent clause.

Because some students work part-time while taking a full load of courses, **they have very little free time.**

(2) Delete the subordinator (*because*).

Some students work part-time while taking a full load of classes.

2. For example, the increase in the cost of renting an apartment.
To live and work for at least a year in a foreign country.

PROBLEM Neither sentence has a verb.

To CORRECT Rewrite each sentence so that it has a verb.

For example, the increase in the cost of renting an apartment **is** one reason for more people being homeless.

To live and work for at least a year in a foreign country **has** always **been** my dream.

3. Teachers who give too much homework.

PROBLEM This is a noun (*teachers*) + an adjective clause (*who give too much homework*). The noun is the beginning of an independent clause that was never finished.

To CORRECT Finish the independent clause.

Teachers who give too much homework **are unpopular.**

Always check your own writing for sentence fragments. Pay particular attention to sentences beginning with subordinators (*although, since, because, if, before,* and so on). These are DANGER WORDS! Make sure that every clause beginning with these words is attached to an independent clause.

PRACTICE 2

Rewriting Sentence Fragments

A. Read the following sentences. Mark them *Frag.* if they are sentence fragments, or *Comp.* if they are complete sentences. On a separate sheet of paper, rewrite each fragment to make a complete sentence.

_____ 1. The desire of all humankind to live in peace and freedom, for example.

_____ 2. Second, a fact that men are physically stronger than women.

_____ 3. The best movie I saw last year.

_____ 4. *Titanic* was the most financially successful movie ever made, worldwide.

_____ 5. For example, many students have part-time jobs.

_____ 6. Although people want to believe that all men are created equal.

_____ 7. Finding a suitable marriage partner is a challenging task.

_____ 8. Many of my friends who did not have the opportunity to go to college.

_____ 9. Working during the morning and attending classes during the afternoon.

_____ 10. Because I do not feel that grades in college have any value.

_____ 11. A tsunami that occurred in the Indian Ocean in December 2004, killing more than 200,000 people.

_____ 12. The total energy of the tsunami waves was about five megatons of TNT.

_____ 13. More than twice the total explosive energy used during all of World War II, including two atomic bombs, according to one expert.

_____ 14. Evidence that the wave reached a height of 80 feet (24 meters) when coming ashore along the coastline and rose to 100 feet (30 meters) in some areas when traveling inland.

_____ 15. Despite a lag of up to several hours between the earthquake and tsunami, nearly all of the victims were taken completely by surprise.

B. Read the following short essay. Put brackets [ ] around any sentence fragments you find and mark them *Frag*. Then correct the fragments on a separate sheet of paper.

Women Drivers

1   Sexism[1] extends even into the area of automobile driving, it seems. Believing that they are far better drivers than women. Men consider women drivers incompetent, inattentive, and even dangerous behind the wheel.

2   However, statistics prove that women are, in fact, safer drivers than men. For example, insurance rates. Insurance rates for women are 20 percent lower than they are for men. Another proof is that more accidents are caused by male drivers between the ages of 18 and 25 than by any other group. Also, the greater percentage of accidents involving deaths caused by men. Although women are criticized for being too cautious. They are really just being safe drivers.

3   The reasons for women drivers' safer driving habits can perhaps be found in the differing attitudes of the sexes toward automobiles. On the one hand, women drivers who regard the automobile as a convenience. Like a washing machine. On the other hand, men regard the automobile as an extension of their egos. Using it as a weapon when they feel particularly aggressive. Or using it as a status symbol.

4   All in all, women are safer drivers. Because of their attitude. Men can learn to become safe drivers. If they adopt the attitude that an automobile is merely a convenience.

Choppy Sentences

Choppy sentences are sentences that are too short. Short sentences can be effective in certain situations. For instance, when you want to make an impact, use a short sentence.

Despite countless doctors' warnings, news stories, and magazine articles about the importance of eating a nutritious, balanced diet, many people resist developing healthy eating habits. Some people just like junk food.

(*A sentence of 25 words is followed by one of 6 words. The second sentence has greater impact because it is so short.*)

---

[1]**Sexism:** men's belief in male superiority

However, overuse of short sentences is considered poor style in academic writing.

Choppy sentences are easy to correct. Just combine two or three short sentences to make one compound or complex sentence. Your decision to make a compound or a complex sentence should be based on whether the ideas in the short sentences are equal or whether one idea is dependent on the other.

1. If the sentences express equal ideas, use coordination to combine them.

CHOPPY SENTENCES   Wind is an enduring source of power. Water is also an unlimited energy source. Dams produce hydraulic power. They have existed for a long time. Windmills are relatively new.

CORRECTED   Both wind and water are enduring sources of power. Dams have produced hydraulic power for a long time, but windmills are relatively new.

2. If the sentences express unequal ideas, that is, if one sentence expresses a less important idea than the other, use subordination to combine them.

CHOPPY SENTENCES   We must find new sources of energy. Natural sources of energy are decreasing. Solar energy is a promising new source of energy. Solar energy is energy from the sun.

CORRECTED   We must find new sources of energy because natural sources of energy are dwindling. Solar energy, which is energy from the sun, is a promising new source.

| PRACTICE 3 | Improve the following choppy sentences by combining them. |

Rewriting Choppy Sentences

Step 1 Decide what the relationship between the sentences is.

*   Do they express equal ideas? If yes, write a compound sentence. Both sentences present the main idea.

Similar or equal idea	**and**
Negative equal idea	**nor**
Opposite idea	**but**
Alternative possibility	**or**
Surprising continuation	**yet**
Expected result	**so**
Reason	**for**

*   Is one idea more important than another idea? If yes, go on to Steps 2 and 3 and write a complex sentence.

Step 2 Decide which sentence expresses the most important idea. This will be the independent clause.

Step 3 Then decide what the relationship of other sentences to the main idea is and choose a subordinator that expresses that relationship.

Time	**when, after, as soon as,** and so on
Reason	**because, since,** or **as**
Contrast	**although, whereas,** and so on
Descriptive information	**who, which, that,** and so on

The first one has been done for you as an example. As you can see from the example, there may be more than one way to combine the sentences.

1. (a) Gasoline became expensive. (b) Automobile manufacturers began to produce smaller cars. (c) Smaller cars use less gasoline.

   Equal /(Not equal)?
   Main idea?   Sentence (b)
   Relationships: Sentence (a) could be time (when) or reason
                               (because). Sentence (c) could be reason (because) or
                               descriptive information (which).

   Combined sentence: When gasoline became more expensive, automobile
                               manufacturers began to produce smaller cars because
                               they use less gasoline.
                               OR
                               Because gasoline became more expensive, automobile
                               manufacturers began to produce smaller cars, which
                               use less gasoline.

2. (a) Electric cars are powered solely by batteries. (b) The new hybrid vehicles switch between electricity and gasoline.

   Equal / Not equal?
   Main idea?   _____
   Relationship: _____
   Combined sentence: _____
   _____
   _____

3. (a) Government and private agencies have spent billions of dollars advertising the dangers of smoking. (b) The number of smokers is still increasing.

   Equal / Not equal?
   Main idea?   _____
   Relationship: _____
   Combined sentence: _____
   _____
   _____

4. (a) Some students go to a vocational school to learn a trade. (b) Some students go to college to earn a degree.

   Equal / Not equal?
   Main idea?   _____
   Relationship: _____
   Combined sentence: _____
   _____
   _____

5. (a) The grading system at our college should be abolished. (b) The students do not like getting grades. (c) The instructors do not enjoy giving grades.

   Equal / Not equal?

   Main idea?   _____

   Relationship: _____

   Combined sentence: _____

   _____

   _____

6. (a) Education in a free society teaches children how to think. (b) Education in a dictatorship teaches children what to think.

   Equal / Not equal?

   Main idea?   _____

   Relationship: _____

   Combined sentence: _____

   _____

   _____

Run-On Sentences and Comma Splices

A **run-on sentence** is a sentence in which two or more independent clauses are written one after another with no punctuation. A similar error happens when two independent clauses are incorrectly joined by a comma without a coordinating conjunction. This kind of error is called a **comma splice**.

RUN-ON   My family went to Australia then they emigrated to Canada.

COMMA SPLICE   My family went to Australia, then they emigrated to Canada.

The ways to correct these two sentence errors are the same.

1. Add a period:

   My family went to Australia. Then they emigrated to Canada.

2. Add a semicolon:

   My family went to Australia; then they emigrated to Canada.

3. Add a coordinator:

   My family went to Australia, **and** then they emigrated to Canada.

4. Add a subordinator:

   My family went to Australia **before** they emigrated to Canada.

   After my family went to Australia, they emigrated to Canada.

PRACTICE 4

Run-On/Comma Splice Sentences

A. Correct the following run-on/comma splice sentences using the method indicated.

1. A newly arrived international student faces several challenges, for example, he or she has to cope with a new culture.

   a. Add a period: _____

   _____

   b. Add a semicolon: _____

   _____

2. New York City is very cosmopolitan, people from many cultures and ethnic groups live there.

   a. Add a period: _____

   _____

   b. Add a semicolon: _____

   _____

   c. Add a subordinator: _____

   _____

   d. Add a coordinator: _____

   _____

3. Learning a new language is like learning to swim it takes a lot of practice.
   Add a coordinator: _____

   _____

4. Ask for assistance at the reference desk in the library, a librarian is always on duty.
   Add a semicolon: _____

   _____

5. Skiing is a dangerous sport you can easily break your leg or your neck.
   Add a subordinator: _____

   _____

B. Some of the following sentences are run-ons or comma splices, and some are correct. Check each sentence. If it is incorrect, write *RO* or *CS* in the space at the left. If it is correct, leave the space blank. Then, on a separate sheet of paper, correct the incorrect sentences.

   ____RO____ 1. Two letters arrived on Monday a third one came on Wednesday.
   Two letters arrived on Monday; a third one came on Wednesday.

   _____ 2. An encyclopedia is a valuable source of information it contains summaries of every area of knowledge.

   _____ 3. Because of the rapid expansion of human knowledge, it is difficult to keep encyclopedias current.

   _____ 4. A printed encyclopedia becomes out of date almost as soon as it is published also it is quite expensive to purchase.

   _____ 5. Online encyclopedias are available to everyone with access to the Internet.

_____ 6. Articles in encyclopedias are written by experts in each subject, who are often university professors.

_____ 7. An editor of an encyclopedia does not write articles he only collects and edits articles written by subject experts.

_____ 8. To find a book on a certain subject, you used to look in a card catalog, to find a magazine article on a subject, you used to look in a periodical index.

_____ 9. Now, most libraries have thrown away their card catalogs, they have computerized catalogs that are much more efficient to use and update.

_____ 10. Many periodical indexes, which list only titles of magazine articles and indicate where to find them, have been replaced by computer indexes, some of which display abstracts[1] and even entire articles instantly.

_____ 11. If you cannot find any information on a subject, you can always ask a librarian to help you, they are paid to assist students.

C. Locate the run-on/comma splice sentences in the following paragraphs. Mark them by writing *RO* or *CS* above them. Then, on a separate sheet of paper, rewrite both paragraphs, correcting the mistakes that you found. There are four errors.

[1]Teachers at Stone Mountain State College give higher grades than teachers at 12 of the 19 other colleges in the state college system, according to a recent report from the State Institutional Research Committee. [2]This report showed that more than one-third of the undergraduate grades awarded in the spring semester 2005 were A's only 1.1 percent were F's. [3]The percentage of A's awarded to graduate students was even higher, almost two-thirds were A's.

[4]While students may be happy to receive high grades, evidence suggests that this trend is having negative consequences. [5]Investigation of the admissions criteria[2] of some graduate and professional schools indicates that the admissions offices of these schools are discounting high grades on the transcripts of SMSC students, this means that an A from SMSC is not equal to an A from other universities. [6]Grade inflation may, therefore, hurt a student from Stone Mountain State College who intends to apply to a graduate or professional school he or she may not be accepted despite a high grade point average.

Stringy Sentences

A **stringy sentence** is a sentence with too many clauses, usually connected with *and, but, so,* and sometimes *because*. It often results from writing the way you speak, going on and on like a string without an end.

To correct a stringy sentence, divide it and/or recombine the clauses, remembering to subordinate when appropriate.

---

[1]**abstracts:** summaries
[2]**criteria:** standards by which a judgment is made

STRINGY SENTENCE   Many students attend classes all morning, and then they work all afternoon, and they also have to study at night, so they are usually exhausted by the weekend.

CORRECTED   Many students attend classes all morning and work all afternoon. Since they also have to study at night, they are usually exhausted by the weekend.

OR

Because many students attend classes all morning, work all afternoon, and study at night, they are usually exhausted by the weekend.

PRACTICE 5

Stringy Sentences

Improve these stringy sentences.

1. He enrolled in an intermediate calculus class, but he found it too easy, so he dropped it, and he signed up for the advanced class.

   _____

   _____

2. First-born children in a family often have more responsibility than their younger siblings, and they feel pressure to set a good example, so they often become superachievers.

   _____

   _____

3. Last-born children, on the other hand, often have little responsibility, and they may be pampered as the "baby" of the family, but they are the smallest, and they have to get people to like them, so they often develop superior social skills.

   _____

   _____

4. The students in my engineering class could not do the homework, so we got together and worked for several hours, and we finally solved all the problems.

   _____

   _____

5. The lack of rainfall has caused a severe water shortage, so people have to conserve water every day, and they also have to think of new ways to reuse water, but the situation is improving.

   _____

   _____

Review

These are the important points covered in this chapter.

1. Parallelism

Two or more items joined by coordinating conjunctions and paired conjunctions must be parallel in structure. The same is true of contrasts and comparisons of items. If the first item is a noun, make all others nouns; if it is a phrase, make all the others phrases; if it is a clause, make all the others clauses.

Not Parallel	Parallel
Taking a class on a pass/fail basis is sometimes better than to get a grade of C.	Taking a class on a pass/fail basis is sometimes better than getting a grade of C.
My grandmother not only speaks four languages but also she understands six others.	My grandmother not only speaks four languages but also understands six others.

2. Sentence Problems

The main kinds of problem sentences that students may write are fragments, run-ons, comma splices, choppy, and stringy sentences.

Fragments are incomplete sentences.

Fragment	Corrected
The subject I enjoyed the most in high school.	The subject I enjoyed the most in high school was physics.

Run-ons and **comma splices** are incorrectly joined independent clauses.

Run-On	Corrected
Getting married is easy staying married is another matter.	Getting married is easy, but staying married is another matter.
	OR
Comma Splice	
Getting married is easy, staying married is another matter.	Although getting married is easy, staying married is another matter.

Choppy sentences are sentences that are too short.

Choppy	Corrected
My family left our homeland. Then we lived in a refugee camp. We lived there for several months. Then we got our documents. We traveled to Canada. We live there now.	After my family left our homeland, we lived in a refugee camp for several months. As soon as we got our documents, we traveled to Canada, where we live now.

Stringy sentences are sentences with too many independent clauses.

Stringy	Corrected
My family left our homeland, and we lived in a refugee camp for several months, but finally we got our documents, so we traveled to Canada, and we live there now.	After my family left our homeland, we lived in a refugee camp for several months. As soon as we got our documents, we traveled to Canada, where we live now.

Editing Practice

Edit the following paragraphs for errors in parallel structure and other sentence problems. Identify the problem sentences and correct them. Rewrite the paragraphs on a separate sheet of paper. (*Note:* Not every sentence has a problem.)

The United States: Melting Pot or Salad Bowl?

[1]The United States counts its population every 10 years, and each census[1] reveals that the racial and ethnic mix is changing dramatically, so by the year 2050, the "average" person in the United States will not be descended from[2] Europeans, but the majority of U.S. residents will trace their ancestry[3] to Africa, Asia, the Hispanic world, the Pacific Islands, or the Middle East. [2]Once the United States was a microcosm[4] of European nationalities, today the United States is a microcosm of the world. [3]The United States is no longer considered a "melting pot" society by many of its residents. [4]Instead, many people prefer the term "salad bowl." [5]They use this term to describe U.S. society. [6]U.S. society will soon be predominantly nonwhite. [7]"Melting pot" implies that the different ethnic groups blend together into one homogeneous mixture, "salad bowl" implies that nationalities, like the ingredients in a mixed green salad, retain their cultural identities.

[8]Earlier generations of immigrants believed that they had to learn English quickly not only to survive but also for success. [9]Now, many immigrant groups do not feel the same need. [10]Because there are many places in the United States where you can work, shop, get medical care, marry, divorce, and die without knowing English. [11]For example, Chinatown in San Francisco and New York. [12]Also, Los Angeles has many Vietnamese immigrants and immigrants from Mexico. [13]In addition, many immigrant groups want their children to know their own culture. [14]Many Hispanics, for instance, want their children to learn both English and study the Spanish language in school. [15]They are fighting for the right to bilingual education in many communities. [16]In many communities they are in the majority.

---

[1]**census:** population count
[2]**be descended from:** be the children, grandchildren, etc., of
[3]**ancestry:** a person's origins
[4]**microcosm:** small community representing a large one

Noun Clauses

Persian miniature, 1536 A.D.

A **noun clause** is a dependent clause that functions as a noun. A noun clause is often part of an independent clause, where it can be a subject or an object.

> ┌─── SUBJECT ───┐ VERB
> **What the newspaper reported** was incorrect.

> VERB ┌─── OBJECT ───┐
> People once believed **that the world was flat**.

A noun clause can also follow certain adjectives and nouns.

> ADJECTIVE
> We were happy **that the semester was over**.

> NOUN
> Who first challenged the belief **that the world was flat**?

There are three kinds of noun clauses:

1. *that* clauses, which begin with the word *that*
2. *if/whether* clauses, which begin with the words *whether* or *if*
3. question clauses, which begin with a question word, such as *who, what, where, when*, or *how*

We will study each kind in this chapter.

Punctuating Noun Clauses

1. NEVER use a comma to separate a noun clause from the main clause.

   I am sure✕that the address is correct.

2. If the independent clause is a statement, put a period at the end of the entire sentence. If the independent clause is a question, put a question mark at the end of the entire sentence.

Independent Clause	Noun Clause
I am sure	that the address is correct.
Are you sure	that the address is correct**?**

That Clauses

A *that* clause is a dependent noun clause that begins with the word *that*.

The young filmmaker hopes **that his film will be a financial success**.

You can sometimes omit *that* if the meaning is clear without it. However, you can never omit *that* when it is the first word in a sentence.

CORRECT   The young filmmaker hopes that his film will be a financial success.

CORRECT   The young filmmaker hopes his film will be a financial success.

CORRECT   That his film is a critical success is beyond doubt.

INCORRECT   His film is a critical success is beyond doubt.

A *that* clause can appear in different locations.

1. **After the independent clause verb.** The most common position of a noun clause is after the verb of the independent clause, where it functions as the object of that verb.

   ┌─ INDEPENDENT CLAUSE ─┐
   S   V   ┌──────── NOUN CLAUSE (OBJECT) ────────┐
   The catalog states that science courses require a laboratory period.

2. **After certain adjectives.** A *that* clause can also follow certain adjectives such as *happy, glad, proud, pleased, sad, upset, worried, sorry, certain, surprised*, and *sure*. These adjectives describe emotions.

┌─────── INDEPENDENT CLAUSE ───────┐ ┌─────────── NOUN CLAUSE ───────────┐
                    ADJECTIVE
The class was surprised that the instructor canceled the final exam.

3. **After certain nouns.** A *that* clause can follow certain nouns such as *idea, theory, thought, claim, assertion, statement, belief, notion*, and *opinion*.

┌────────── INDEPENDENT CLAUSE ──────────┐ ┌─────────── NOUN CLAUSE ───────────┐
                              NOUN
No one believed Galileo's theory that Earth revolves around the sun.

4. **At the beginning of a sentence.** A *that* clause at the beginning of a sentence functions as the subject of the independent clause verb.

┌─────────── INDEPENDENT CLAUSE ───────────┐
┌──── NOUN CLAUSE (SUBJECT) ────┐ V
That Earth is getting warmer is certain.

Sentences Beginning with *It*

Starting a sentence with a noun clause seems awkward to many English speakers, so they often rewrite such sentences by putting *it* at the beginning and moving the noun clause to the end.

AWKWARD   **That Earth is getting warmer** is certain.

BETTER   **It** is certain **that Earth is getting warmer**.

In addition, the verb following *it* (except *be* or any intransitive verb like *seem* or *appear*) is often written in the passive voice, especially in academic writing.

It is believed that carbon dioxide is responsible for global warming.

It was agreed that the meeting would be postponed until next week.

It has been proven that the world's deserts are expanding.

You can also write these sentences in the active voice:

Many scientists believe that carbon dioxide is responsible for global warming.

The participants agreed that the meeting would be postponed until next week.

Measurements have proven that the world's deserts are expanding.

Note: In general, English writers prefer the active voice because it is more direct. However, they prefer the passive voice in five specific situations.

1. You want to emphasize what happened, not who did it.

    Jack was promoted last month.

2. The performer of the action is unknown.

    The wheel was invented during the Bronze Age.

3. The performer of the action is unimportant.

   Smoking is prohibited on airplanes.

4. You want to be objective, such as in a scientific or technical report.

   With a dropper, 3 ml of HCl were added to the test tube and heated to 37°C.

5. You want to be diplomatic; that is, you don't want to say who did something wrong or made an error.

   I believe a mistake has been made on our bill.

PRACTICE 1

That *Clauses 1*

A. Complete each sentence with a *that* clause. The first one has been done for you as an example.

1. A comparison of the size of glaciers and icebergs over the past hundred years reveals <u>that they are shrinking in size.</u>
2. Scientists believe _____
3. Environmentalists warn _____
4. People living near seacoasts and on low-lying islands are worried _____

   _____

5. _____ has been proven.
6. The idea _____ is nonsense.
7. Our teacher was very proud _____

B. Write each sentence so that it begins with *it* and ends with a *that* clause. The first one has been done for you as an example.

1. That air temperatures are rising is significant.

   <u>It is significant that air temperatures are rising.</u>
2. That ocean levels are rising is undeniable.

   _____

3. That burning fossil fuels is a cause of global warming has been well documented.

   _____

4. Rewrite sentence 5 from Part A.

   _____

Special Verb Tenses in *That* Clauses

Reported Speech

One of the most common uses of noun clauses in academic writing is to report what someone else has said or written. This kind of noun clause is called *reported speech, indirect speech*, or *indirect quotation*. Verb tenses in reported speech follow special rules.

- If the main clause verb is simple present, present perfect, or future, the verb in the noun clause is in the tense that expresses the meaning that the main clause intends.

    The prime ministers **agree** that global warming **is** a serious world problem.

    They **hope** that all nations **will be** responsible for solving this problem.

    Scientists **report** that atmospheric warming **has** already **begun**.

    Measurements **have indicated** that the average temperature of Earth **has risen** in the past hundred years.

    Further research **will prove** that carbon dioxide **is** largely responsible.

- If the main clause verb is in past tense, the verb in the noun clause is usually in a past form.

    The prime ministers **agreed** that global warming **was** a serious world problem.

    They **hoped** that all nations **would be** responsible for finding a solution.

    An international group of scientists **reported** that Earth's temperature **had risen** 1.1°F (0.6°C) in the last century.

    Their report **stated** that carbon dioxide **was** largely responsible.

    Exception: The verb in the noun clause stays in the present tense when it reports a fact or a general truth:

    Researchers in the field **verified** that icebergs and glaciers **are** melting.

For more examples and practice, refer also to Indirect Quotations and Sequence of Tenses Rules in Chapter 3, page 48.

PRACTICE 2
That *Clauses II*

Step 1 Read the following article.
Step 2 Write sentences containing *that* clauses. Use the prompts and information from the article to form your sentences.
- When the prompt begins with *it*, use the passive voice in the independent clause.
- Use an appropriate verb tense in both clauses.

The first two have been done for you as examples.

Who Are Smarter—Men or Women?

Neither sex is more intelligent than the other; their brains are just different. For example, a certain area of the brain controls language, and women have more brain cells in that area than men do. Therefore, women learn language more easily than men do. However, women's superior language skills certainly do not mean that women are more intelligent than men. Indeed, men generally show superior ability at math and reasoning.

Another difference between the sexes involves spatial tasks. Men are better at reading maps, but women are better at remembering the location of objects. Perhaps men's and women's brains developed different spatial skills because of the different tasks they performed in prehistoric times. In those days, men were the hunters. They had to be able to track prey, make a kill, and then find their way back to the camp. Women, on the other hand, were the gatherers. They were responsible for finding edible leaves, roots, and berries, so they had to remember the location of particular trees and plants. Thus, men's brains were programmed to follow routes and women's to remember locations.

1. Experts/agree

   <u>Experts agree that neither sex is more intelligent than the other.</u>

2. It/know/for a long time

   <u>It has been known for a long time that women learn languages more easily</u>
   <u>than men do.</u>

3. Researchers/prove/a long time ago

   _____

4. Scientists/reassure/men

   _____

5. It/often observe

   _____

6. It/think/by many scientists

   _____

Write two sentences of your own.

7. _____

8. _____

Subjunctive Noun Clauses

After certain independent clause verbs and adjectives, you must use the subjunctive form of the verb in the following noun clause. The subjunctive form of a verb is the same as the base form—*be, go, come, do,* and so on.

The verbs and adjectives that require the subjunctive form in the noun clauses that follow indicate urgency, advisability, necessity, and desirability.

Verbs			Adjectives	
advise	insist	request	advisable	mandatory
ask	order	require	desirable	necessary
command	prefer	suggest	essential	urgent
demand	propose	urge	important	vital
direct	recommend			

The company president **urged** that the marketing department **be** more aggressive.

It is **necessary** that each salesperson **work** longer hours.

Make a subjunctive verb negative by putting the word *not* in front of it

She **insisted** that the company **not lose** any more customers to its competitors.

The subjunctive also occurs when the independent clause verb is in the passive voice.

It **was recommended** that the department **not hire** new staff at this time.

Step 1 Read the following information.

Step 2 Write complex sentences containing subjunctive noun clauses.
- Rewrite each question as a main clause.
- Use the information from the proposed restrictions to write a subjunctive noun clause.
- Combine the two clauses to make a new complex sentence.

The first one has been done for you as an example.

Background Information

A three-year drought has caused a serious water shortage in the fictitious country of Sunnyland. As a result, Sunnyland's water department has recommended restrictions on water use.

Sunnyland County Water Department

Sunnyland County, Texas

Due to the recent drought in our region, the County of Sunnyland is imposing restrictions on water use, effective immediately. Violators will be subject to penalties.

Restrictions on Water Use

a. All citizens must conserve water wherever possible.
b. Every individual must decrease water use.
c. Every family must reduce its water use by 40 percent.
d. In the cities, everyone must limit showers to 5 minutes.
e. In the countryside, farmers must cut their water use by 25 percent.
f. Every farmer should install a drip irrigation system.
g. People in the suburbs must not use water to wash cars, sidewalks, or streets.

1. What does the water department recommend?

   <u>The water department recommends that all citizens conserve water</u>
   <u>wherever possible.</u>

2. What will the water department demand?

   _____

3. What is necessary?

   _____

4. What does the water department propose for city dwellers?

   _____

5. What is required of farmers?

   _____

6. What is suggested for farmers?

   _____

7. What does the water department urge for people living in suburban areas?

   _____

Write three sentences of your own using a different verb or adjective from the chart in the independent clause.

8. _____

9. _____

10. _____

If/Whether Clauses

An *if/whether* clause is a dependent noun clause that begins with the subordinator *whether* or *if*. *Whether* is more formal than *if*. The optional phrase *or not* may be added in two places with *whether* and in one place with *if*. Therefore, there are five possible patterns:

The patient wanted to know **whether Dr. Chen practices acupuncture**.

The patient wanted to know **whether or not Dr. Chen practices acupuncture**.

The patent wanted to know **whether Dr. Chen practices acupuncture or not**.

The patient wants to know **if Dr. Chen practices acupuncture**.

The patient wants to know **if Dr. Chen practices acupuncture or not**.

Notice that *if/whether* clauses are statements, not questions, even though they are made from *yes/no* questions (questions that can be answered *yes* or *no*). *If/whether* clauses use statement word order (subject-verb) and do not contain *do, does,* or *did*.

To change a question into an *if/whether* clause, add a subordinator (*if* or *whether*), change the word order to statement word order, and delete *do, does,* and *did* if necessary.

Question	Sentence with *if/whether* clause
Is the test easy?	The students want to know if ⌐is⌐ ⌐the test⌐ easy.
Does he know the answer?	I want to know whether ~~does~~ he know ˄the answer.

Follow the sequence of tenses rules if necessary. (If the independent clause verb is in a past tense, the verb in the noun clause should also be in a past tense.)

John asked if the test ~~is~~ ^was^ hard.

PRACTICE 4

If/Whether Clauses

Imagine that you are doing research on acupuncture. In addition to getting information from the library and the Internet, you have decided to write a letter to Dr. Robert Hsu, a leading authority in the field. Here are the questions you wish to ask Dr. Hsu:

1. Is acupuncture a risky medical procedure?
2. Are the needles made of stainless steel or of some other metal?
3. Do the needles hurt when they are inserted?
4. Has the effectiveness of acupuncture in relieving back pain ever been documented?
5. Can acupuncture strengthen the immune system?
6. Does acupuncture use the body's energy to promote healing?
7. Did you study acupuncture in China or in the United States?
8. Have you ever used acupuncture during an operation?

Add two questions of your own.

9. _____

10. _____

Complete the letter to Dr. Hsu. Change each of the ten questions into an *if/whether* clause. Add an *if/whether* clause to each incomplete sentence.

- Change the word order to SV statement order.
- Delete *do, does*, and *did* if necessary.
- Observe the sequence of tenses rules.

The first one has been done for you as an example. Use the blank lines at the end of the letter for your own questions.

415 Burleigh Avenue
Norfolk, VA 23505
July 8, 2006

Robert Hsu, M.D.
1200 South Eliseo Drive
Los Angeles, CA 90034

Dear Dr. Hsu:

I am a prenursing student at a community college in Norfolk, Virginia. I am doing research about the practice of acupuncture in China and the United States. I hope you will be kind enough to answer a few questions.

   The first thing I would like to know is (1) <u>whether or not acupuncture is a risky</u> <u>medical procedure</u>. Also, can you please tell me (2) _____ _____?
People who have never had acupuncture are curious to find out (3) _____ _____. Since I have frequent backaches, I am personally interested in learning (4) _____ _____.

   I also have two questions about the way acupuncture works in the body. Can you say for certain (5) _____? I also wonder (6) _____.

   About your own background, I would like to ask (7) _____ _____.

   Finally, I have heard that acupuncture is used as an anesthetic during surgery in China, and I am wondering (8) _____ _____.

(9) _____
_____

(10) _____
_____

Thank you sincerely for your time.

Very truly yours,

Marvin Lemos

Marvin Lemos

Question Clauses

A question clause is a dependent noun clause that begins with a subordinator such as *who, what, when, where, why, how, how much, how long,* and so on. There are two possible patterns. In the first pattern, the subordinator is the subject of the clause.

SUBJECT/SUBORD. V

The police do not know **who** committed the robbery.

In the second pattern, the subordinator is not the subject of the clause.

SUBORD.   ⌐SUBJECT¬   V

The police do not know **when** the robbery happened.

Notice that the word order in question clauses is statement order (subject + verb), not question order (verb + subject). Also, question clauses do not contain *do, does,* or *did* because they are not questions even though they begin with a question word.

To change a question into a question clause, change the word order to statement word order and delete *do, does,* and *did* if necessary.

Question	Sentence with Question Clause
What time is it?	Please tell me what time ⌊is⌋⌊it⌋.
How did the robbers enter the apartment?	The police want to know how ~~did~~ the robbers enter the apartment.

In the second example, *ed* is added above the word *enter*.

Follow the sequence of tenses rules if necessary. (If the independent clause verb is in a past tense, the verb in the noun clause should also be in a past tense.)

The victims **did not know** how the robbers **had entered** the apartment.

PRACTICE 5

Question Clauses

Imagine that you are working as a summer intern at your local newspaper, the "Fog City News." A well-known rock group, Behind Bars, is in town to give a concert. Your boss has asked you to write an article about the group for the Sunday entertainment section. However, when you try to interview the group, they are not very helpful.

Here is a list of questions that you have prepared for the interview.

1. When and where will the concert take place?
2. When did you last perform in Fog City?
3. How many years have you been together as a group?
4. Who writes your songs?
5. Where do you practice on the road?
6. How many songs have you recorded?
7. Which company produces your CDs?
8. How many Grammys do you have?

Add two questions of your own.

9. _____
10. _____

Complete the memo that follows. Explain to your boss why you cannot write the article. Change each of the ten questions into a question clause. Add a question clause to each incomplete sentence.

- Change the word order to SV statement order.
- Delete *do, does*, and *did* if necessary.
- Observe the sequence of tenses rules.

The first one has been done for you as an example. Use the blank lines at the end of the memo for your own questions.

Interoffice Memorandum

Date: _____, 2005

To: Warren Carreiro, Editor
     Sunday Entertainment Section

From: _____, Summer Intern

Re: Proposed article about Behind Bars rock band

Unfortunately, I will not be able to write an article for the Sunday entertainment section because my interview with Behind Bars was not very successful.

I began the interview by asking (1) <u>when and where the concert would take place</u>_____. Then I asked (2) _____

In my next question, I tried to find out (3) _____

_____. They did

not give me any information at all. For instance, they did not reveal (4) _____

_____.

They also did not tell me (5) _____

_____. No one remembered

(6) _____.

They told me to ask their manager (7) _____

_____. The entire group was silent when I asked them

(8) _____ they had. Finally, I asked them

(9) _____.

They ended the interview without even telling me (10) _____

_____.

_____
    (your signature)

_____
    (your name)

Review

These are the important points covered in this chapter.

1. A noun clause is a dependent clause that acts like a noun.

   ┌─ NOUN ─┐ ┌────────── NOUN CLAUSE ──────────┐
   John asked a **question**. John asked **which chapters the exam would cover**.

2. A noun clause can act as a subject, an object, or a subject complement. *That* clauses can also follow certain adjectives and nouns. The most common position of a noun clause is after the verb of the main (independent) clause.

3. Starting a sentence with a noun clause is awkward. English speakers usually rewrite these sentences so that they begin with *it* and end with the noun clause.

   That the professor canceled the exam surprised us.

   It surprised us **that the professor canceled the exam**.

   Whether the professor will reschedule the exam is uncertain.

   It is uncertain **whether the professor will reschedule the exam**.

4. Passive voice is often used in these kinds of sentences, especially in academic writing.

   It **was** once **believed** by many that Earth was flat.

5. When a noun clause reports what someone asked or said, you must follow the sequence of tenses rules for reported speech.

6. Following verbs and adjectives indicating urgency, advisability, necessity, and desirability, use the base form of the verb in the noun clause. This kind of noun clause is called a subjunctive noun clause.

   It is necessary that students **be** on time for the final exam.

7. Noun clauses use statement word order even when they begin with a question word. They also do not contain *do, does,* or *did* because they are not questions.

8. Commas are not used with noun clauses.

Types of Noun Clauses

That clauses • formed from statements • introduced by subordinator *that* • *that* can be omitted	The Russian president and his wife told the press **(that) they were enjoying their visit.**
Subjunctive noun clauses • verb in base form • occur after verbs and adjectives of urgency, advisability, necessity, and desirability	The president of the United States suggested **that Russia open its doors to U.S. business.**
Question clauses • formed from *wh-* questions; *wh-* words are the subordinators: *who, where, which, how,* etc. • use SV statement word order • *do, does, did* disappear	Do you know **who the interpreter for the Russian leader was?** The reporter asked **which companies planned to do business in Russia.**
If/Whether clauses • formed from *yes/no* questions • introduced by subordinator *if* or *whether.* *Whether* is more formal than *if.* • *or not* may be added • use SV statement word order • *do, does, did* disappear	The question is **whether (or not) U.S. and European companies understand the Russian business environment (or not).** No one knows **if the experiment will succeed (or not).**

Editing Practice

Edit the composition that follows on page 208 for errors in noun clauses. You should make 21 changes. Look for these kinds of errors:

INCORRECT WORD ORDER

We do not know who ~~is she~~ she is.

MISSING SUBORDINATOR AND INCORRECT WORD ORDER

Λ careful shopper asks ~~is there~~ if there is a warranty on a product before buying it.

SEQUENCE OF TENSES RULES NOT FOLLOWED

The newspaper reported that world leaders ~~have~~ had failed to agree at the conference.

SUBJUNCTIVE VERB NOT USED

Environmentalists urged that carbon dioxide emissions ~~are~~ be decreased immediately.

INCORRECT PUNCTUATION

Everyone wonders when world peace will become a reality. Everyone hopes that peace will come soon.

A College Lecture

[1]Professor Sanchez gave a lecture on transistors last Tuesday. [2]First, he explained what are transistors. [3]He said, that they are very small electronic devices used in telephones, automobiles, radios, and so on. [4]He further explained that transistors control the flow of electric current in electronic equipment. [5]He wanted to know which popular technological invention cannot operate without transistors. [6]Most students agreed, it is the personal computer. [7]Professor Sanchez then asked if the students know how do transistors function in computers. [8]He said that the transistors were etched[1] into tiny silicon microchips and that these transistors increase computers' speed and data storage capacity. [9]Then he asked the class when had transistors been invented? [10]Sergei guessed that they were invented in 1947. [11]The professor said that he is correct. [12]Professor Sanchez then asked what was the importance of this invention? [13]Many students answered that it is the beginning of the information age. [14]At the end of the lecture, the professor assigned a paper on transistors. [15]He requested that each student chooses a topic by next Monday. [16]He suggested that the papers are typed.

Writing Practice

Imagine that you are going to graduate from the university a year from now, and you are interested in seeing what kinds of positions employers are offering to graduates in your field (business, engineering, teaching, and so on). You could look in your local newspaper to see what job opportunities are available. The following are examples of ads that you might find.

College Grad

Do you have a B.A. or B.S. degree in accounting or business? No experience necessary. Training program in national firm. Inquiries welcomed. Write: Billings, Goodwill, and Rush Accountants, Inc., 354 Waterfront Center, Suite 3790, New York, New York, 10017. Affirmative Action Employer.

Engineering Graduates

Must possess degree in electrical/chemical/industrial engineering. Company is expanding. Job opportunities on U.S. West or East Coasts and in Middle East. Letters of inquiry are welcome. Write: Frank Memry, MHC Engineering, Inc., 475 Evanston Drive, Santa Clara, CA 94301. Equal Opportunity Employer.

---

[1]**etched:** cut into the surface

If you are planning to become an accountant or an engineer, you might answer one of these ads. If you have a different career preference, look in your local newspaper for an ad that fits your needs, and attach the ad to your assignment.

Write a letter of inquiry using noun clauses. Use *that* clauses to state information that you already know ("Your ad stated that your company was seeking . . . "). Use *wh-* word clauses and *if/whether* clauses to ask for information. You might want to inquire about the size of the company, travel requirements, salary, benefits, number of employees, advancement opportunities, support for further education, and so on.

Use the letter in Practice 4 on page 203 as a model. Notice the punctuation in the addresses and the greeting and closing. Also note the capitalization of proper nouns, of the word *Dear*, and of the first word of the closing. Study the line spacing between different parts of the letter. When you write your own letter, follow this format exactly.

Adverb Clauses

Woodcut from *Canterbury Tales*, 1490 edition

An **adverb clause** is a dependent clause that functions as an adverb. It can tell *when, where, why, how, how long, how far, how often*, and *for what purpose* something happened. An adverb clause can also express a contrast.

An adverb clause always begins with a subordinating conjunction that expresses the relationship between the adverb clause and the independent clause.

Relationship	Adverb Clause	Independent Clause
Time	SUBORDINATOR **As soon as** a baby opens its eyes,	it begins to observe its surroundings.
Contrast	SUBORDINATOR **Although** some people are more productive in the morning,	others work better at night.

Kinds of Adverb Clauses

These are the various kinds of adverb clauses. In the pages that follow, you will study and practice each kind.

- **Time clauses** answer the question "When?"
- **Place clauses** answer the question "Where?"
- **Clauses of manner** answer the question "How?"
- **Distance clauses** answer the question "How far?"
- **Frequency clauses** answer the question "How often?"
- **Purpose clauses** answer the question "For what intention?"
- **Result clauses** answer the question "For what effect?"
- **Conditional clauses** answer the question "Under what circumstance?"
- **Contrast clauses of direct opposition** show how one thing differs from another.
- **Contrast clauses of concession** show an unexpected result.

Punctuation of Adverb Clauses

The punctuation of an adverb clause depends on the order of the clauses. When an adverb clause comes first in a sentence, put a comma after it. When an adverb clause follows an independent clause, do not separate the clauses with a comma.

ADVERB CLAUSE   INDEPENDENT CLAUSE
Because humans are curious animals, they constantly explore their world.

INDEPENDENT CLAUSE   ADVERB CLAUSE
Humans constantly explore their world **because they are curious animals.**

Time Clauses

An **adverb time clause** tells when the action described in the independent clause took place. The action in a time clause can occur at the same time or at a different time. Be aware that verbs in time clauses often take forms that you do not expect. For example, the verb in a future time clause uses a present form, not a future form. Consult a grammar book to learn about these special situations.

A time clause can come before or after an independent clause.

A time clause is introduced by one of the subordinators in the following chart.

Time Subordinators	
when: a specific time	**When people had to hunt for food,** they moved from place to place.
whenever: at any time	**Whenever food became scarce in one area,** they moved to another area.
while: at the same time	The men hunted game **while the women gathered plants.**
as soon as: soon after	Eating habits changed **as soon as people stopped moving from place to place in search of food.**
after: later	**After people learned how to grow their own food,** they settled in villages.
since: from that time	**Since the United States changed from an agricultural to an industrial society,** eating habits there have changed.
as: at the same time	People in the United States started eating more processed convenience foods **as their lives became busier.**
before: earlier	**Before people in the United States moved to cities,** they grew most of their own food.
until: up to the time	Women had time to cook meals "from scratch"[1] **until they went to work in factories and offices.**

PRACTICE 1

Time Clauses

A. **Step 1** Form an adverb time clause by adding a time subordinator to the appropriate sentence in each pair. Use a different time subordinator in each clause.

Step 2 Write a new sentence by combining the adverb clause with the independent clause in each pair. Add a comma if necessary. Write your sentences on a separate sheet of paper.

Step 3 Copy your sentences to make a paragraph on the lines provided on page 213 and circle the subordinators.

The first one has been done for you as an example.

1. Everyone should know what to do. An earthquake strikes.
2. If you are inside, move away from windows, and get under a desk or table, or stand in a doorway. You feel the floor begin to shake.
3. Try to stay calm. The earthquake is happening.
4. Do not move. The floor stops shaking.

---

[1]**from scratch:** not using convenience foods (such as cake mixes) that have been previously prepared

5. You are sure the earthquake is over. You may begin to move around. You have checked carefully for fallen power lines. You may go outside.

Everyone should know what to do (when) an earthquake strikes.

_____

_____

_____

_____

_____

B. Choose either topic 1 or 2 and write an original paragraph on a separate sheet of paper. Use adverb time clauses in your paragraph. Use a variety of time subordinators, and circle them.

1. Tell someone what to do in the event of a house fire, an auto accident, a boat sinking, or any other dramatic event.
2. Create a story (real or imaginary) about a dramatic event that happened to you in the past.

Place Clauses

An **adverb place clause** tells where the action described by the main verb took place. The subordinators *wherever, everywhere,* and *anywhere* are similar in meaning and are interchangeable. You can begin a sentence with *wherever, everywhere,* and *anywhere* clauses, but usually not with a *where* clause. (Expressions such as the following are exceptions: *Where there is lightning, there is thunder. Where there is smoke, there is fire.*)

Place Subordinators	
where: a specific place	Most people shop **where they get the lowest prices**.
wherever: any place	I pay by credit card **wherever I can**.
everywhere: every place	Can you use an ATM card **everywhere you shop?**
anywhere: any place	**Anywhere you go,** you hear people talking on their cell phones.

PRACTICE 2
Place Clauses

A. **Step 1** Form an adverb place clause by replacing the word *there* with a place subordinator in the appropriate sentence in each pair. Use all four subordinators at least once.

Step 2 Write a new sentence by combining the adverb clause with the independent clause. Add a comma if necessary.

Step 3 Circle the subordinators.

The first one has been done for you as an example.

1. People prefer to shop/credit cards are accepted there

   <u>People prefer to shop (where) credit cards are accepted.</u>

2. Consumers tend to buy more/credit cards are accepted for payment of merchandise there.

   _____

3. You cannot use credit cards/you shop there.

   _____

4. There are a few places of business/a credit card is not accepted there.

   _____

5. Travelers can use credit cards in foreign countries/they are accepted there.

   _____

B. ATM machines and cell phones are two common objects that did not exist 50 years ago. Choose something that your grandmother might not have seen but that is everywhere today.

Write a short paragraph on your topic. Use at least three adverb place clauses in your paragraph. Circle the subordinators. (If you cannot write a whole paragraph on one topic, write at least four sentences on different topics.)

Suggested topics: cell phones, ATM machines, people walking around with headphones, Starbucks stores, litter, homeless people, people eating in their cars, no-smoking signs, recycling bins, bumper stickers.

Distance, Frequency, and Manner Clauses

Adverb clauses of distance answer the question "How far?" **Adverb clauses of frequency** answer the question "How often?" **Adverb clauses of manner** answer the question "How?" Distance, frequency, and most (but not all) manner clauses follow the independent clause.

Distance, Frequency, and Manner Subordinators	
as + *adverb* + as: distance	Fire had destroyed the trees in the forest **as far as the eye could see**.
as + *adverb* + as: frequency	I do not visit my parents **as often as they would like me to**.
as: manner	We mixed the chemicals exactly **as the lab instructor had told us to**.
as + *adverb* + as: manner	Our instructor asked us to fill out the questionnaire **as carefully as we could**.
as if, as though: manner	The bus's engine sounds **as if/as though** it is going to stall at any moment.

Notes

1. In informal spoken English, people often use *like* in place of *as if* and *as though*. *Like* is not correct in formal written English, so use only *as if* and *as though* in your writing.

FORMAL   It looks **as if** it is going to rain.

INFORMAL   It looks **like** it is going to rain.

2. In very formal written English, the verb takes the same form as it does in conditional clauses when the information in the *as if/as though* clause is untrue (or probably untrue). However, many English speakers use normal verb forms in this situation.

FORMAL   John acts as if he **were** the Prince of Wales.

INFORMAL   John acts as if he **is** the Prince of Wales.

PRACTICE 3

Distance, Frequency, and Manner Clauses

A. Form a sentence containing an adverb clause by adding a distance, frequency, or manner subordinator and completing the clause. Use each subordinator at least once. The first one has been done for you as an example.

1. People should try to recycle _____*as often as they can*_____. (frequency)
2. Most people want to move_____. (distance)
3. We should not consume our natural resources _____. (manner)
4. Should teenagers have the right to dress _____? (manner)
5. No nation in the world can afford to act _____. (manner—use *as if* or *as though*)

B. Answer the questions with sentences containing a clause of distance, frequency, or manner. Make sure that your answer contains two complete clauses, an independent clause and an adverb clause. (*Hint*: A phrase such as *as fast as possible* is not a clause.) The first one has been done for you as an example.

1. How does your writing instructor want you to write your essays?
   Our writing instructor wants us to write our essays as thoughtfully as we can.

2. How should you act when you see an enraged elephant running toward you?

   _____

3. How can you overcome stage fright[1]? (Use *as if* or *as though* in your sentence.)

   _____

_____

[1]**stage fright:** fear of performing on a stage

4. How can you perfect your pronunciation of a foreign language?

_____

5. When the teacher catches you sleeping in class, how can you avoid embarrassment? (Use *as if* or *as though* in your sentence.)

_____

Reason Clauses

An **adverb reason clause** answers the question "Why?" A reason clause can come before or after the independent clause in a sentence.

Reason Subordinators	
because	Europeans are in some ways better environmentalists than North Americans **because they are more used to conserving energy.**
since	**Since many Europeans live, work, and shop in the same locale,** they are quite accustomed to riding bicycles, trains, and streetcars to get around.
as	**As the price of gasoline has always been quite high in Europe,** most Europeans drive high-mileage automobiles that use less fuel.

PRACTICE 4

Reason Clauses

A. **Step 1** Form an adverb clause by adding a reason subordinator to the appropriate sentence in each pair. Do not change the order of the clauses.

Step 2 Write a new sentence by combining the adverb clause with the independent clause. Add a comma if necessary.

Step 3 Circle the subordinator.

The first one has been done for you as an example.

1. Electricity is expensive. Europeans buy energy-saving household appliances such as washing machines that use less water.
   Since electricity is expensive, Europeans buy energy-saving household appliances such as washing machines that use less water.

2. Europeans experienced hardship and deprivation[1] during and after World War II. They are used to conserving.

_____

_____

---

[1]**deprivation:** lack of necessities for living

3. Coal pollutes the air and gives off a lot of carbon dioxide. Most European nations have switched to natural gas or nuclear power to produce electricity.

_____

_____

4. In the United States, in contrast, 56 percent of the nation's electricity is generated by burning coal. Coal is cheap and plentiful.

_____

_____

5. The parliamentary system in Europe is different. A European head of government has more power than a U.S. president to force industry to make environmentally responsible changes.

_____

_____

B. Imagine that you have a summer job as an administrative assistant to a company manager. One of your duties is to write letters for the manager to sign. Some of the letters to the company's clients and employees contain good news, and some contain bad news. Complete the following first sentences in each letter with reason clauses. Use all three subordinators at least once. Also, vary the order of the clauses, sometimes putting the reason clause first and sometimes last. The first one has been done for you as an example.

Good News Letters

Dear _____:

I am pleased to inform you that . . .

1. . . . you have won the salesperson of the year award . . .
   because your sales have shown such outstanding growth over the past
   12 months, you have won the salesperson of the year award.

2. . . . we are increasing the limit on your credit card to $5,000 . . .

   _____

   _____

3. . . . the company has decided to offer you a raise . . .

   _____

   _____

4. . . . we have decided to extend the time limit for repayment of your loan . . .

   _____

   _____

Bad News Letters

Dear _____ :

I regret to inform you that . . .

1. . . . the company has decided not to renew your car insurance policy . . .

    _____

    _____

2. . . . we are unable to offer you employment at this time . . .

    _____

    _____

3. . . . we have decided not to extend the time limit for repayment of your loan . . .

    _____

    _____

Result Clauses

An adverb result clause expresses the effect or consequence of the information in the independent clause. A result clause follows the independent clause in a sentence.

Result Subordinators	
so + *adjective/adverb* + that	Joanna's cookie business is **so** successful **that she hired three new employees last week.** New orders are coming in **so** rapidly **that she has expanded her production facilities.**
such a(n) + *noun* + that	Joanne's cookies are **such** a success **that she is considering franchising the business.**
so much/many + *noun* + that	Running the business takes **so much** time now **that Joanne no longer does the baking herself.** There were **so many** orders for her holiday cookies **that her workers were baking 24 hours a day.**
so little/few + *noun* + that	Now Joanne has **so little** free time **that she has not taken a vacation in months.** Her cookies contain **so few** calories **that even people on diets can enjoy them.**

PRACTICE 5

Result Clauses

A. Step 1 Form an adverbial clause by adding a result subordinator to the appropriate sentence in each pair.
Step 2 Write a new sentence by combining the adverb clause with the independent clause. Add a comma if necessary.
Step 3 Circle the subordinator.

The first one has been done for you as an example.

1. Anthropological museums have realistic displays. A visitor can gain insight into the lifestyles of ancient people.
   Anthropological museums have (such) realistic displays (that) a visitor can gain insight into the lifestyles of ancient people.

2. The Ancient Peru exhibit was popular. It was held over for two weeks.
   _____
   _____

3. The artifacts[1] were of historic value. Anthropologists from several universities came to study them.
   _____
   _____

4. The exhibits were precious. A museum guard was posted in every room.
   _____
   _____

5. Computer graphics allowed the exhibit's curators[2] to present the lives of ancient Peruvians realistically. You felt you were actually there.
   _____
   _____

6. There were many exhibits. We could not see all of them.
   _____
   _____

B. Complete the sentences in this story with an appropriate result clause.

Last week our biology class went on a field trip to a local science museum. Our appointment was for 9:00 a.m. We went there by bus, but the bus driver got lost. In fact, we were (1) ____so____ lost that we almost turned around and drove back to school.

At long last, we arrived at the museum. The curator met us and took us to see the snake exhibit. In one room, a man was sitting on a chair with a very large boa constrictor around his neck. He was feeding the snake its weekly meal of mice. A few of the students started shrieking when they saw the first cute little mouse disappear into the boa constrictor's open jaws. They were shrieking (2) _____ loudly _____.

---

[1] **artifacts:** objects such as tools, weapons, pottery, and clothing
[2] **curators:** keepers of museums who plan, design, care for, manage, and build exhibits and collections

After the boa constrictor had finished his meal, the curator asked if any of us would like to hold it. It was (3) _____ a large and heavy snake _____. The few students who were brave enough to hold it said that its skin was surprisingly dry and smooth.

Next, we visited the insect room. Well, there must have been a million bugs in that place! There were (4) _____ many different _____. Our teacher had assigned each student an insect to draw in detail. It was almost lunchtime. I spent (5) _____ time trying to find my assigned insect among the millions _____.

By the time I had found my insect and sketched it, I was starved. In fact, I was (6) _____ hungry _____!

Purpose Clauses

An adverb purpose clause states the purpose of the action in the independent clause. A purpose normally follows the independent clause, but you may put it at the beginning of a sentence if you want to especially emphasize it.

Purpose Subordinators	
so that	Farmers use chemical pesticides **so that they can get higher crop yields.**[1]
in order that	**In order that consumers can enjoy unblemished**[2] **fruits and vegetables,** farmers also spray their fields.

Notes

1. *In order that* is formal.
2. The modals *may/might, can/could, will/would,* or *have to* usually occur in a purpose clause.
3. We often use the phrase *in order to* + a base verb or simply *to* + a base verb when the subjects of both the independent clause and the purpose clause are the same person or thing. We prefer *to* + verb over *in order to* + verb because it is shorter. The first example above could be written as follows because the two subjects (*farmers* and *they*) refer to the same people.

Farmers use chemical pesticides **in order to get** higher crop yields.

Farmers use chemical pesticides **to get** higher crop yields.

In the second example, the two subjects (*farmers* and *consumers*) are different, so it is not possible to use an *in order to* + verb or a *to* + verb phrase.

---

[1]**crop yields:** amounts of a crop that a farmer can sell
[2]**unblemished:** perfect, without spots or marks

PRACTICE 6
Purpose Clauses

A. **Step 1** Match the ideas in the two columns.
Step 2 Add a purpose subordinator to one of the sentences in each matched pair to form a purpose clause.
Step 3 Write a new sentence by combining the adverb clause with the independent clause. Add a comma if necessary.
Step 4 Circle the subordinator.

The first one has been done for you as an example.

<u>e</u> 1. Chemists create food products in the laboratory.

2. For example, an artificial food called "bacon bits" was invented.

3. Chemicals are added to many foods.

4. Most farmers use chemical fertilizers and pesticides.

5. Some farmers use only natural pest control methods.

6. People like to buy organic farm produce.

a. They can avoid food with chemicals.

b. They can increase crop yields.

c. They can produce organic[3] crops.

d. The foods will stay fresh longer.

e. Consumers can have substitutes for scarce, expensive, or fattening natural foods.

f. Consumers could enjoy the taste of bacon without the fat.

1. <u>Chemists create food products in the laboratory (so that) consumers can have substitutes for scarce, expensive, or fattening natural foods.</u>

2. _____

_____

3. _____

_____

4. _____

_____

5. _____

_____

6. _____

_____

---

[3]**organic:** grown without chemicals

B. Look at Part A and decide which three sentences you can rewrite using *in order to* + simple verb or *to* + simple verb. Write the new sentences on the lines provided.

1. _____

   _____

2. _____

   _____

3. _____

   _____

Contrast Clauses

There are two types of adverb clauses that express contrast: direct opposition clauses and concession clauses.

Direct Opposition Clauses

In this type, the information in the adverb clause and the information in the independent clause are in direct contrast.

Direct Opposition Subordinators	
whereas	San Francisco is cool during the summer, **whereas Los Angeles is generally hot**.
while	**While most homes in San Francisco do not have air conditioning,** it is a necessity in Los Angeles.

Notes
1. *While* and *whereas* have the same meaning and are interchangeable.
2. Use a comma between the two clauses no matter which order they are in. (This is an exception to the comma rule for adverb clauses.)
3. Since the two ideas are exact opposites, you can put the subordinator with either clause, and the clauses can be in either order. Thus, the examples can be written in four ways with no change in meaning:

San Francisco is cool during the summer, whereas Los Angeles is generally hot.

Whereas Los Angeles is generally hot during the summer, San Francisco is cool.

Whereas San Francisco is cool during the summer, Los Angeles is generally hot.

Los Angeles is generally hot during the summer, whereas San Francisco is cool.

Concession (Unexpected Result) Clauses

A concession clause means "This idea is true, but the idea in the independent clause is more important."

These clauses are sometimes called "unexpected result" clauses because the information in the independent clause is surprising or unexpected based on the information given in the concession clause.

Concession Subordinators	
although	**Although I had studied all night,** I failed the test.
even though	Our house is quite comfortable **even though it is small**.
though	**Though the citizens had despised the old regime,** they disliked the new government even more.

Notes

1. *Although, even though*, and *though* have almost the same meaning. *Though* is less formal. *Even though* is a little stronger than *although*.
2. Some writers follow the normal comma rule for adverb clauses: Use a comma only when the concession clause comes before the independent clause. Other writers use a comma between the two clauses no matter which order they are in.
3. Be careful about which clause you use the subordinator with. Sometimes you can use it with either clause, but not always.

CORRECT — He loves sports cars, although he drives a sedan.

CORRECT — Although he loves sports cars, he drives a sedan.

CORRECT — I went swimming, even though the water was freezing.

NOT POSSIBLE — Even though I went swimming, the water was freezing.

Don't forget that there are other ways to express contrast. Refer to the section on contrast signal words in Chapter 7, pages 119–120.

PRACTICE 7
Contrast Clauses

A. **Step 1** Decide whether the two clauses in each item express direct opposition or concession. (There are four of each.)

Step 2 Add an appropriate contrast subordinator to one of the clauses. Use each subordinator at least once. (You will use *while* and *whereas* twice each.)

Step 3 Write a new sentence by combining the clauses, and add a comma.

Step 4 Circle the subordinator.

The first one has been done for you as an example.

1. Modern Olympic equestrian[1] events emphasize style. The ancient Greek events emphasized speed.

   <u>Modern Olympic equestrian events emphasize style, (whereas) the ancient</u>
   <u>Greek events emphasized speed.</u>

2. Both the common cold and the flu are caused by viruses. Only the flu can be prevented through immunization.

3. A cold develops gradually, and any fever that develops will be low-grade (101°F or less). The flu often comes on abruptly, with a sudden high fever.

4. Ludwig van Beethoven became totally deaf in midlife. He wrote some of the Western world's greatest music.

5. South Korea is becoming an economic superpower. It is a small country with few natural resources.

6. The Northwest rainfall averages hundreds of inches annually. The Southwest averages less than 12 inches per year.

7. Scientists know why earthquakes happen. They are still not able to predict them.

8. Smokers claim the right to smoke in public places. Nonsmokers claim the right to breathe clean air.

B. Read the following paragraph, which describes an experiment to test the healing power of placebos.[2] Fill in the blanks with an appropriate contrast subordinator. One sentence requires a direct opposition and the other a concession subordinator.

---

[1] **equestrian:** horse-related

[2] **placebo:** substance given to a patient instead of medicine, without telling him or her it is not real, either because the person is not really sick or because the placebo is part of a test of the effectiveness of real medicine. Sometimes patients who receive placebos improve.

Tor Wager, a psychologist at Columbia University, led a recent study in which test subjects were told that one skin cream would reduce pain, (1) _____ another wouldn't. Wager put the creams on two spots on the subjects' arms and then applied enough heat to produce a burning sensation. Brain scans and verbal reports indicated that subjects perceived less pain with the cream that "really worked," (2) _____ the creams were identical.[3]

C. Complete the sentences. In some pairs, you will have to add an independent clause. In others, simply complete the dependent clause. The first two have been done for you as examples.

1. a. A robot cannot think creatively, even though *it can make logical decisions based on input data.*

   b. A robot cannot think creatively, *whereas a human worker can.*

2. a. Though it seldom snows in the desert, _____
   _____

   b. While it seldom snows in the desert, _____
   _____

3. a. The IT (information technology) manager did not submit next year's budget on time, although _____
   _____

   b. The IT (information technology) manager did not submit next year's budget on time, whereas _____
   _____

4. a. In recent years, Asian medical techniques such as acupuncture have gained acceptance in the West, even though _____
   _____

   b. In recent years, Asian medical techniques such as acupuncture have gained acceptance in the West, while _____
   _____

5. a. Even though SUVs are dangerous to drive, _____
   _____

   b. Whereas SUVs are dangerous to drive, _____
   _____

Conditional Clauses

A conditional clause states a condition for a result to happen or not happen. In the sentence *If it rains tomorrow, we will not go to the beach,* the condition is the weather. The result is going or not going to the beach. A conditional clause can come before or after an independent clause.

---

[3]Achenbach, Joel. "Medicine: Please Pass the Sugar." *National Geographic* Aug. 2004:1.

Conditional Subordinators	
if	**If you study,** you will get good grades. The mayor would have lost the election **if the labor unions had not supported him**.
unless	**Unless you study,** you will not get good grades. The mayor cannot govern **unless the labor unions support him**.

Notes

1. There are four basic patterns of conditional sentences. Each pattern has a different combination of verb forms depending on whether the time is present, future, or past, and on whether the condition is true or not true. The following chart summarizes the four patterns. There are many variations to these basic patterns; consult a grammar book for more complete information.

Pattern	Verb form in the *if* clause	Verb form in the independent clause
1. Present time, true condition	present If (when) you have a college education,	present you earn more money.
2. Future time, true condition	present If you get at least 90% on the final exam,	future you will get an A in the course.
3. Present or future time, untrue condition	simple past If Paul were not so lazy, (*Paul is lazy.*)	*would* + base form he would get better grades.
4. Past time, untrue condition	past perfect If the test had been easier, (*The test was hard.*)	*would have* + past participle all of us would have gotten A's.

2. *Unless* means "if not."

> You cannot get a refund **unless you have a receipt**. (You cannot get a refund if you do not have a receipt.)

> **Unless you get at least 90% on the final exam**, you will not get an A in the class. (You will not get an A if you do not get at least 90% on the final exam.)

PRACTICE 8
Conditional Clauses

A. Complete the sentences. In some sentences, you will have to add an appropriate independent clause. In others, just complete the conditional clause. If necessary, refer to the preceding chart to select verb tenses. The first one has been done for you as an example.

1. The company will have to declare bankruptcy unless <u>its sales improve soon.</u>

2. If the company does not increase it profits, _____

   _____

3. The company would increase its profits if _____

   _____

4. Unless _____ ,
   all the employees will lose their jobs.

5. The company president would not have resigned if _____

   _____

6. The vice president will also resign unless _____

   _____

B. Everyone makes decisions in their lives that affect their lives. On a separate sheet of paper, write six sentences using conditional clauses. Write three sentences about decisions you are facing now or that you will face in the near future and three sentences about decisions you made in the past.

Examples

<u>If I get married, I will not be free to travel as much as I want to.</u>

<u>If I had not finished high school, I would still be working at a minimum-wage job.</u>

Review

These are the important points covered in this chapter.

1. An adverb clause is a dependent clause that answers questions such as *Where? When? Why? How? For what purpose?* and *Under what conditions?* Adverb clauses can also express two kinds of contrast.

2. Place an adverb clause either before or after an independent clause. If an adverb clause comes before an independent clause, put a comma after it. If it comes after an independent clause, do not use a comma. (*Exception:* Always use a comma with *while* and *whereas.* Also, many writers always use a comma with *although, though,* and *even though.*)

Adverb Clause Subordinators		
Time	**when, whenever, while, as soon as, after, since, as, before, until**	**Whenever I had to speak in front of people,** I was paralyzed by fear.
Place	**where, wherever, everywhere, anywhere**	I saw unfriendly, critical faces **everywhere I looked.**
Distance	**as + *adverb* + as**	She runs on the beach **as far as she can.**
Frequency	**as + *adverb* + as**	He visits his family **as often as he can.**
Manner	**as, as + *adverb* + as, as if/as though**	I tried to act **as if I were not afraid.**
Reason	**because, since, as**	**Since I need to make speeches for career advancement,** I enrolled in a speech class.
Purpose	**so that, in order that**	I took a speech class **so that I could overcome my fear of public speaking.**
Result	**so + *adjective/adverb* + that such a(n) + *noun* + that so much/little + *noun* + that so many/few + *noun* + that**	At first, making a speech made me **so** nervous **that I got a stomachache before every class.** During the semester, I made **so many** speeches **that I lost some of my fear.**
Concession (unexpected result)	**although, even though, though**	**Even though I am a successful business executive,** I still do not enjoy speaking in public.
Contrast (direct opposition)	**while, whereas**	At social events, I like to talk quietly with one or two people, **whereas my girlfriend enjoys being in the center of a crowd.**
Conditional	**if, unless**	**If I hadn't taken that speech class in college,** I wouldn't be able to do my job well. **Unless I have to give an impromptu speech on a topic I know nothing about,** I feel quite confident in front of any audience.

Editing Practice

Edit the essay on page 229 for errors in adverb clauses. There are 13 errors. Look for the following kinds of mistakes.

INCORRECT SUBORDINATOR
    so that
I made an appointment with my history professor, ~~so~~ I could ask his advice about graduate schools.

TOO MANY CONNECTORS
Even though I am studying five hours a night, ~~but~~ I am still getting low grades.
OR
~~Even though~~ I am studying five hours a night, but I am still getting low grades.

COMMA ERROR
He does not eat meat,/because he is a vegetarian.

WRONG SUBORDINATOR
  If
~~Unless~~ his father were not the owner of the store, he would not be working here.

Net[1] Addiction

[1]A lot of people enjoy surfing the Net.[2] [2]They look for interesting Web sites and chat with people all over the world. [3]However, some people spend such many hours online that they are Internet addicts. [4]Although an average person spends about eight to twelve hours per week, but an addict spends eight to twelve hours per day online. [5]Because addicts spend so much time interacting with the computer so their lives are negatively affected. [6]They become social recluses,[3] because they stop going out and talking to people face-to-face. [7]They avoid real-life social situations, preferring instead to be in a dimly lit room with only the glowing screen to light up their lives.

[8]Internet addiction affects not only the addicts themselves but also the people around them. [9]For example, John's marriage to Marta broke up until he insisted on spending so many hours on the Net. [10]As soon as he arrived home from work he was at his computer. [11]While he finished dinner, he would disappear into his computer room again. [12]He paid so little attention to her, that she finally divorced him.

[13]Since college students are especially technologically skilled they can easily become nonstop Net-surfers. [14]Most colleges provide computers at several locations around campus, so that students can use them at any time day or night. [15]As a result, students can spend too much time surfing the Net instead of "surfing" their textbooks. [16]Last semester, nine freshmen at Berkshire College flunked out[4] although they became Internet addicts. [17]In short, even though the Internet is an excellent source of information and entertainment, but we must not let it take over our lives.

Writing Practice

Practice using adverb clauses to enliven your writing. Choose one of the following topics and write two to three paragraphs about it. Use at least eight adverb clauses in your paragraph. Use a variety of clause types—time, reason, contrast, purpose, result, frequency, conditional, and so on. (Bonus points to anyone who can use all eleven types!)

Topic Suggestions
My life will be different from my parents' lives
A memorable vacation/trip/adventure
Why I want to become a _____

---

[1]**Net:** shortened from Internet
[2]**surfing the Net:** exploring the Internet
[3]**recluses:** people who withdraw from the world and live in isolation
[4]**flunked out:** left school because of failing grades

Adjective Clauses

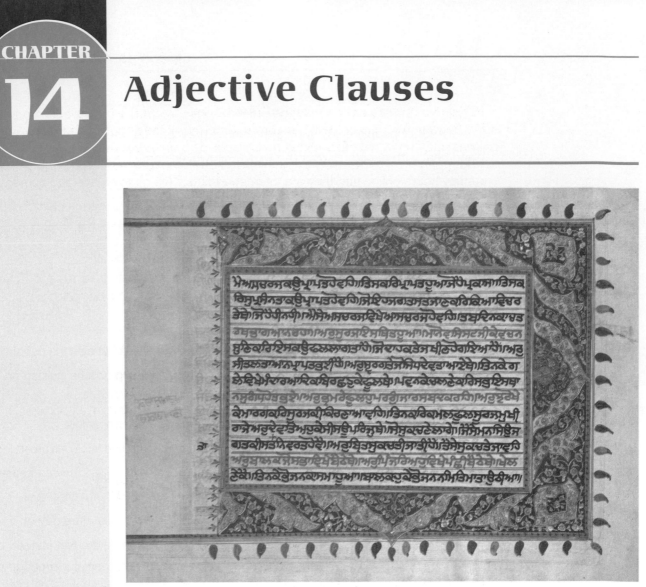

Hindu calligraphy

An **adjective clause** is a dependent clause that functions as an adjective. That is, it modifies (gives more information about) a noun or pronoun.

> ADJECTIVE CLAUSE
>
> The first thanksgiving feast in the United States, **which took place in 1621**, lasted three days.

> ADJECTIVE CLAUSE
>
> Everyone **who studied for the exam** passed it easily.

> ADJECTIVE CLAUSE
>
> The award **that Mario received** was for his volunteer work.

In the first sentence, *which took place in 1621* is an adjective clause that gives more information about the noun phrase *the first thanksgiving feast in the United States*. This noun phrase is called the **antecedent** of the adjective clause.

What is the adjective clause in the second sentence? What is the antecedent? Is the antecedent a noun or a pronoun? What is the adjective clause in the third sentence? What is the antecedent?

Adjective clauses are one way to improve your writing style because they use subordination to connect ideas. Subordination, rather than coordination (using lots of *and*s and *but*s to connect ideas) is the mark of a mature writing style. However, take care not to use too many adjective clauses. A paragraph or essay that is filled with too many *who*'s and *which*'s is not good either.

Relative Pronouns and Adverbs

An adjective clause begins with a **relative pronoun** or **relative adverb**.

PRONOUNS	**who, whom, whose, that**	refer to people
	which, whose, that	refer to animals and things
ADVERBS	**when, where**	refer to a time or a place

Position of Adjective Clauses

To avoid confusion, an adjective clause should come right after its antecedent.

CONFUSING

He left the gift in his friend's car **that he had just bought**.

(It is not clear whether the adjective clause modifies car or gift.)

CORRECTED

He left the gift **that he had just bought** in his friend's car.

(The adjective clause clearly modifies gift.)

In the following examples, notice that the adjective clause comes immediately after the antecedent *scientists* no matter where *scientists* appears in the sentence.

Scientists **who study fossils** are called paleontologists.

The government awards large contracts each year to scientists **who do research for the government.**

Occasionally, other words may come between the antecedent and the adjective clause.

Recently, a friend of mine at the University of Toronto, **who is majoring in electrical engineering,** received a government grant to study airport runway lighting.

Yesterday I spent an hour in the library reading the article from <u>Scientific American</u> **that the instructor had put on reserve**.

Sometimes an adjective clause modifies an entire sentence. In this case, it comes at the end of the sentence. The relative pronoun is always *which*, and the clause is always nonrestrictive.

The team won the championship, which shocked the opponents.

Verb Agreement in Adjective Clauses

The verb in an adjective clause agrees in number with its antecedent. Compare these two sentences:

An employee **who works part-time** usually receives no benefits.

(*The verb **works** is singular to agree with the singular antecedent* employee.)

Employees **who work part-time** usually receive no benefits.

(*The verb **work** is plural to agree with the plural antecedent* employees.)

Punctuation of Adjective Clauses

Adjective clauses are either **restrictive** (necessary) or **nonrestrictive** (unnecessary).

- A restrictive clause is necessary because it identifies its antecedent for the reader. Do not use commas with restrictive clauses.
- A nonrestrictive clause is not necessary to identify its antecedent; it merely gives the reader some extra information about it. Because you can omit a nonrestrictive clause without loss of meaning, separate it from the rest of the sentence with commas.
- The relative pronoun *that* is used in restrictive clauses only. *Which* is used in nonrestrictive clauses only. The other relative pronouns and adverbs can be used in both restrictive and nonrestrictive clauses.

Restrictive (necessary): no commas

The professor **who teaches my biology class** won a Nobel Prize two years ago.

(*Which professor won a Nobel Prize two years ago? The clause **who teaches my biology class** is necessary to identify the professor.*)

He won the prize for research **that might lead to a cure for AIDS**.

(*For which research did he win the prize? We need the clause **that might lead to a cure for AIDS** to tell us.*)

Nonrestrictive (unnecessary): commas

Professor Jones, **who teaches my biology class**, won a Nobel Prize two years ago.

(*The person who won a Nobel Prize is identified by his name, so the clause **who teaches my biology class** is extra, unnecessary information about Professor Jones. If it were omitted, we would still know which person won the Nobel Prize.*)

He won the prize for his research into the structure of T-cells, **which might lead to a cure for AIDS**.

(*We already know which research he won the prize for: his research into the structure of T-cells. The information **which might lead to a cure for AIDS** is not necessary to identify the research; it merely gives us extra information about it.*)

Identify and punctuate sentences with adjective clauses.

PRACTICE 1

Restrictive and Nonrestrictive Clauses

Step 1 Underline the adjective clause or clauses in each sentence. (Some sentences have two.)

Step 2 In the space next to the sentence, write *R* for a restrictive and *NR* for a nonrestrictive clause.

Step 3 Add commas to the nonrestrictive clauses.

The first two have been done for you as examples.

  R   1. Families <u>whose incomes are below a certain level</u> pay no income tax.

 NR   2. My family, <u>whose income is more than $50,000,</u> pays about 25 percent income tax.

_____ 3. The sun which in 40 minutes can produce enough solar energy to meet humankind's needs for a year is one of Earth's potential sources of power.

_____ 4. We are at the beginning of a medical computer revolution, according to an article that appeared in *Time* magazine

_____ 5. A medical computer is a machine that analyzes the results of laboratory tests and electrocardiograms.

_____ 6. A physician who feeds a patient's symptoms into a computer receives a list of diseases that fit the symptoms of that patient.

_____ 7. Laser beams which are useful in both medicine and industry were first predicted in science fiction stories 75 years ago.

_____ 8. The country that has the highest per capita[1] income is not the United States which is in third place.

_____ 9. Kuwait which is a small country in the Middle East is in first place.

_____ 10. It was a thrilling experience to meet the author of the book that we had been reading all semester.

_____ 11. The public is highly critical of the tobacco industry whose profits have been increasing in spite of the health risks of smoking.

_____ 12. Carbohydrates which are composed of carbon, hydrogen, and oxygen are organic compounds.

_____ 13. People who use body language[2] to express themselves are interesting to watch.

_____ 14. My brother-in-law who is from Italy moves his hands a lot when he is talking.

_____ 15. The man whom the president nominated to the Supreme Court is an experienced and respected judge.

_____ 16. X-ray machines are gradually being replaced by machines that can provide clearer, more detailed images of the human body, its tissues, and its organs.

_____ 17. X-ray machines are gradually being replaced by CAT scanners and MRI devices which can provide clearer, more detailed images of the human body, its tissues, and its organs.

_____ 18. The company promised to reimburse[3] everyone who had bought a defective[4] product.

_____ 19. Students whose grade point averages fall below 2.0 will be placed on probation.

_____ 20. She plans to marry her childhood sweetheart whom she has known since they were five years old.

---

[1]**per capita:** per person (literally, "per head" in Latin)
[2]**body language:** communication by body movements
[3]**reimburse:** pay money back to
[4]**defective:** flawed, not in working condition

Kinds of Adjective Clauses

There are different types of adjective clauses. In each different type, the relative pronoun has a different function. It may be a subject or an object in its own clause, or it may replace a possessive word.

Relative Pronouns as Subjects

A relative pronoun can be the subject of its own clause.

Subject Relative Pronouns	
who, which, that	American football, **which is** the most popular sport in the United States, began at Harvard University.

In this pattern, *who, which*, and *that* can be either singular or plural. Make the verb agree with the antecedent.

I have not read the **magazine** that **is lying** on the coffee table.

(*The verb **is lying** is singular to agree with the singular antecedent* magazine.)

I have not read the **magazines** that **are lying** on the coffee table.

(*The verb **are lying** is plural to agree with the plural antecedent* magazines.)

The following examples show you how to combine two sentences to make a new sentence containing a subject pattern adjective clause.

For People	

Restrictive who, that	People save time and energy. ~~They~~ use microwave ovens.
	    People **who use microwave ovens** save time and energy.
	    People **that use microwave ovens** save time and energy. (*informal*)

Nonrestrictive who	Microwave cooking is not popular with most professional chefs.
	~~Professional chefs~~ say that fast cooking does not allow flavors
	to blend.
	    Microwave cooking is not popular with most professional chefs, **who**
	    say that fast cooking does not allow flavors to blend.

For Animals and Things	

Restrictive that	Ovens are capable of cooking food quickly. ~~They~~ use microwave energy.
	    Ovens **that use microwave energy** are capable of cooking foods
	    quickly.

Nonrestrictive which	An electron tube in the oven produces microwaves. ~~Microwaves~~ cook
	by agitating[1] the water molecules in food.
	    An electron tube in the oven produces microwaves, **which cook by**
	    agitating the water molecules in food.

---

[1]**agitating:** moving very quickly

PRACTICE 2

Relative Pronouns as Subjects

A. Combine the two sentences in each pair to make a new complex sentence containing an adjective clause in the subject pattern.

Step 1 Change the subject of the second sentence to a relative pronoun. Use *who, which,* or *that* as appropriate.

Step 2 Combine the two sentences, placing the adjective clause as close to its antecedent as possible.

Step 3 Add commas if necessary.

The first one has been done for you as an example.

1. John Fish explained the complex structure of DNA. He is a research chemist.
   <u>John Fish, who is a research chemist, explained the complex structure of DNA.</u>

2. While he lectured, he showed us a slide. The slide diagrammed the double helix structure of DNA.

   _____

   _____

3. Words in English are often difficult for foreigners to pronounce. They begin with the consonants *th*.

   _____

   _____

4. Foreigners also have difficulty with English spelling. English spelling is not always consistent with its pronunciation.

   _____

   _____

5. Anyone must have a logical mind. He or she wants to be a computer programmer.

   _____

   _____

6. Fans quickly lose interest in a sports team. The team loses game after game.

   _____

   _____

B. Write six sentences that contain adjective clauses in the subject pattern. Use the following prompts. The first one has been done for you as an example.

1. I do not know anyone who <u>does not like chocolate ice cream.</u>

2. My father, who _____

3. _____ is a sport that _____

4. _____ is soccer, which _____

5. The school subject that _____

6. The school subjects that _____

Relative Pronouns as Objects

A relative pronoun can be an object in its own clause.

Object Relative Pronouns	
whom, **which, that,** Ø (no pronoun)	The address **that he gave me** was incorrect.

Note: You can omit *that* in object pattern clauses only.

The address **he gave me** was incorrect.

The following examples show you how to combine two sentences to make a new sentence containing an object pattern adjective clause.

For People	
Restrictive **whom, that, Ø**	The professor is chair of the English Department. You should see ~~the professor~~. The professor **whom you should see** is chair of the English Department. The professor **that you should see** is chair of the English Department. (*informal*) The professor **you should see** is chair of the English Department.
Nonrestrictive **whom**	Dr. White is an ecologist. You met ~~Dr. White~~ in my office. Dr. White, **whom you met in my office,** is an ecologist.
For Animals and Things	
Restrictive **that, Ø**	The book was written in German. The professor translated ~~the book~~. The book **that the professor translated** was written in German. The book **the professor translated** was written in German.
Nonrestrictive **which**	Environmental science is one of the most popular courses in the college. Dr. White teaches ~~environmental science~~. Environmental science, **which Dr. White teaches,** is one of the most popular courses in the college.

PRACTICE 3

Relative Pronouns as Objects

A. Combine the two sentences in each pair to make a new sentence containing an adjective clause in the object pattern.

Step 1 Change the object in the second sentence to a relative pronoun. Use *whom, which, that,* or no pronoun, as appropriate. Move the relative pronoun to the beginning of its clause.

Step 2 Combine the two sentences, placing the new adjective clause as close to its antecedent as possible.

Step 3 Add commas if necessary.

Step 4 Write the sentences as a paragraph in the space provided.

The first one has been done for you as an example.

1. Albert Einstein was a high school dropout. The world recognizes him as a genius.
2. As a young boy, Einstein had trouble in elementary and high school. He attended these schools in Germany.
3. He did poorly in certain subjects such as history and languages. He disliked them.
4. The only subjects were mathematics and physics. He enjoyed them.
5. He developed theories. We use his theories to help us understand the nature of the universe.
6. Einstein is best known for his general theory of relativity. He began to develop this theory while living in Switzerland.

> Albert Einstein, whom the world recognizes as a genius, was a high school dropout.

_____

_____

_____

_____

_____

_____

_____

_____

B. Write five sentences of your own that contain adjective clauses in the object pattern. Use the prompts given, and then write two sentences of your own. Write both restrictive and nonrestrictive clauses.

1. My mother, whom _____

_____

2. _____ the homework that _____

_____

3. _____ someone whom _____

_____

4. The islands of Hawaii, which _____

_____

5. The television program that _____

_____

Possessive Adjective Clauses

In possessive adjective clauses, the relative pronoun *whose* replaces a possessive word such as *Mary's, his, our, their, the company's,* or *its.* Possessive adjective clauses can follow the subject or the object pattern.

In the subject pattern, the *whose* + noun phrase is the subject of the adjective clause. In the object pattern, the *whose* + noun phrase is the object in the adjective clause.

Notes

1. Some writers feels that *whose* should be used to refer only to people. For animals and things, they recommend using *of which.* Compare:

   I returned the book **whose cover** was torn.

   I returned the book, **the cover of which** was torn.

   Other writers use *whose* in all but the most formal writing (such as legal documents).

2. You have learned that the verb in an adjective clause agrees with the antecedent.

   The **student** who **is working** alone is a friend of mine.

   The **students** who **are working** together are also friends of mine.

   Now learn the exception: When *whose* + noun is the subject of an adjective clause, the verb agrees with that noun.

   She takes care of two children whose mother **works** at night.
   (*The verb* **works** *is singular to agree with* mother.)

   She takes care of two children whose parents **work** at night.
   (*The verb* **work** *is plural to agree with* parents.)

The following examples show you how to combine two sentences to make a new sentence containing a subject pattern possessive adjective clause.

For People, Animals, and Things: Subject Pattern	
Restrictive **whose**	Opportunities are increasing for graduates. ~~Graduates'~~ degrees are in computer engineering. Opportunities are increasing for graduates **whose degrees are in computer engineering**.
Nonrestrictive **whose**	Santa Claus is the symbol of Christmas gift-giving. ~~His~~ jolly figure appears everywhere during the Christmas season. Santa Claus, **whose jolly figure appears everywhere during the Christmas season,** is the symbol of Christmas gift-giving.

The following examples show you how to combine two sentences to make a new sentence containing an object pattern possessive adjective clause.

For People, Animals, and Things: Object Pattern	
Restrictive **whose**	The citizens protested. The government had confiscated[1] ~~their~~ property. The citizens **whose property the government had confiscated** protested.
Nonrestrictive **whose**	*Consumer Reports* magazine publishes comparative evaluations of all kinds of products. Shoppers trust ~~the magazine's~~ research. *Consumer Reports*, **whose research shoppers trust,** publishes comparative evaluations of all kinds of products.

PRACTICE 4

Possessive Adjective Clauses

A. Combine the two sentences in each pair to make a new sentence containing a possessive adjective clause in the subject pattern.

Step 1 Find a possessive expression in the second sentence and change it to *whose*.

Step 2 Combine the two sentences, placing the new adjective clause as close to its antecedent as possible.

Step 3 Add commas if necessary.

1. Maya Angelou tells about her early life in her book *I Know Why the Caged Bird Sings*. Her childhood was difficult.

   <u>Maya Angelou, whose childhood was difficult, tells about her early life in her book I Know Why the Caged Bird Sings.</u>

2. Securities Corporation's president is a man. His expertise[2] on financial matters is well known.

   _____

   _____

3. First National Bank tries to attract female customers. The bank's president is a woman.

   _____

   _____

4. Companies conduct market research to discover trends among consumers. Consumers' tastes change rapidly.

   _____

   _____

5. A manufacturer can offer lower prices. Its costs are lower because of mass production.

   _____

   _____

---

[1]**confiscated:** taken by an authority, such as a government, teacher, or parent, without payment
[2]**expertise:** skill, knowledge

B. Follow the steps in Part A to combine the two sentences in each pair to make a new sentence containing a possessive adjective clause in the object pattern.

1. Maya Angelou is one of the most famous female poets in the United States. We have been reading Maya Angelou's poetry in our English class.
   <u>Maya Angelou, whose poetry we have been reading in our English class, is one of the most famous female poets in the United States.</u>

2. John is dating a girl. I keep forgetting the girl's name.
   _____
   _____

3. Any company has a better chance of success. Consumers easily recognize its logo or symbol.
   _____
   _____

4. McDonald's has restaurants all around the globe. Most people recognize its golden arches.
   _____
   _____

C. Write three sentences containing possessive adjective clauses in either the subject or the object pattern. Use the following prompts.

1. the lost child, whose photograph
   _____
   _____

2. my cousin, whose car
   _____
   _____

3. teachers whose classes
   _____
   _____

Relative Pronouns as Objects of Prepositions

A relative pronoun can be the object of a preposition in its own clause.

Object Relative Pronouns	
whom, which, that, Ø (no pronoun)	The address to which I sent my application was incorrect.

These adjective clauses are formed in two ways: the formal way and the informal way.

(a) In the formal way, the preposition and relative pronoun are together at the beginning of the clause:

for whom I did a favor   **to which** I sent my application

with whom I shared a secret   **in which** the gift was wrapped

(b) In the informal way, the pronoun comes at the beginning and the preposition at the end of the clause:

whom I did a favor **for**   **which** I sent my application **to**

whom I shared a secret **with**   **that** the gift was wrapped **in**

When should you use the informal way, and when should you use the formal way? In all but the most formal writing (master's theses, Ph.D. dissertations, legal documents, or business reports, for example), the informal pattern is probably acceptable. English has no academic or governmental authority that issues rules about correctness. Standards vary. In your classes, some teachers will require you to write only formal English, while others will accept informal usage. Always ask if you are not sure.

The following examples show you how to combine two sentences to make a new sentence containing an adjective clause. Sentence (a) is formal; all of the (b) sentences are informal.

For People	
Restrictive **whom, that, Ø**	The candidate lost the election. I voted for ~~the candidate~~. (a) The candidate **for whom I voted** lost the election. (b) The candidate **whom I voted for** lost the election. The candidate **that I voted for** lost the election. The candidate **I voted for** lost the election.
Nonrestrictive **whom**	Mayor Pyle lost the election. I voted for ~~Mayor Pyle~~. (a) Mayor Pyle, **for whom I voted**, lost the election. (b) Mayor Pyle, **whom I voted for**, lost the election.
For Animals and Things	
Restrictive **which, that, Ø**	No one had read the book. He quoted from the ~~book~~. (a) No one had read from the book **from which he quoted**. (b) No one had read the book **which he quoted from**. No one had read the book **that he quoted from**. No one had read the book **he quoted from**.
Nonrestrictive **which**	The President's Scholarship was awarded to someone else. John had applied for ~~the President's Scholarship~~. (a) The President's Scholarship, **for which John had applied**, was awarded to someone else. (b) The President's Scholarship, **which John had applied for**, was awarded to someone else.

The friend, whom I talk with / last topic of conversation

PRACTICE 5

*Relative
Pronouns
as Objects
of Prepositions*

A. Combine sentences to make a new sentence containing an adjective clause.

Step 1 Change the sentence with the underlined prepositional phrase to an adjective clause.

Step 2 Combine it with the first sentence. Write each new sentence twice, (a) in the formal pattern and (b) in any of the possible informal patterns.

The first one has been done for you as an example.

1. Finding reasonably priced housing in big cities is a problem. Many young people are concerned <u>about the problem.</u>
    (a) <u>Finding reasonably priced housing in big cities is a problem about</u>
        <u>which many young people are concerned.</u>
    (b) <u>Finding reasonably priced housing in big cities is a problem that many</u>
        <u>young people are concerned about.</u>

2. Affordable apartments are scarce. Young people would like to live <u>in them</u>.
    (a) _____
    (b) _____

3. Of course, many young people share apartments, but they have to take care in choosing the people. They will share living space and expenses <u>with these people</u>.
    (a) _____
    (b) _____

4. Living with people can be stressful, but it can also be fun. You are not related <u>to the people.</u>
    (a) _____
    (b) _____

5. In many countries, young people continue to live with their parents in the same house. They grew up <u>in that house</u>.
    (a) _____
    (b) _____

6. In the United States, young people do not want to live with their parents. They typically declare their independence <u>from their parents</u> at age 18.
    (a) _____
    (b) _____

B. Now write sentences of your own. Write two sentences in the informal pattern and two in an formal pattern. Use the prompts suggested.

1. Informal pattern
    (a) The package that _____ for finally arrived.
    (b) Uncle Charlie, whom _____ with, is going to spend Thanksgiving with his friends this year.

2. Formal pattern
   (a) I have received no response from your Customer Service Department, to which _____
   (b) The person to whom _____ called me yesterday with a job offer.

Relative Pronouns in Phrases of Quantity and Quality

A relative pronoun can occur in phrases of quantity and quality.

Quantity Relative Pronouns	
some of whom all of whom each of which both of which, etc.	He gave two answers, **both of which were correct.** The top students, **all of whom graduated with honors,** received scholarships.
Quality Relative Pronouns	
the best of whom the oldest of whom the most important of which, etc.	She has three daughters, **the oldest of whom is studying abroad.** The comedian's jokes, **the funniest of which I had heard before,** were about politics.

These adjective clauses can follow either the subject or the object pattern, and they are always nonrestrictive; that is, they are always used with commas.

The following examples show you how to combine two sentences to make a new sentence containing an adjective clause with an expression of quantity or quality. Notice that the relative pronoun is always *of whom* or *of which*.

For People	
Nonrestrictive **of whom**	The citizens of Puerto Rico are well educated. Ninety percent of ~~them~~ are literate.[1] The citizens of Puerto Rico, **ninety percent of whom are literate,** are well educated.
For Animals and Things	
Nonrestrictive **of which**	There are many delicious tropical fruits in Puerto Rico. I have never tasted most of ~~them~~ before. There are many delicious tropical fruits in Puerto Rico, **most of which I have never tasted before.**

---

[1] **literate:** able to read and write

PRACTICE 6

Adjective clauses with Phrases of Quantity and Quality

A. Change the second sentence in each pair to an adjective clause, and combine it with the first sentence. The first one has been done for you as an example.

1. There is a chain of islands in the Caribbean Sea. The most charming of the islands is Puerto Rico.

   <u>There is a chain of islands in the Caribbean Sea, the most charming of which is Puerto Rico.</u>

2. Puerto Rico attracts thousands of visitors. Most of them come for the sunny weather, the beautiful beaches, and the Spanish atmosphere.

   _____

   _____

3. Puerto Rico has many historic sites. The most famous of them are in the Old San Juan area of the capital city.

   _____

   _____

4. Puerto Rico's economy is growing. The most important sector[1] of the economy is clothing manufacturing.

   _____

   _____

5. Puerto Ricans have strong ties to the United States. All of them are U.S. citizens.

   _____

   _____

6. Puerto Rico has three political parties. One of them favors Puerto Rico's becoming a state.

   _____

   _____

B. Complete the sentences.

1. The presidential candidate spoke about his qualifications, the most impressive of which_____

2. The doctors in the free clinic, most of whom_____

   _____

Adjective Clauses of Time and Place

Adjective clauses can also be introduced by the relative adverbs *when* and *where*.

Relative Adverbs	
when, where	Ramadan is the month **when devout Muslims fast.**
	The Saudi Arabian city of Mecca, **where Mohammed was born,** is the holiest city in Islam.

---

[1]**sector:** part, division

These clauses refer to a time or a place, and they can be restrictive or nonrestrictive. In the following examples, notice how *when* and *where* replace entire prepositional phrases such as *during that night* and *in Berlin*.

Time	
Restrictive **when**	The lives of thousands of Germans suddenly changed on the night. East German soldiers began building the Berlin Wall ~~during that night~~. The lives of thousands of Germans suddenly changed on the night **when East German soldiers began building the Berlin Wall**.
Nonrestrictive **when**	On November 9, 1989, their lives changed again. The wall was torn down ~~on November 9, 1989~~. On November 9, 1989, **when the wall was torn down,** their lives changed again.
Place	
Restrictive **where**	The city was suddenly divided. Citizens had lived, worked, and shopped relatively freely ~~in the city~~. The city **where citizens had lived, worked, and shopped relatively freely** was suddenly divided.
Nonrestrictive **where**	Berlin was suddenly divided. Citizens had lived, worked, and shopped relatively freely ~~in Berlin~~. Berlin, **where citizens had lived, worked, and shopped relatively freely,** was suddenly divided.

It is also possible to write time and place clauses with the relative pronoun *which, that,* or Ø and a preposition. The following patterns are possible.

March 31, 1980, was the day
{
when I was born.
on which I was born.
which I was born on.
that I was born on.
I was born.
}

Cody, Wyoming, is the town
{
where I grew up.
in which I grew up.
which I grew up in.
that I grew up in.
I grew up in.
}

PRACTICE 7

*Adjective Clauses
of Time and Place*

A. Combine the two sentences in each pair, changing the second sentence into an adjective clause of time or place. Add commas if necessary. The first one has been done for you as an example.

1. Germany had been divided into two countries since 1945. It was defeated in World War II in 1945.

   Germany had been divided into two countries since 1945, when it was defeated in World War II.

2. 1989 was the year. The Berlin Wall was torn down in that year.

   _____

   _____

3. In 1990, Germany became one country again. East and West Germany were reunited in 1990.

   _____

   _____

4. East Germany became part of the Federal Republic of Germany. People had lived under communist rule in East Germany.

   _____

   _____

5. There was rejoicing in areas. Germans looked forward to reunification with their fellow citizens in some areas.

   _____

   _____

6. There was anxiety in places. People feared losing their jobs in some places.

   _____

   _____

B. Write four sentences containing adverbial adjective clauses, two sentences using *when* and two sentences using *where*. Try to write both restrictive and nonrestrictive clauses. Use the prompts given for sentences 1 and 2. Invent your own sentences in 3 and 4.

1. My grandmother enjoys telling about the time when _____

   _____

2. _____ my hometown, where _____

   _____

3. _____

   _____

4. _____

   _____

Review

These are the important points covered in this chapter.

1. An adjective clause is a dependent clause that functions as an adjective; that is, it gives more information about a noun or pronoun in the independent clause. The modified noun or pronoun is called the antecedent.
2. An adjective clause begins with a relative pronoun or a relative adverb.
3. Place an adjective clause after its antecedent and as close to it as possible to avoid confusion of meaning.
4. The verb in an adjective clause should agree in number with its antecedent.
5. Adjective clauses are either restrictive (necessary) or nonrestrictive (unnecessary). Add commas before and after nonrestrictive clauses.

				Relative Pronouns
who	refers to people	subject in its own clause	restrictive	The professor **who teaches my biology class** won a Nobel Prize two years ago.
			or nonrestrictive	Professor Jones, **who teaches my biology class,** won a Nobel Prize two years ago.
whom	refers to people	object in its own clause	restrictive	She loaned her car to someone **whom she did not know.**
			or nonrestrictive	Professor Jones, **whom I have for biology,** won a Nobel Prize two years ago.
whose	refers to people, animals, and things; shows possession	subject or object in its own clause	restrictive	I studied algebra with a professor **whose name I have forgotten.**
			or nonrestrictive	Apple Computer, **whose Macintosh computer changed computing,** was started by two men working in a garage.
which	refers to animals and things	subject or object in its own clause	nonrestrictive only	She teaches biology, **which is my favorite subject.**
				Her husband teaches algebra, **which I enjoy the least.**
that	refers to animals and things; informally, refers to people	subject or object in its own clause; if *that* is an object, it may be omitted	restrictive only	The class **that meets in the next room** is very noisy.
				The subject **that I enjoy the least** is algebra.
				The subject **I enjoy the least** is algebra.
				The salesman **that sold me my car** was fired. (*informal*)

Relative Adverbs				
when	refers to a time		restrictive	I work full time on days **when I do not have classes**.
			or nonrestrictive	I did not work last week, **when I had my final exams**.
where	refers to a place		restrictive	She has never returned to the city **where she was born**.
			or nonrestrictive	First City Bank, **where I have a checking account,** was robbed last week.

Editing Practice

Edit the following essay for errors in adjective clauses. You should make 14 changes. Look for the following kinds of errors.

INCORRECT RELATIVE PRONOUN

DISAGREEMENT OF VERB AND ANTECEDENT

INCORRECT REPETITION OF NOUNS OR PRONOUNS

INCORRECT COMMA USAGE

                whose
I telephoned the student ~~who his~~ wallet I found in the parking lot.

       live
People who ~~lives~~ in earthquake zones need earthquake insurance.

My friend whom I loaned my car to ~~him~~ returned it with several dents.

Electronic pagers, which always seem to beep at inappropriate times, should be turned off during concerts, lectures, and naps. (*Two commas added.*)

El Niño

[1] Scientists have been studying an ocean event who is the cause of drastic changes in weather around the world. [2] This event is an increase in the temperature of the Pacific Ocean that appear around Christmas off the coast of Peru. [3] Hence, the Peruvian fishermen whom first noticed it named it El Niño, a name that means "the Christ child" in Spanish. [4] The causes of this rise in ocean temperatures are unknown, but its effects are obvious and devastating.

[5] One of El Niño's far-reaching effects is that it threatens Peru's vital anchovy harvest, which could mean higher prices for food. [6] The warm water of El Niño keeps the nutrient-rich cold water which provides anchovies with food down at the bottom of the ocean. [7] Anchovies are the primary source of fish meal which is the main ingredient in livestock and chicken feed.

[8]In addition, guano[1] from birds who feed off the anchovies is a major source of fertilizer for farmers. [9]As a result of decreasing supplies of anchovies and guano, the prices of chicken feed, livestock feed, and fertilizer rise. [10]This causes farmers, who they must pay more for feed and fertilizer, to charge more for the food they produces. [11]The prices of eggs, meat, and even bread have soared as a result of El Niños in past years.

[12]El Niño has other global effects. [13]It can cause heavy rains, floods, and mudslides along the coasts of North and South America and droughts in other parts of the world. [14]In the 1982–1983 El Niño, West Africa suffered a terrible drought, which caused crop failures and food shortages. [15]Lack of rain also created problems for Indonesia, whose forests burned for months during the 1997–1998 El Niño. [16]Winds spread smoke from these fires as far north as Malaysia and Singapore, resulting in choking smog, that closed schools and caused pedestrians to wear masks.

[17]Indeed, El Niño is an unpredictable and uncontrollable phenomenon of nature, that we need to study it and understand it in order to prepare for and perhaps lessen its devastating effects in the future.

Writing Practice

Practice using adjective clauses in your writing. Choose one of the topics suggested, or write on a topic of your own choice. Write a short paragraph in which you use at least five adjective clauses. Use different patterns if possible.

1. Write about a favorite toy from your childhood.
2. Write about a childhood memory.
3. Describe a room in a house that you have lived in.
4. Retell the plot of a movie you have recently seen.
5. Describe a photograph or advertisement from a magazine.

---

[1]**guano:** droppings of seabirds and bats

15 Participial Phrases

Chinese calligraphy, 4th century

Participles

A **participle** is an adjective formed from a verb. There are two kinds of participles: *-ing* participles (called present participles) and *-ed* participles (called past participles).

a **sleeping** baby   a **used** car

a **frightening** experience   a **frightened** child

The two kinds of participles come from either active or passive voice verbs.

- An active voice verb becomes an *-ing* participle.

Verbs	*-ing* Participles
The custom **fascinates** me.	The **fascinating** custom has been the subject of many books.
The essay **won** an award.	Jacob wrote the **winning** essay.
The baby **will sleep** until eight.	Try not to wake a **sleeping** baby.

- A passive voice verb becomes an *-ed* participle.

Verbs	*-ed* Participles
Some movies **are rated X**.	Children should not see **X-rated** movies.
My leg **was broken** in three places.	My **broken** leg is healing slowly.

- There are also perfect forms.

Verbs	Perfect Participles
The students **had solved** most of the problems without any help.	**Having solved** most of the problems without any help, the students were exhilarated.

The most commonly used participle forms are shown in the following chart.

Participle Forms

Description	*-ing* Forms	*-ed* Forms
The **general forms** do not indicate time. Time is determined by the main clause verb.	verb + *ing* **opening**	verb + *ed, en, t, d* **opened** **taken** **bought** **sold**
The **perfect forms** emphasize that the action happened before the time of the main clause verb.	*having* + past participle **having opened**	

Participial Phrases

A **participial phrase** contains a participle + other words. Use participial phrases to modify nouns and pronouns.

Students **planning to graduate in June** must make an appointment with the registrar.

Airport security will question anyone **found with a suspicious object in their baggage**.

Participial phrases can be formed by reducing adjective clauses and adverb clauses. For this reason, they are sometimes called **reduced clauses**.

Reduced Adjective Clauses

You can reduce a subject pattern adjective clause as follows.

1. Delete the relative pronoun (*who, which,* or *that*).
2. Change the verb to a participle.
3. Keep the same punctuation (commas or no commas).
4. Put the word *not* at the beginning of a participial phrase to make it negative.

Adjective Clauses	Participial Phrases
A pedestrian **who had been hit by a speeding taxi** was lying in the street.	A pedestrian **hit by a speeding taxi** was lying in the street.
An ambulance **that was summoned by a bystander** came quickly.	An ambulance **summoned by a bystander** came quickly.
The taxi driver, **who did not realize what had happened**, continued on.	The taxi driver, **not realizing what had happened**, continued on.

Position and Punctuation of Participial Phrases

Participial phrases, like adjective clauses, can be restrictive (necessary) or nonrestrictive (unnecessary). If the original clause is nonrestrictive, the phrase is nonrestrictive also. A nonrestrictive phrase is separated from the rest of the sentence by commas. Restrictive phrases use no commas.

The position of a participial phrase in a sentence depends on whether it is restrictive or nonrestrictive, or whether it modifies an entire clause.

1. A restrictive participial phrase can only follow the noun it modifies and does not have commas.

RESTRICTIVE   A woman **hurrying to catch a bus** tripped and fell.

2. A nonrestrictive participial phrase can precede or follow the noun it modifies and is separated by a comma or commas from the rest of the sentence.

NONRESTRICTIVE   Teresa, **hurrying to catch a bus**, stumbled and fell.

Hurrying to catch a bus, Teresa stumbled and fell.

CAUTION! When you begin a sentence with a participial phrase, make certain that the phrase modifies the subject of the sentence. If it does not, your sentence is incorrect.

INCORRECT   Hoping for an A, my exam grade disappointed me.

(*The participial phrase* Hoping for an A *cannot modify* my exam grade. *A grade cannot hope.*)

CORRECT   Hoping for an A, I was disappointed in my exam grade.

3. Sometimes a participial phrase modifies an entire independent clause. In this case, it follows the clause and requires a comma.

The team won the championship, **shocking their opponents**.

General Form -*ing* Participial Phrases

A general form -*ing* participle may come from present, past, or future tense verbs.

Verb Tense	Sentence with Adjective Clause	Sentence with Participial Phrase
Simple present	Many students **who study at this university** are from foreign countries.	Many students **studying at this university** are from foreign countries.
Present continuous	Students **who are taking calculus** must buy a graphing calculator.	Students **taking calculus** must buy a graphing calculator.
Simple past	The team members, **who looked happy after their victory,** were cheered by the fans.	The team members, **looking happy after their victory,** were cheered by the fans.
Past continuous	The crowd, **which was cheering wildly as the game ended,** would not leave the stadium.	**Cheering wildly as the game ended,** the crowd would not leave the stadium.
Future	Everyone **who will take the TOEFL next month** must preregister.	Everyone **taking the TOEFL next month** must preregister.

PRACTICE 1

-*ing Participial Phrases*

A. Rewrite each sentence, reducing the adjective clause to a participial phrase. Rewrite sentences 4 and 5 each in two ways: once with the participial phrase before and once with it after the noun it modifies. Add commas to sentences with nonrestrictive phrases. The first one has been done for you as an example.

1. Robotics is a complex field that combines electronics, computer science, and mechanical engineering.

   Robotics is a complex field combining electronics, computer science, and mechanical engineering.

2. The number of students who are studying robotics is growing.

   _____

   _____

3. Soon, robots that work in assembly plants will be able to follow voice commands.

   _____

   _____

4. Robots, which have the ability to withstand extreme temperatures and radiation levels, can perform jobs that are too dangerous for humans.

   a. _____

   _____

   b. _____

   _____

5. Robots, which do not need to eat, sleep, or take breaks, can work nonstop.

   a. _____

   _____

   b. _____

   _____

B. Fill in the blank with an *-ing* phrase formed from the words in parentheses. Add commas if necessary. The first one has been done for you as an example.

1. The industries ___using the most robots___ are those with assembly lines, such as automobile manufacturing. (**use/the most robots**)

2. In the field of medicine, it will soon be normal to find robots _____ _____. (**perform/surgery**)

3. With one kind of robotic device, a human surgeon _____ directs the robot. (**sit/in front of a video screen**)

4. The surgeon controls three robotic arms _____ _____ with joysticks similar to those used in video games. (**hold/surgical tools/above/patient**)

5. _____ robots are very valuable for surgery on infants. (**allow/surgeons to make tiny incisions and to use small tools**)

General Form *-ed* Participial Phrases

The general form *-ed* participle is the past participle or third form of a verb: *opened, spoken, sold, caught*. A general form *-ed* participle comes from both present and past tense passive voice verbs.

Verb Tense	Sentence with Adjective Clause	Sentence with Participial Phrase
Simple present	Lab reports **that are not handed in by Friday** will not be accepted.	Lab reports **not handed in by Friday** will not be accepted.
Simple past	The proposed law, **which was opposed by the majority of the people,** did not pass.	The proposed law, **opposed by the majority of the people,** did not pass.

PRACTICE 2

-ed Participial Phrases

A. Rewrite each sentence, reducing the adjective clause to a participial phrase. Retain the commas in sentences containing them. The first one has been done for you as an example.

1. Cigarette companies, which have been long[1] criticized for their advertising tactics, have been looking for new ways to sell their products.
   Cigarette companies, long criticized for their advertising tactics, have been looking for new ways to sell their products.

2. One company plans to try out a new approach that is aimed at young adults.

   _____

   _____

---

[1]**long:** for a long time

3. The new approach suggests that smokers, who are often scorned for continuing to smoke despite health risks, are daring rebels.

_____

_____

4. The company hopes that the image that is projected by the new marketing campaign will succeed half as well as the Marlboro Man image succeeded in the 1950s.

_____

_____

5. The Marlboro Man, who was pictured in hundreds of ads over the years, was a ruggedly handsome cowboy smoking a Marlboro cigarette.

_____

_____

B. Fill in the blanks with a participial phrase containing an -*ed* participle. Use the words in parentheses to make the phrase, and add commas if necessary.

1. The languages _____*spoken most widely in Switzerland*_____ are German, French, and Italian. (**speak / most widely in Switzerland**)

2. Switzerland _____ has tried to remain neutral throughout its history. (**situate / between four sometimes warring countries**)

3. Children _____ have an advantage over monolingual children. (**raise / in bilingual families**)

4. A new treatment for malaria

_____ will soon be available.

(**develop / ABC Pharmaceutical Company**)

5. _____ the public responded generously. (**ask / to donate food and clothing to the hurricane victims**)

Perfect Form Participial Phrases

Perfect forms emphasize the completion of an action that takes place before the action of the main verb.[2] You can change both present perfect and past perfect verbs into perfect participles.

Verb Tense	Sentence with Adjective Clause	Sentence with Participial Phrase
Present perfect	The secrets of the universe, **which have fascinated people for centuries,** are slowly being revealed.	The secrets of the universe, **having fascinated people for centuries,** are slowly being revealed.
Past perfect	The senator, **who had heard that most people opposed the new law,** voted against it.	**Having heard that most people opposed the new law,** the senator voted against it.

_____

[2]There is also an -*ed* perfect form (*having been* + a past participle). However, the perfect -*ed* form is often shortened to the general -*ed* form with no difference in meaning. In the following example, *having been elected* becomes *elected*: *The president, (having been) elected by a large majority, promised to lower taxes.*

PRACTICE 3

*Perfect Form
Participial
Phrases*

A. Rewrite each sentence by changing the adjective clause to a participial phrase. Since all of the clauses in these sentences are nonrestrictive, use commas. For practice, write at least two of the sentences with the participial phrase at the beginning of the sentence, as in the second example in the chart on page 255. The first one has been done for you as an example.

1. Women around the world, who have traditionally been without political power, are beginning to gain influence in politics and government.
   <u>Having traditionally been without political power, women around the world are</u>
   <u>beginning to gain influence in politics and government.</u>
   OR
   <u>Women around the world, having traditionally been without political power, are</u>
   <u>beginning to gain influence in politics and government.</u>

2. Ireland, which had never chosen a woman leader in its entire history, has elected two consecutive female presidents in recent years. (Put *never* in front of the participle.)

   _____

   _____

3. India and the Philippines, which have elected women prime ministers in the past, are more progressive in this area than the United States.

   _____

   _____

4. Voters in the United States, who have had little experience with strong female leaders at the national level, may never choose a female president.

   _____

   _____

B. Fill in the blanks with a phrase containing a perfect form participle. Use the words in parentheses to make the phrase, and add commas.

1. _____<u>Having saved for many years,</u>_____ the young couple could finally buy their first home. (**save / for many years**)

2. The New York Yankees baseball team _____

   _____ is the best baseball team in the United States. (**win / The World Series more times than any other team**)

3. Janice _____ decided to hide one in a potted plant outside her front door. (**forget / her house key for the third time in a week**)

4. _____, my father found it difficult to quit. (**smoke / for 40 years**)

Participial Phrases and Writing Style

Use participial phrases to improve your writing style.

- If you write sentences with a lot of *which*'s, *who*'s, and *that*'s, consider reducing some adjectives clauses to participial phrases.
- If you write short, choppy sentences, consider combining them by using participial phrases.
- Vary your sentence openings by occasionally starting a sentence with a participial phrase.

SHORT, CHOPPY SENTENCES

First-born children are often superachievers. They feel pressure to behave well and to excel in school.

IMPROVED

First-born children, who feel pressure to behave well and to excel in school, are often superachievers.

First-born children, feeling pressure to behave well and to excel in school, are often superachievers.

Feeling pressure to behave well and to excel in school, first-born children are often superachievers.

PRACTICE 4
Sentence Combining

A. Write sentences containing participial phrases by combining sentences.

Step 1 Match the ideas in the two columns.
Step 2 Change the sentence in the right column to a participial phrase.
Step 3 Write a new sentence that combines the two parts, and add commas if necessary.

The first one has been done for you as an example. (There is more than one possible way to combine some of the sentences.)

_d_ 1. Eskimos are distant cousins of modern Asians.	a. A problem is being discussed by the Alaskan government.
___ 2. Eskimos have adapted well to their harsh environment.	b. Eskimos want to improve their standard of living.
___ 3. A problem concerns the rights of native Alaskans.	c. Eskimos want to preserve their traditional way of life.
___ 4. Some Eskimos reject the ways of the modern world. (Delete *some* in your sentence.)	d. Eskimos had migrated across a land bridge from Asia.
___ 5. On the other hand, some Eskimos hope that they can combine both worlds—old and new. (Delete *some* in your sentence.)	e. Eskimos have lived in Alaska for thousands of years.

1. <u>Having migrated across a land bridge from Asia, Eskimos are distant cousins of modern Asians.</u>

2. _____

3. _____

4. _____

5. _____

B. Follow the same procedure for these sentences. (There is more than one possible way to combine some of the sentences.)

_____ 6. Alaska became the 49th state of the United States in 1959.

_____ 7. The purchase of Alaska was at first criticized.

_____ 8. The people of the United States called it "Seward's Folly."[1]

_____ 9. The state is now separated from Asia by only a few miles of water.

f. The people did not understand the value of the purchase.

g. Alaska was purchased from Russia in 1867.

h. Alaska was once connected to Asia by a land bridge.

i. The purchase was negotiated by Secretary of State William H.Seward.

6. _____

7. _____

8. _____

9. _____

Reduced Adverb Clauses

You can reduce some adverb clauses to -*ing* and -*ed* phrases.

Sentence with Adverb Clause	Sentence with -*ing* or -*ed* Phrase
When you enter a theater, you should turn off your cell phone.	**When entering a theater,** you should turn off your cell phone.
Because he had read that the company needed workers, John applied for a job.	**Having read** that the company needed workers, John applied for a job.

An -*ing* or -*ed* phrase from an adverb clause may occupy several positions in a sentence. If a participial phrase from a reduced adverb clause comes in front of or in the middle of the independent clause, punctuate it with commas. If it comes after the independent clause, do not use commas.

---

[1]**folly:** silly act; foolishness

To reduce an adverb clause, follow these steps.[2]

Step 1 Make sure that the subject of the adverb clause and the subject of the independent clause are the same.

While **technology** creates new jobs in some sectors of the economy, **it** takes away jobs in others.

Step 2 Delete the subject of the adverb clause. If necessary, move it to the subject position in the independent clause.

While **technology** creates new jobs in some sectors of the economy, ~~it~~ takes away jobs in others.

Step 3 Change the adverb clause verb to the appropriate participle.

While **creating** new jobs in some sectors of the economy, technology takes away jobs in others.

Step 4 Delete or retain the subordinator according to the following rules:
a. Retain *before*, and retain *since* when it is a time subordinator.
b. Delete *as* when it is a time subordinator.
c. Delete all three reason subordinators *because, since,* and *as.*
d. Retain *after, while,* and *when* if the participial phrase follows the independent clause. When the phrase is in another position, you may either retain or delete these subordinators.

Retain

before   Before a student chooses a college, he or she should consider several factors.

Before choosing a college, a student should consider several factors.

A student should consider several factors **before choosing a college.**

since (time)   Carlos has not been back home since he came to the United States three years ago.

Since coming to the United States three years ago, Carlos has not been back home.

Carlos has not been back home **since coming to the United States three years ago.**

---

[2]*Note*: There are many instances in which the rules given in the four steps do not apply. The rules are general guidelines and do not cover every situation.

Delete

because **since** **as** (reason)	Because (Since/As) Carlos came from a very conservative family, he was shocked at the U.S. system of coed[1] dormitories.

Coming from a very conservative family, Carlos was shocked at the U.S. system of coed dormitories.

(Placing the -ing phrase at the end of the sentence does not work well in this example: **Carlos was shocked at the American system of coed dormitories coming from a very conservative family.** *It sounds as if the dormitories come from a conservative family.)*

as (time)	As he gradually got used to the way of life in the United States, he became less homesick.

Gradually getting used to the way of life in the United States, he became less homesick.

Retain or Delete

after	After he had passed the TOEFL exam, he became a freshman in college.

After passing the TOEFL exam, he became a freshman in college.

(The perfect form, **After having passed the TOEFL exam,** *is not necessary because the word* after *already indicates the time relationship.)*

Having passed the TOEFL exam, he became a freshman in college.

He became a freshman in college **after passing the TOEFL exam.**

while	While he was preparing for the TOEFL, he lived with a family.

While preparing for the TOEFL, he lived with a family.

Preparing for the TOEFL, he lived with a family.

He lived with a family **while preparing for the TOEFL**

when	When he was asked about his life in the United States, he said that he was enjoying himself but that he was a little homesick.

When asked about his life in the United States, he said that he was enjoying himself but that he was a little homesick.

(Placing the -ing phrase at the end of sentence results in awkwardness: **He said that he was enjoying himself but that he was a little homesick when asked about his life in the United States.** *It sounds as if he is homesick only when he is asked about his life in the United States.)*

Asked about his life in the United States, he said that he was enjoying himself but that he was a little homesick.

---

[1]**coed:** coeducational, shared by men and women

PRACTICE 5

Reducing Adverb
Clauses

A. Rewrite the following sentences, changing the adverb clause in each to a participial phrase. If possible, write the sentence in more than one way. The first one has been done for you as an example.

1. After I had received my B.A., I went to graduate school for two years.
   <u>After receiving my B.A., I went to graduate school for two years.</u>
   <u>Having received my B.A., I went to graduate school for two years.</u>

2. I enjoyed living in a big city while I was studying at the University of Chicago.
   _____
   _____

3. Before I left home, I promised my parents that I would return.
   _____
   _____

4. Because I am the eldest son, I am responsible for taking care of my parents.
   _____
   _____

5. Since they have spent most of their savings to send me and my sisters to college, my parents may not have enough money for their retirement.
   _____
   _____

B. Complete the following sentences by adding a participial phrase in the blanks. Use the words in parentheses to make the phrase, and add commas if necessary.

1. _____ automobile manufacturers want to replace assembly line workers with robots. (**hope / to save labor costs**)

2. Labor unions _____ are resisting the introduction of robots into factories. (**fear / loss of jobs for their members**)

3. Union members _____ went on strike. (**protest / loss of jobs**)

Review

These are the important points covered in this chapter

1. Participles are adjectives formed from verbs. Some participles are from active voice verbs:

   The baby cried.   . . . the **crying** baby

   The speaker bored the audience.   . . . the **boring** speaker

Some participles are from passive voice verbs:

| The soldier was wounded. | . . . the **wounded** soldier |
| The audience was bored by the speaker | . . . the **bored** audience |

The most commonly used participle forms and the times they indicate are shown in the following chart.

Participle Forms

Description	*-ing*	*-ed*
General: no time indicated	**talking**	**talked**
Perfect: time before that of the main verb	**having talked**	

2. You can form a participial phrase by reducing an adjective clause.

> The audience, **which was listening intently to the music,** failed to notice the fire.

> The audience, **listening intently to the music**, failed to notice the fire.

- A nonrestrictive participial phrase may precede or follow the noun it modifies and is set off by commas.

> The audience, **listening intently to the music**, failed to notice the fire.

> **Listening intently to the music**, the audience failed to notice the fire.

- A restrictive participial phrase must follow the noun it modifies and is not set off by commas.

> The audience failed to notice the fire **starting to smolder[1] in the back of the auditorium.**

- A nonrestrictive participial phrase may also modify an entire sentence, in which case it comes at the end of the sentence and is set off by a comma.

> The building collapsed, **killing three firefighters**.

3. Participial phrases may also be reduced from time and reason adverb clauses.

- Participial phrases reduced from time clauses may occupy various positions in a sentence, and the time subordinators are sometimes deleted and sometimes retained.

Time Clauses	Participial Phrases
Since I arrived . . .	**Since arriving** . . .
After they had finished . . .	**Having finished** . . .
	After finishing . . .

---

[1]**smolder:** burn without flame

- Participial phrases reduced from reason clauses may come before or after the independent clause in a sentence. Reason subordinators are always deleted.

Reason Clauses	Participial Phrases
Because I wanted . . .	**Wanting** . . .
As we did not know . . .	**Not knowing** . . .

Editing Practice

Improve the following short essay by changing the underlined adjective and adverb clauses to participial phrases. Rewrite the essay on a separate sheet of paper.

Global Warming

[1]One of the biggest problems <u>that faces humankind in the next few decades</u> is the problem of global warming. In the past 150 years, global temperatures have risen approximately 1°C (1.8°F). The year 1998 was the warmest year <u>that has ever been recorded</u>. If temperatures continue to rise, the consequences could be catastrophic. As Earth's temperature rises, polar ice will melt, <u>which will cause the water level of the oceans to rise</u>. Rising ocean levels, in turn, will cause flooding along the coasts. Global warming will also cause major changes in climate that will affect agriculture. For example, crops <u>that were previously grown in Guatemala</u> may not do so well because it will become too hot.

[2]<u>Because they believe</u> that the increase in carbon dioxide in Earth's atmosphere is the primary cause of global warming, scientists have urged immediate action to decrease CO_2 levels. They are asking the world's governments to write an agreement <u>that will control the amount of CO_2 that is released into the atmosphere</u>. <u>After each government signs such an agreement,</u> each government will have to enforce it. Brazilians, for example, will have to stop burning their rain forests, and Americans will have to stop driving their gas-guzzling SUVs.

Writing Practice

A. Write eight sentences about yourself or members of your family, using a participial phrase in each. Try to use all three participle forms shown in the chart on page 262.

Examples

<u>Having six older brothers, I have always been interested in sports.</u>

<u>My father always had time to play with us, even after working 12-hour days in his small shop.</u>

B. Write a short autobiography and include at least three participial phrases. You may write facts about your family background, your education, and your career goals, or you may write more personal information, such as your characteristics, your likes and dislikes, and your dreams and goals. Use the paragraph below as a model.

MODEL

A Short Autobiography

Born on November 12, 1980, in a medium-sized town in the mountains of Peru, I learned responsibility at an early age. My family, consisting of my father, my mother, and seven younger brothers and sisters, is quite large. Being the oldest daughter, I had many responsibilities. I helped my mother at home with the cooking and cleaning, and I was almost like a second mother to my younger siblings. By the time I was 10 years old, I had learned how to soothe a crying baby, how to bandage an injured knee or elbow, and especially how to get a bored schoolchild to finish his or her homework. Having helped my brothers and sisters with their homework for so many years, I have developed a love of teaching. I hope to get a college degree in elementary education and teach either math or science in my hometown in Peru.

A The Process of Academic Writing

Academic writing, as the name implies, is the kind of writing that you are required to do in college or university. It differs from other kinds of writing, such as personal, literary, journalistic, or business writing. Its differences can be explained in part by its particular **audience, tone**, and **purpose**.

Whenever you write, consider your specific **audience**, that is, the people who will read what you have written. In academic writing, your audience is primarily your professors or instructors. Second, consider the **tone** of your writing, your style or manner of expression. It is revealed by your choice of words and grammatical structures and even the length of your sentences. The tone of a piece of writing can be, for example, serious, amusing, personal, or impersonal. Academic writing is formal and serious in tone. Finally, the **purpose** of a piece of writing determines its organizational pattern. A persuasive essay will be organized in one way and a comparison-contrast essay in another way.

Writing is a process of creating, organizing, writing, and polishing. In the first step of the process, you create ideas. In the second step, you organize the ideas. In the third step, you write a rough draft. In the final step, you polish your rough draft by editing it and making revisions.

The Writing Process, Step 1: Creating (Prewriting)

The first step in the writing process is to choose a topic and collect information about it. This step is often called **prewriting** because you do the step *before* you start writing.

Step 1A: Choosing and Narrowing a Topic

If you are given a specific writing assignment (such as an essay question on an examination), then what you can write about is limited. However, when you can choose your own topic, here are two tips for making a good choice.

1. Choose a topic that interests you.
2. Choose a topic that fits the assignment.

If you are not sure what interests you, pay attention to what kinds of newspaper and magazine articles you read. Do your eyes stop at stories about new discoveries in science? Do you turn immediately to the travel, sports, or entertainment sections of newspapers? If you spend time watching television or exploring the Internet, what captures your interest when you are flipping through TV channels or surfing the Net?

Suppose you are interested in the environment, which is a very large topic. You must narrow the topic—perhaps to environmental pollution, if that is your interest. Environmental pollution, however, is still a large topic, so you must narrow the topic further—perhaps to one type of environmental pollution, such as pollution of the oceans.

Writing about ocean pollution is still too large because it includes pollution by oil, chemicals, sewage, and garbage. Therefore, you must narrow your topic further—perhaps to oil as a source of ocean pollution. You could make this topic even narrower by writing only about the effects of oil spills on sea life. This is an appropriate topic for a college assignment, perhaps a ten-page paper. For an essay-length paper, you should narrow the topic further, perhaps to just one kind of sea life—corals or sea birds or shellfish.

The diagram illustrates the process of narrowing a topic.

GENERAL TOPIC

VERY SPECIFIC TOPIC

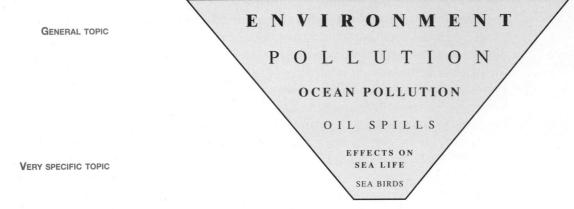

E N V I R O N M E N T

P O L L U T I O N

OCEAN POLLUTION

OIL SPILLS

EFFECTS ON
SEA LIFE

SEA BIRDS

PRACTICE 1

*Choosing and
Narrowing
a Topic*

Individually, in a small group, or with your whole class, narrow each of the general topics below to one specific topic below that you could write about in a college assignment.

School   Entertainment   Sports   Food

Step 1B: Generating Ideas

After you have chosen a topic and narrowed it, the next prewriting step is to collect information and develop ideas. For some writing tasks, you will need to go to outside sources, such as newspapers, magazines, library books, or the Internet. For other assignments, you can interview friends, classmates, and neighbors to get their ideas and opinions. For still other writing tasks, you can search your own brain and life experiences. Four useful techniques for exploring within yourself are *journal writing*, *listing*, *freewriting*, and *clustering*.

Journal Writing

In journal writing, you can record your daily experiences, or you can write down quotations that are meaningful to you. You might write about a dream you had. You might have a conversation with yourself on paper during which you discuss a problem or an idea. The advantage of writing a journal is that you are writing only for yourself. You can write down your thoughts and explore ideas without worrying what other people will think. A personal journal can be a very rich source of ideas.

Three other brainstorming techniques are *listing*, *freewriting*, and *clustering*. Learn how to do each of them and then decide which is the most productive for you.

Listing

Listing is a brainstorming technique in which you think about your topic and quickly make a list of whatever words or phrases come into your mind. Your purpose is to produce as many ideas as possible in a short time, and your goal is to find a specific focus for your topic. Follow this procedure:

1. Write down the general topic at the top of your paper.
2. Make a list of every idea that comes into your mind about the topic. Don't stop writing until you have filled a page. Keep the ideas flowing. Try to stay on the general topic; however, if you write down information that is completely off the topic, don't worry about it because you can cross it out later.
3. Use words, phrases, or sentences, and don't worry about spelling or grammar.

Here is an example of the listing technique on the topic of the culture shock experienced by international students in the United States.

MODEL

Listing

Culture Shock

communication problems	homeless people shocking sight
poor verbal skills	American students
children are disrespectful	classroom environment
new language	unclear expressions
American family life	public transportation is not good
families seldom eat together	need a car
lack vocabulary	use first names with teachers
show affection in public	college professors wear jeans
Americans talk too fast	students ask questions
they are friendly	no formal dress code
people are always in a hurry	no one takes time to cook good meals
use slang and idioms	professor's role
families don't spend time together on weekends and holidays	children spend more time with friends than with parents
children are "kings"	use incomplete sentences
lack confidence	poor pronunciation
American food is unhealthy	Americans difficult to understand
everyone eats fast food	students can challenge professors

4. Now rewrite your list and group similar ideas together. Cross out items that don't belong or that are duplications.

Group A

(communication problems)
poor verbal skills
new language
lack vocabulary
~~show affection in public~~
Americans talk too fast
~~they are friendly~~
~~people are always in a hurry~~
use slang and idioms
lack confidence
use incomplete sentences
poor pronunciation
Americans difficult to understand
unclear expressions

Group B

~~homeless people shocking sight~~
American students

(classroom environment)
~~public transportation is not good~~
~~need a car~~
use first names with teachers
college professors wear jeans
students ask questions
no formal dress code
~~no one takes time to cook good meals~~
professor's role
students can challenge professors

Group C

(American family life)
children are "kings"
families seldom eat together
children are disrespectful
families don't spend time together on weekends and holidays
children spend more time with friends than with parents
~~Americans food is unhealthy~~
~~everyone eats fast food~~

PRACTICE 2

Brainstorming by Listing

Now there are three lists, each of which has a central focus. The central focus in each new list is circled: *communication problems, classroom environment*, and *American family life*. The writer can choose one list to be the basis for a single paragraph or all three for an essay.

With your class, in a small group, or individually, brainstorm by listing ideas on one of the following topics. Follow the four steps.

Characteristics of a good student/employee/boss/friend
Differences between generations
Gender differences
Changes in everyday life caused by new technology
One of the topics from Practice 1: Choosing and Narrowing a Topic on page 266

Freewriting

Freewriting is a brainstorming activity in which you write freely about a topic because you are looking for a specific focus. While you are writing, one idea will spark another idea. As with listing, the purpose of freewriting is to generate as many ideas as possible and to write them down without worrying about appropriateness, grammar, spelling, logic, or organization. Remember, the more you freewrite, the more ideas you will have. Don't worry if your mind seems to "run dry." Just keep your pencil moving. Follow this procedure:

1. Write the topic at the top of your paper.
2. Write as much as you can about the topic until you run out of ideas. Include such supporting items as facts, details, and examples that come into your mind about the subject.
3. After you have run out of ideas, reread your paper and circle the main idea(s) that you would like to develop.
4. Take each main idea and freewrite again.

In the following model, the student is supposed to write a paragraph about one major problem at his college. The student has no idea what to write about, so he starts freewriting about some of the problems that come to mind.

MODEL

Freewriting 1

Problems at Evergreen College

What is the biggest problem at Evergreen College? Well, I really don't know. In fact, I can't think of one particular problem although I know there are many problems. For one thing, (the classrooms are usually overcrowded.) At the beginning of this semester, Science Hall 211 had 45 students although there were only 31 desks. A few of the seats attached to the desks were broken, so about 20 had to sit on the floor. Besides, (the classrooms are poorly maintained.) In several of my classes, there are broken chairs and litter on the floor. Students even leave their dirty cups and other garbage on the desks. So the rooms are messy. The library is too small and always crowded with students. Not all students really study in the library. Sometimes they talk a lot, and this is really quite distracting to me and other serious students who want and need a quiet place to study. So the present library should be expanded or a new library should be built. Oh yes, I think that (another problem is parking near the campus.) The

> college has a big parking lot across from the west side of campus, but it is always full. So many times students have to park their cars in the residential areas, which can be so far away from the campus that they have to run to class to make it. Yes, parking is a big problem that many students face every day. I have a car, and many of my friends have one. We really have a problem. So I think the biggest problem at Evergreen College is not enough parking spaces near the college campus . . .

After he finished freewriting, the student reread his paper and circled the main ideas, one of which he will consider as the major problem at Evergreen College.

Let's say that the student has decided to choose parking as the major problem at Evergreen College. Now that the student knows the topic he wants to write about, he will again brainstorm by freewriting, this time on the parking problem only. His freewriting paper might look like this.

MODEL

Freewriting 2

> ### The Parking Problem at Evergreen College
> I think finding a parking space close to the campus at Evergreen College is a major problem. There are not enough parking lots for students to park their cars. Therefore, students have to come early to get a parking space, and even then, sometimes they are unlucky and can't get a good parking space. Once I couldn't find a space in the west-side parking lot, and I had to drive in the streets for a half hour before I found one. So I was late for class. Some students are late to class almost every time the English class meets. Some even drop the class, not because they can't handle it, but because they can't find a place to park close to the campus. The teacher warns them time and time again not to be late, but they can't help it. What is the solution to the parking problem? Maybe the college should spend some funds to construct a multilevel parking lot that will accommodate three times as many cars as the present parking lot holds.

The student can do this freewriting activity several times until he has enough material to develop into a paragraph or essay.

Brainstorm by freewriting on one of the following topics.

PRACTICE 3

Brainstorming by Freewriting

Advertising   Diets   Health foods   Automobiles

Clustering

Clustering is another brainstorming activity you can use to generate ideas. To use this technique, first, write your topic in the center of your paper and draw a "balloon" around it. This is your center, or core, balloon. Then write whatever ideas come to you in balloons around the core. Think about each of these ideas and make more balloons around them.

For example, suppose you are writing about the changes technology is making in the way we communicate. Using the clustering technique to get ideas, you might end up with the following.

MODEL

Clustering

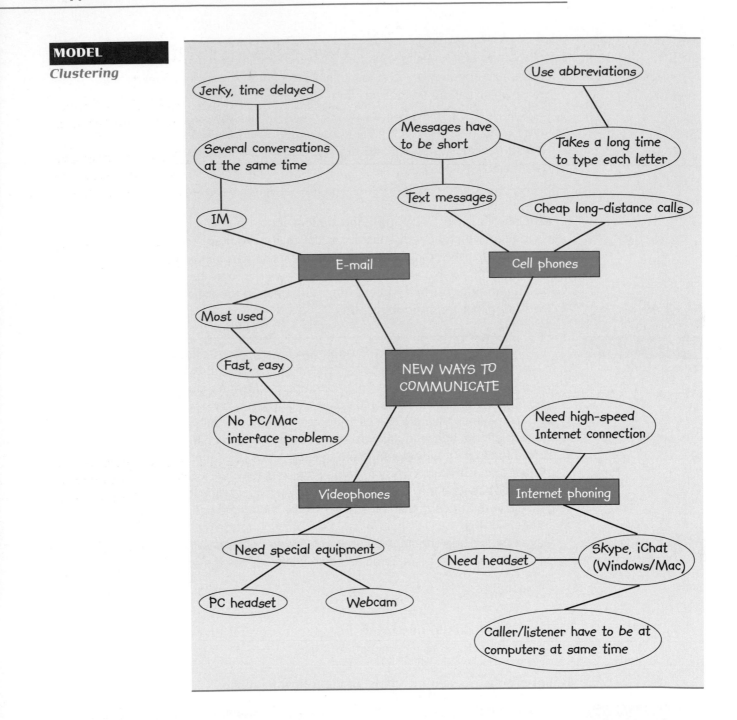

PRACTICE 4

Brainstorming by Clustering

Use the clustering technique to generate ideas about the way technology has changed one area of daily living (housework, education, or money management, for example).

The Writing Process, Step 2: Planning (Outlining)

In Step 1, you chose topics and narrowed them, and you generated ideas by brainstorming. In Step 2 of the writing process, the planning stage, you organize the ideas into an **outline**.

Turn back to the model about culture shock on page 267. The writer developed three different lists of ideas: *communication problems, classroom environment*, and *American family life*. Imagine that you are the student and that your assignment is to write a single paragraph.

Step 2A: Making Sublists

As a first step toward making an outline, divide the ideas in the *communication problems* list further into sublists and cross out any items that do not belong or that are not useable.

MODEL

Sublists

Communication Problems

(1)   poor verbal skills
      lack vocabulary
      ~~new language~~
      poor pronunciation
      ~~lack confidence~~

(2)   Americans difficult to understand
      use incomplete sentences
      unclear expressions
      Americans talk too fast
      use slang and idioms

The two sublists are (1) items that describe international students (*poor verbal skills*) and (2) items that describe Americans (*Americans difficult to understand*). *New language* and *lack confidence* do not fit in either sublist, so cross them out. The remaining items fit under 1 or 2. Now you have created a rough outline.

MODEL

Rough Outline

Communication Problems

A. poor verbal skills
     —lack vocabulary
     —poor pronunciation
B. Americans difficult to understand
     —use incomplete sentences
     —use unclear expressions
     —talk too fast
     —use slang and idioms

Step 2B: Writing the Topic Sentence

Finally, write a topic sentence. The topic is clearly communication problems. A possible topic sentence might be as follows.

One problem that many international students face in the United States is communication with Americans.

OR

International students in the United States face communication problems with Americans.

Step 2C:
Outlining

An outline is a formal plan for a paragraph. You may never need to prepare a formal outline, but if you do, this is what one looks like.

MODEL

Formal Outline

> **Communication Problems**
>
> TOPIC SENTENCE — One problem that international students face in the United States is communication with Americans.
>
> SUPPORTING POINT — **A.** International students have poor verbal skills.
> SUPPORTING DETAIL —   1. lack vocabulary
> SUPPORTING DETAIL —   2. have poor pronunciation
> SUPPORTING POINT — **B.** Americans are difficult to understand.
> SUPPORTING DETAIL —   1. use incomplete sentences
> SUPPORTING DETAIL —   2. use unclear expressions
> SUPPORTING DETAIL —   3. talk too fast
> SUPPORTING DETAIL —   4. use slang and idioms
>
> CONCLUDING SENTENCE — Because of their own poor verbal skills and because of Americans' way of speaking, international students have a hard time communicating when they first arrive in the United States.

With this outline in front of you, it should be relatively easy to write a paragraph. There is a topic sentence, two main supporting points, supporting details, and since this is a stand-alone paragraph, a concluding sentence.

PRACTICE 5

Outlining

Follow the three steps described above and develop outlines for one of the other groups from the brainstorming list on culture shock, *classroom environment* or *American family life*. Each outline should contain a topic sentence, main supporting points, and supporting details.

The Writing Process, Step 3: Writing

Step 3 in the writing process is **writing** the rough draft. Follow your outline as closely as possible, and don't worry about grammar, punctuation, or spelling. A rough draft is not supposed to be perfect.

Above all, remember that writing is a continuous process of discovery. As you are writing, you will think of new ideas that may not be in your brainstorming list or outline. You can add or delete ideas at any time in the writing process. Just be sure that any new ideas are relevant.

A rough draft that a student wrote from her outline follows.

MODEL

First Rough Draft

Communication Problems

[1]International students in the United States face communication problems with Americans. [2]It is a kind of culture shock to them. [3]They soon realize that their verbal skills are poor. [4]They lack vocabulary, and they have poor pronounciation. [5]American people don't understand them. [6]They also speak too softly because they are shy. [7]Students don't feel confidence when speaking English. [8]Is difficult for foreign people to understand Americans. [9]Americans use incomplete sentences, and often they use unclear expressions. [10]Americans talk too fast, so it is often imposible to catch their meaning. [11]Americans also use a lot of slangs and idioms. [12]People do not know their meaning.

The Writing Process, Step 4: Polishing

The fourth and final step in the writing process is **polishing** what you have written. This step is also called revising and editing. Polishing is most successful if you do it in two stages. First, attack the big issues of content and organization (revising). Then work on the smaller issues of grammar and punctuation (editing).

Step 4A: Revising

After you write the rough draft, the next step is to revise it. When you revise, you change what you have written to improve it. You check it for content and organization, including unity, coherence, and logic. You can change, rearrange, add, or delete, all for the goal of communicating your thoughts more clearly, more effectively, and in a more interesting way.

During the first revision, do not try to correct grammar, sentence structure, spelling, or punctuation; this is proofreading, which you will do later. During the first revision, be concerned mainly with content and organization.

- Read over your paragraph carefully for a *general* overview. Focus on the *general* aspects of the paper and make notes in the margins about rewriting the parts that need to be improved.
- Check to see that you have achieved your stated purpose.
- Check for general logic and coherence. Your audience should be able to follow your ideas easily and understand what you have written.
- Check to make sure that your paragraph has a topic sentence and that the topic sentence has a central (main) focus.
- Check for unity. Cross out sentences that are off the topic.
- Check to make sure that the topic sentence is developed with sufficient supporting details. Does each paragraph give the reader enough information to understand the main idea? If the main point lacks sufficient information, make notes in the margin such as "add more details" or "add an example."
- Check your use of transition signals.
- Finally, does your paragraph have or need a concluding sentence? If you wrote a final comment, is it on the topic?

Now rewrite your paragraph, incorporating all the revisions. This is your second draft.

MODEL

Revisions to Rough Draft

Communication Problems

¹International students in the United States face communi-

(COMBINE SENTENCES) cation problems with Americans. ²It is a kind of culture shock

to them. ³They soon reallize that their verbal skills are poor. (T) (ADD EXAMPLES)

⁴They lack vocabulary, and they have poor pronounciation.

⁵American people doesn't understand them. ⁶They also speak

too softly because are shy. ⁷~~Students don't feel confidence~~

(T) ~~when speaking English~~. ⁸Is difficult for foreign people to

understand Americans. ⁹Americans use incomplete sentences,

(T) ~~and often they use unclear expressions~~. ¹⁰Americans talk too

(T) fast, so it is often imposible to catch their meaning. ¹¹Americans

also use a lot of slangs and idioms. ¹²People do not know their

meaning. (ADD CONCLUDING SENTENCE)

Notice the revisions the student marked on her rough draft.

1. She checked to make sure that her paragraph matched the assignment. The assigned topic was "culture shock." Although her second sentence mentions culture shock, her topic sentence does not, so she decided to combine sentences 1 and 2.
2. The writer checked the paragraph for unity and decided that sentence 6, which she had added while writing the rough draft, was a good addition. However, she decided that sentence 7 was off the topic, so she crossed it out.
3. She checked to see if there were enough supporting details, and she decided that there were not. She decided to add examples of poor pronunciation, an incomplete sentence, and an idiom. She could not think of an example of an unclear expression, so she crossed out her reference to unclear expressions in sentence 9.
4. She also decided to add transition signals such as *first of all, for example,* and *also* to make her paragraph more coherent.
5. She decided to add a concluding sentence.

Then the student wrote her second draft.

PRACTICE 6

Revising

By yourself, with a partner, or in a group, revise the following rough draft. Suggest or make revisions to the content and organization only. The assignment was to write one paragraph on the topic of culture shock.

American Classrooms (Rough Draft)

The classroom environment in American schools is very surprising to me. I am from a culture where teachers and students behave more formally. In this country, students can be very relaxed in classroom without getting into trouble. Students can ask questions and even disagree with the professors. This would never happen in schools in my culture. Teachers are different too. In my culture, there is a formal dress code for students and teachers. In the United States, teachers and students wear casual clothes to school. Most surprising of all, sometimes students call their professors by their first names. This seems disrespectful to me. American schools are easier, too. Here, they study a foreign language for only two years, and most students don't take advanced math. Teachers are a lot stricter in schools in my culture. They are not friendly to students.

Step 4B: Editing (Proofreading)

The second step in polishing your writing is proofreading your paper for possible errors in grammar, sentence structure, spelling, and punctuation.

- Check each sentence for correctness and completeness. You should have no fragments and no choppy or run-on sentences.
- Check each sentence for a subject and a verb, subject-verb agreement, correct verb tenses, noun plurals, articles, and so on.
- Check the mechanics: punctuation, spelling, and capitalization.
- Check for incorrectly used or repeated words.
- Check for contractions (*can't, isn't, I'll*, and so on). (Some writing instructors permit them, but others do not. Find out your instructor's preference.)

The student edited her paragraph as shown in the following model.

MODEL

Proofreading

Communication Problems

[1]One kind of culture shock faced by international students in the United

~~when they first arrive in the United States.~~

States is the difficulty they have communicating with Americans. [2]They soon

sp

reallize that their verbal skills are poor. [3]First of all, they lack vocabulary, and

, so   *don't* *do not*

they have poor pronunciation [4]American people doesn't understand them.

[5]For example, a few days ago, I asked an American student how to get to the

did not

library, but because I have trouble pronouncing *r*'s and *l*'s, the student didn't

had   *International students*

understand me. [6]I finally have to write it on a piece of paper. [7]They also speak

they   *It is*

too softly because are shy. [8]Is difficult for foreign people to understand

Americans, too. [9]Americans use incomplete sentences, such as "Later" to mean

I will

"I'll see you later," and "Coming?" to mean "Are you coming?" [10]Also,

sp   *understand*   *them*

Americans talk too fast so it is often imposible to catch their meaning. [11]In

whose meaning nonnative speakers

addition, Americans also use a lot of slangs and idioms. [12]People do not know

their meaning. [13]For example, the other day someone said to me, "That drives

me up the wall," and I could not imagine what he meant. [14]I had a picture in my

driving   *did not*

mind of him sitting in his car driving up a wall. [15]It didn't make sense to me.

[16]In short, communication is probably the first problem that international

students face in the United States. [17]After a while, however, their ears get used

abilities

to the American way of speaking, and their own verbal skills improve.

Following are the corrections the student made.

Sentence structure
1. This student knows that one of her writing problems is sentences that are sometimes too short, so she tried to find ways to lengthen her short sentences in this paragraph.
    - She added *When they first arrive in the United States* to sentence 2.
    - She combined sentences 3 and 4.
    - She combined sentences 11 and 12.
2. She crossed out three words in sentence 1 and changed *sitting in his car driving up a wall* to *driving his car up a wall* in sentence 14 to make these sentences more concise.

Coherence
3. It was not clear who *They* referred to in sentence 7 (Americans or international students?), so she changed it to *International students*.

Grammar
4. This student knows that she occasionally makes mistakes with verbs and omits subjects, so she checked carefully for these problems.
    - She needed to correct *doesn't* in sentence 4 and *have* in sentence 6.
    - She needed to add *they* in sentence 7 and *It* in sentence 8.

Mechanics
5. The student writer found two spelling errors and added a missing comma.
6. She also eliminated contractions.

Vocabulary
7. In sentence 10, because *catch their meaning* is not standard English and because she did not want to use the word *meaning* in consecutive sentences, she changed the phrase to *understand them*.
8. In sentence 11, *slang* is uncountable, so she crossed out the *-s*.
9. In sentence 12, *people* is not very specific. *Nonnative speakers* is more appropriate.
10. In the concluding sentence she did not want to repeat the phrase *verbal skills*, so she wrote *verbal abilities* instead.

Then the student wrote the final copy to hand in.

Editing Practice

By yourself, with a partner, or in a group, edit the following second draft. Suggest or make improvements to the sentence structure, and correct any mistakes you find in grammar, punctuation, and mechanics. Look for incorrect sentence structure (sentence fragments and run-ons) and places to combine short sentences. Look for subject-verb agreement errors and verb tense errors. Look for missing articles (*a, an, the*) and other missing words. Look for incorrect forms after the word *enjoy*. Finally, look for errors in capitalization and noun plurals, and eliminate contractions.

American Family Life (Second Draft)

[1]One culture shock that I experience when I first arrive in U.S. is American families lifes. [2]In my culture, family is most important. [3]Is more important than work, school, and friends. [4]We enjoy to spend time together. [5]Mother cook a nice dinner every night for family. [6]When we come home from work or school. [7]Every member sit around the table and eat and talk. [8]We joke and tease and enjoy this time together. [9]In U.S., on the other hand, sometimes family never eat dinner together. [10]The children busy with after-school sports or clubs. [11]The father work late. [12]The mother often work too. [13]So she doesn't have time to cook nice meal. [14]Maybe she bring home already-prepared food from a restaurant such as pizza. [15]Or maybe she cook a fast-food dinner in the microwave. [16]In addition, my family enjoys to spend time together on weekends and holidays. [17]For example, on sundays we often having big barbecue, invite Aunts, Uncles, cousins, Grandparents. [18]We spend whole day together. [19]It gives nice feeling. [20]In U.S., in contrast, children have their own activities, parents have different activities, teenagers prefer to be with their own friends. [21]In fact, children spend more time with friends than with parents. [22]Families here don't live close to one another. [23]Children don't know their aunts and uncles. [24]They don't become close their cousins. [25]As we do in my culture. [26]It's too bad, I think, for close family is lasting treasure.

Step 4C: Writing the Final Copy

Now you are ready to write the final copy to hand in. Your instructor will expect it to be written neatly and legibly in ink or typed on a computer. Read it once more, and don't be surprised if you decide to make changes. Remember that writing is a continuous process of writing and rewriting until you are satisfied with the final product.

Following is the final copy of the paragraph about communication problems.

MODEL

Final Copy

Communication Problems

One kind of culture shock faced by international students in the United States is difficulty communicating with Americans. When they first arrive in the United States, they soon realize that their verbal skills are poor. First of all, they lack vocabulary, and they have poor pronunciation, so American people do not understand them. For example, a few days ago, I asked an American student how to get to the library, but because I have trouble pronouncing *r*'s and *l*'s, the student did not understand me. I finally had to write it on a piece of paper. International students also speak too softly because they are shy. It is difficult for foreign people to understand Americans, too. Americans use incomplete sentences, such as "Later" to mean "I'll see you later," and "Coming?" to mean "Are you coming?" Also, Americans talk too fast, so it is often impossible to understand them. In addition, Americans also use a lot of slang and idioms whose meanings nonnative speakers do not know. For example, the other day someone said to me, "That drives me up the wall," and I could not imagine what he meant. I had a picture in my mind of him driving his car up a wall. It did not make sense to me. In short, communication is probably the first problem that international students face in the United States. After a while, however, their ears get used to the American way of speaking, and their own verbal abilities improve.

Punctuation Rules

Using correct punctuation is important because punctuation conveys meaning just as words do. Consider these two sentences:

Eat children.

Eat, children.

Both sentences are commands, but the first sentence would be correct only in a society of cannibals[1]! Learn and practice the rules of punctuation until you are confident about using them correctly.

Commas[2]

Commas are sometimes troublesome to learners of English because they are used differently in other languages. There are many comma rules in English, but you may remember them more easily if you realize that they can be organized into just four main groups: **introducers, coordinators, inserters**, and **tags**. Each group of commas relates to independent clauses in a particular way, except the coordinator group. Coordinator commas link not just independent clauses but *any* coordinate (equal) elements in a sentence.

Study the examples for each comma group, and notice the kinds of elements that can be introducers, coordinators, inserters, and tags.

Introducer Commas

An introducer comma follows any element that comes in front of the first independent clause in a sentence.

WORDS

Therefore, I plan to quit smoking.
Nervously, I threw away my cigarettes.

PHRASES

As a result, I feel terrible right now.
After 16 years of smoking, it is not easy to quit.
Having smoked for 16 years, I find it difficult to quit.

DEPENDENT CLAUSES

Because I have a chronic cough, my doctor recommended that I quit immediately.

DIRECT QUOTATIONS

"Stop smoking today," she advised.

---

[1]**cannibals:** people who eat human flesh
[2]Thanks to Anne Katz of ARC Associates, Oakland, California, for permission to adapt her presentation of comma rules.

Coordinator Commas

Together with a coordinating conjunction, a comma links coordinate (equal) elements in a sentence.

COMPOUND SENTENCE WITH
2 INDEPENDENT CLAUSES:

She has a good job, yet **she is always broke.**
They were tired, so **they went home early.**

SERIES OF 3 OR MORE
WORDS

He does not enjoy **skiing, ice-skating,** or **sledding.**
Cecille speaks **English, Spanish, French,** and **Creole.**

(*No comma with only two items: Chen speaks Mandarin and Taiwanese.*)

SERIES OF 3 OR MORE
PHRASES

A nurse has to work **at night, on weekends,** and **on holidays.**
We **ran into the airport, checked our luggage, raced to the boarding gate, gave the attendant our boarding passes,** and **collapsed in our seats.**

Inserter Commas

An inserter comma is used before and after any element that is inserted into the middle of an independent clause.

WORDS

My uncle, **however,** refuses to quit smoking.

PHRASES

My father, **on the other hand,** has never smoked.
There is no point in living, **according to my uncle,** if you do not do what you enjoy.

NONRESTRICTIVE PHRASES
AND CLAUSES

My aunt, **his wife,** died of lung cancer.
My cousins, **grieving over their mother's death,** resolved never to smoke.
My mother, **who just celebrated her fiftieth birthday,** enjoys an occasional cigarette.

REPORTING VERBS IN
DIRECT QUOTATIONS:

"I have tried to quit dozens of times," **she says,** "but I can't."

Tag Commas

A tag comma is used when adding certain elements to the end of a sentence.

WORDS

My uncle believes in drinking a daily glass of wine, **too.**[3]
He appears to be in good health, **however.**

PHRASES

He swims for an hour every day, **for example.**
He also plays tennis, **beating me most of the time.**

TAG QUESTIONS

It is not logical, **is it**?

DIRECT QUOTATIONS

He laughs as he says, **"I will outlive all of you."**

PRACTICE 1

Using Commas

Step 1 Add commas wherever they are necessary. (Not all sentences need them, and some sentences need more than one.)

Step 2 Name the function of each comma (introducer, coordinator, inserter, or tag) on the line.

---

[3]Many writers do not use a comma before *too.*

The first one has been done for you as an example.

<u>Inserter</u>   1. The advertising industry, which is one of the largest industries in the United States, employs millions of people and spends billions of dollars.

_____   2. A company that wants to be successful must spend a great deal of money to advertise its products.

_____   3. Advertising is essential to the free enterprise system yet it can sometimes be very annoying.

_____   4. Every minute of the day and night people are exposed to ads on television on billboards in the newspapers and in magazines.

_____   5. You cannot even avoid advertising in the privacy of your own car or your own home for advertisers have begun selling their products in those places too.

_____   6. In the last few years advertising agencies have started to hire young people to hand out circulars on street corners and in parking lots.

_____   7. You can often find these circulars stuck on your windshield thrust through the open windows of your car stuffed in your mailbox or simply scattered on your front doorstep.

_____   8. Because Americans are exposed to so much advertising they have become immune to it.

_____   9. As a result advertisers have to make louder commercials use brighter colors and hire sexier models to catch the public's attention.

_____   10. Many people object to commercials that use sex as a sales strategy.

_____   11. Sexy commercials that sell everything from toothpaste to automobiles seem to imply that you will become sexier if you buy the product.

_____   12. Sex is used in many cigarette and liquor ads for example.

_____   13. The women in such ads are often dressed in revealing clothes and are surrounded by handsome men and the men in such ads are always extremely handsome and virile.

_____   14. As everyone knows smoking and drinking do not make you sexy or virile.

_____   15. On the contrary drinking makes you fat and smoking makes you sick.

_____   16. Recently smoking was banned in most public places in the United States.

_____ 17. Many people opposed the law but it finally passed.
_____ 18. Smoking is now prohibited in hospitals airports stores offices and restaurants.
_____ 19. In many other countries however smoking is still allowed.
_____ 20. Antismoking groups want to ban smoking in those countries too.

Semicolons

Using **semicolons** is not difficult if you remember that a semicolon (;) is more like a period than a comma. It is a very strong punctuation mark. Semicolons are used in three places:

1. Between two sentences that are closely connected in idea
2. Before conjunctive adverbs and some transition phrases when they are followed by an independent clause
3. Between items in a series when the items themselves contain commas

Between Sentences

Use a semicolon at the end of a sentence when the following sentence is closely connected in meaning. You could also use a period, but when the sentences are connected in meaning, a semicolon indicates the connection.

Independent clause; independent clause.

Andrew did not accept the job offer; he wants to go to graduate school.
Computer use is increasing; computer crime is, too.
The meeting ended at dawn; nothing had been decided.

Before Connectors

Use a semicolon before conjunctive adverbs such as *however, therefore, nevertheless, moreover*, and *furthermore*. Also use a semicolon before transition phrases such as *for example, as a result, that is*, or *in fact* when they are followed by an independent clause.

conjunctive adverb,
Independent clause;   OR   **independent clause.**
transition phrase,

Skiing is dangerous; nevertheless, millions of people ski.
I have never been to Asia; in fact, I have never been outside the country.

Between Items in a Series

Semicolons are used to separate items in a series when some of the items already contain commas.

> I cannot decide which car I like best: the Ferrari, with its quick acceleration and sporty look; the midsize Ford Taurus, with its comfortable seats and ease of handling; or the compact Geo, with its economical fuel consumption.

PRACTICE 2

Using Semicolons and Commas

A. Step 1 The following sentences need semicolons; some also need commas. Add the correct punctuation in the appropriate places.

Step 2 On the line at the left, indicate whether the semicolon is
1. before two closely connected sentences.
2. before a conjunctive adverb or a transition phrase.
3. between items in a series if the items already contain commas.

The first one is done for you as an example.

__2__ 1. Professor Smith is at a conference; however, Dr. Jones, who is the department chairman, will be glad to see you.

____ 2. Grace works for a prestigious law firm she is their top criminal lawyer.

____ 3. My favorite leisure-time activities are going to movies especially musicals reading novels especially stories of love and adventure listening to music both rock and classical and participating in sports particularly tennis and volleyball.

____ 4. The future of our wild animals is uncertain for example illegal shooting and chemical poisoning threaten many birds.

____ 5. Homework is boring therefore I never do it.

____ 6. The freeways are always crowded during the busy rush hours nevertheless people refuse to take public transportation.

____ 7. The Smiths' marriage should succeed they share the same interests.

____ 8. Hoping that he would pass the course he stayed up all night studying for the final exam unfortunately he overslept and missed the test.

____ 9. In general I enjoy my English class the amount of homework our teacher assigns is definitely not enjoyable however.

____ 10. If you are a college student, an average day is filled with challenges: you have to avoid running into Professor Jones whose class you missed because you overslept you have to race across the campus at high speed to reach your next class which is always at the other side of the campus and you have to secretly prepare your homework assignment during class hoping all the time that the teacher will not catch you.

B. Punctuate the following sentences by adding semicolons and commas. Use semicolons wherever possible.

1. My bus was late therefore I missed my first class.
2. The politician was discovered accepting bribes as a result his political career was ruined.
3. My father never cries in fact he never shows any emotion at all,
4. The restaurant was closed consequently we went home to eat.
5. Some people feel that grades are unnecessary on the other hand some people feel that grades motivate students.
6. Technology is changing our lives in harmful ways for example the computer is replacing human contact.
7. The computer dehumanizes business nevertheless it has some real advantages,
8. Writing essays is easy it just takes a little practice.
9. North Americans love pets every family seems to have at least one dog or cat.
10. The life expectancy of North Americans is increasing for example the life expectancy of a person born in 2000 was 77.2 years which is an increase of almost 30 years since 1900.
11. Your proposal is a good one however I do not completely agree with your final suggestion.
12. Efficiency is a highly prized quality among North Americans it has almost attained the status of a moral attribute.

C. Write one original sentence for each of the three rules for using semicolons.

1. Between closely connected sentences

_____

2. Before conjunctive adverbs and some transition phrases

_____

3. Between items in a series

_____

Colons

Using a **colon** at the end of an independent clause focuses attention on the words following the colon. After a colon, we often write lists, appositives, and direct quotations.

Before Lists
Use a colon to introduce a list.

Libraries have two kinds of periodicals: bound periodicals and current periodicals.

I need the following groceries: eggs, milk, and coffee.

The causes of the U.S. Civil War were as follows: the economic domination of the North, the slavery issue, and the issue of states' rights versus federal intervention.

Caution

1. Do not use a colon to introduce a list after the verb *to be* unless you add *the following* or *as follows*.

INCORRECT   To me, the most important things in life are: good health, a happy home life, and a satisfying occupation.

CORRECT   To me, the most important things in life **are** good health, a happy home life, and a satisfying occupation.

CORRECT   To me, the most important things in life **are the following:** good health, a happy home life, and a satisfying occupation.

2. Do not use a colon after a preposition. Use a colon only at the end of an independent clause.

INCORRECT   After a long day at work, I look forward to: enjoying a quiet dinner at home, playing with my children, and watching a little TV.

CORRECT   After a long day at work, I look forward to enjoying a quiet dinner at home, playing with my children, and watching a little TV.

Before Appositives

Use a colon after an independent clause to direct attention to an appositive (a word or word group that renames another word or word group).

He had one great love in his life: himself.

A doctor has two important abilities: the ability to listen and the ability to analyze.

Before Long Quotations

Use a colon to introduce a quotation longer than three lines. This type of quote is indented on both sides, and no quotation marks are used.

As Albert C. Baugh and Thomas Cable state in their book *The History of the English Language*:

> There is no such thing as uniformity in language. Not only does the speech of one community differ from that of another, but the speech of different individuals of a single community, even different members of the same family, is marked by individual peculiarities.

Before Subtitles

Use a colon between the main title and the subtitle of a book, article, or play.

A popular book on nonverbal communication is Samovar and Porter's *Intercultural Communication: A Reader.*

The title of an article from the *New York Times* is "Man on Mars: Dream or Reality?"

In Expressions of Time or Day

Use a colon between the numbers for hours and minutes when indicating the time of day.

Helen left the class at 12:30.

Their plane arrived at 1:40 a.m., six hours late.

After Formal Salutations

Use a colon after the salutation of a formal letter.

Dear Professor Einstein:

Dear Customer Relations:

Dear Ms. Smith:

To Whom It May Concern:

In informal letters, use a comma.

Dear Mom,

Dear Mark,

PRACTICE 3

Using Punctuation Marks

A. Add commas, semicolons, and colons to the following.

1. The library offers many special services the Student Learning Center where students can receive individual tutoring special classes where they can improve their math reading writing and computer skills and group study rooms where they can meet with classmates to discuss assignments.

2. Dear Dr. Patterson
   Dear Jacob
   Dear Mr. Carter

3. To check a book out of the library you should follow this procedure Write down the call number of the book find the book take it to the circulation desk fill out the card and show your student I.D.

4. The principal sources of air pollution in our cities are factories airplanes and automobiles.

5. I have a dental appointment at 330 today. Please pick me up at 300.

B. Write a sentence in which you list two pieces of advice that you have received from someone older, such as your parents or a teacher. Use a colon to direct attention to them.

_____

_____

C. Write the title and subtitle of the following book correctly. Remember to underline the full title.

TITLE   SUBTITLE
Paris   A Visitor's Guide to Restaurants

Quotation Marks

Quotation marks ("...") have three basic uses: to enclose direct quotations, to enclose unusual words, and to enclose titles of short works.

Around Direct Quotations

Use quotation marks around a direct quotation that is shorter than three lines. A direct quotation states the *exact* words of a speaker and is usually introduced by a reporting phrase such as *he said* or *as the report stated*.

Punctuation with quotation marks can be a little tricky. Here are some rules to follow:

1. Separate a quoted sentence from a reporting phrase with a comma.

   The receptionist said, "The doctor is unavailable right now. Please wait."

   "We have already been waiting for an hour," we answered.

2. Periods and commas go inside the second quotation mark of a pair.

   "I thought he was responsible," he said, "but he isn't."

3. Colons and semicolons go outside quotation marks.

   "Give me liberty or give me death": these are famous words.

4. Exclamation points (!) and question marks (?) go inside quotation marks if they are a part of the quotation; otherwise, they go outside.

   "Is it eight o'clock?" she asked.

   Did she say, "It is eight o'clock"?

5. Begin each quoted sentence with a capital letter. When a quoted sentence is divided into two parts, the second part begins with a lowercase letter unless it is a new sentence.

   "I thought he was responsible," he said, "but he isn't."

   "I think he is responsible," he said. "Look at his fine work."

6. Use single quotation marks ('...') to enclose a quotation within a quotation.

   As John F. Kennedy reminded us, "We should never forget the words of Martin Luther King, Jr., who said, 'I have a dream.'"

Around Unusual Words

Use quotation marks around words with an unusual, especially ironic, meanings.

The "banquet" consisted of hot dogs and soft drinks.

The little girl proudly showed her "masterpiece": a crayon drawing of a flower.

Around Titles of Short Works

Use quotation marks around the titles of articles from periodical journals, magazines, and newspapers; chapters of books; short stories; poems; and songs.

> In the article "The Future of Manned Space Travel," published in the July 19, 2004, issue of *Space*, the authors explore the problems of a manned flight to Mars.

> The *Times* of London recently published an article entitled "Who Needs the Monarchy?" in which the relevancy of the English monarchy was discussed.

Note: <u>Underline</u> or *italicize* titles of books, journals, magazines, newspapers, and movies.

PRACTICE 4

Using Quotation Marks

Write five sentences about any article in a newspaper or magazine that you enjoy reading. Include a quotation, the name of the newspaper or magazine, and the title of the article in each sentence. (For practice in using quotation marks, see Chapter 3, Practice 2, page 46.)

Editing Practice

Add punctuation to the following paragraphs.

Aging

1 ¹People are more likely to live long enough to get old in wealthy countries than in poor countries. ²In rich countries people have nutritious food modern medical care good sanitation and clean drinking water but poor countries lack these things. ³As a result the mortality rate especially infant mortality is very high. ⁴Citizens of Ethiopia and Yemen which are two of the world's poorest countries have an average life expectancy of 35–39 years. ⁵Citizens of Japan Hong Kong Singapore Australia Iceland and Sweden in contrast have an average life span of more than 80 years. ⁶Japan has the highest Yemen has the lowest. ⁷One exception is Saudi Arabia one of the world's wealthiest nations. ⁸Having an average life expectancy of 45–49 years Saudi Arabians live about as long as Bangladeshis and Cambodians. ⁹Surprisingly the United States is not among the highest rated nations having an average life expectancy of only 77 years.

2 ¹⁰Compared to other mammals humans have a relatively long life span. ¹¹The average life span of elephants is 70 years of dogs 18 years of cats 14 years and of horses 20 years. ¹²The life spans of other species are as follows eagles parrots and owls 60 years parakeets 12 years guppies 5 years and box tortoises 100 years. ¹³Some plants such as trees live much longer than animals. ¹⁴Redwood trees for example live more than 3,000 years and bristlecone pine trees can live over 4,000 years.

3   [15]The life expectancy of people who live in industrialized societies is increasing rapidly in fact it has doubled in the past hundred years. [16]When comparing males and females one finds that women generally live longer than men. [17]The oldest person in the world until recently was a French woman Jeanne Calment. [18]At her death Madame Calment was both blind and deaf but had not lost her sharp wit for which she had become quite famous. [19]Asked what kind of future she expected she replied A very short one. [20]Bragging about her smooth skin she said I've only had one wrinkle in my life and I'm sitting on it.

C Charts of Connecting Words and Transition Signals

Coordinating Words

Coordinating conjunctions

Coordinating conjunctions connect grammatically equal elements. Coordinating conjunctions are sometimes called the "Fan Boys" conjunctions—For, And, Nor, But, Or, Yet, So.

Conjunction	Function	Example
for	Connects a reason to a result	I am a little hungry, **for** I didn't eat breakfast this morning.
and	Connects equal similar ideas	John likes to fish **and** hunt.
nor	Connects two negative sentences	She does not eat meat, **nor** does she drink milk.
but	Connects equal different ideas	I like to eat fish **but** not to catch them.
or	Connects two equal choices	Do you prefer coffee **or** tea?
yet	Connects equal contrasting ideas	It is sunny **yet** cold.
so	Connects a result to a reason	I did not eat breakfast this morning, **so** I am a little hungry.

Paired (correlative) conjunctions

Correlative conjunctions are always in pairs. Like coordinating conjunctions, they connect grammatically equal elements. (Please also read the section Parallelism on pages 179–181.)

Conjunction Pairs	Example
both . . . and	**Both** San Francisco **and** Sydney have beautiful harbors.
not only . . . but also	Japanese food is **not only** delicious to eat **but also** beautiful to look at.
either . . . or	Bring **either** a raincoat **or** an umbrella when you visit Seattle.
neither . . . nor	My grandfather could **neither** read **nor** write, but he was a very wise person.
whether . . . or	The newlyweds could not decide **whether** to live with her parents **or** to rent an apartment.

Subordinating Words

A subordinating word is the first word in a dependent clause. Common subordinating words include the following.

Subordinating Conjunctions for Adverb Clauses

Time (When?)	
after	**After** we ate lunch, we decided to go shopping.
as, just as	**Just as** we left the house, it started to rain.
as long as	We waited **as long as** we could.
as soon as	**As soon as** the front door closed, I looked for my house key.
before	I thought I had put it in my coat pocket **before** we left.
since	I have not locked myself out of the house **since** I was 10 years old.
until	**Until** I was almost 12, my mother pinned the key to my coat.
when	**When** I turned 12, my mother let me keep the key in my pocket.
whenever	I usually put the key in the same place **whenever** I come home.
while	**While** I searched for the key, it rained harder and harder.

Subordinating Conjunctions for Adverb Clauses (continued)

Place (Where?)	
where	I like to shop **where** prices are low.
wherever	I try to shop **wherever** there is a sale.
anywhere	You can find bargains **anywhere** you shop.
everywhere	I use my credit card **everywhere** I shop.
Manner (How?)	
as, just as	I love to get flowers(,) **as** most women do.*
as if	You look **as if** you didn't sleep at all last night.
as though	She acts **as though** she doesn't know us.
Distance (How far? How near? How close?)	
as + *adverb* + as	We will hike **as far as** we can before it turns dark. The child sat **as close as** she could to her mother. The child sat **as close** to her mother **as** she could.
Frequency (How often?)	
as often as	I call my parents **as often as** I can.
Reason (Why?)	
as	I can't take evening classes(,) **as** I work at night.*
because	I can't take evening classes **because** I work at night.
since	I can't take evening classes **since** I work at night.
Purpose (For what purpose?)	
so that	Many people emigrate **so that** their children can have a better life.
in order that	Many people emigrate **in order that** their children can have a better life.
Result (With what result?)	
so + *adjective* + that	I was **so tired** last night **that** I fell asleep at dinner.
so + *adverb* + that	She talks **so softly that** the other students cannot hear her.
such a(n) + *noun* + that	It was **such an easy test that** most of the students got A's.
so much/many/little/few + *noun* + that	He is taking **so many classes that** he has no time to sleep.

*This is an exception to the usual rule for commas. Many writers use a comma before *as*.

Subordinating Conjunctions for Adverb Clauses (continued)

Condition (Under what condition?)	
if	We will not go hiking **if** it rains.
unless	We will not go hiking **unless** the weather is perfect.
Partial contrast	
although	I love my brother **although** we disagree about almost everything.
even though	I love my brother **even though** we disagree about almost everything.
though	I love my brother **though** we disagree about almost everything.
Contrast (Direct opposites)	
while	My brother likes classical music, **while** I prefer hard rock.
whereas	He dresses conservatively, **whereas** I like to be a little shocking.

Subordinating Words for Adjective Clauses

To refer to people	
who, whom, whose, that (informal)	People **who** live in glass houses should not throw stones.
	My parents did not approve of the man **whom** my sister married.
	An orphan is a child **whose** parents are dead.
To refer to animals and things	
which	My new computer, **which** I bought yesterday, stopped working today.
that	Yesterday I received an e-mail **that** I did not understand.
To refer to a time or a place	
when	Thanksgiving is a time **when** families travel great distances to be together.
where	An orphanage is a place **where** orphans live.

Subordinating words for noun clauses

That Clauses	
that	Do you belive **that** there is life in outer space?
If/Whether Clauses	
whether	I can't remember **whether** I locked the door.
whether or not	**whether or not** I locked the door.
whether . . . or not	**whether** I locked the door **or not**.
if	I can't remember **if** I locked the door.
if . . . or not	**if** I locked the door **or not**.
Question Clauses	
who, whoever, whom	**Whoever** arrives at the bus station first should buy the tickets.
which, what, where	Do you know **where** the bus station is?
when, why, how	We should ask **when** the bus arrives.
how much, how many	Do not worry about **how much** they cost.
how long, how often, etc.	He didn't care **how long** he had to wait.

Notice that some subordinating conjunctions can introduce different kinds of dependent clauses. *That* can introduce either noun clauses or adjective clauses, and *where* can introduce either a noun, an adjective, or an adverb clause. It normally is not important to know the kind of clause.

> I can't remember **where** I put the house key. (noun clause; direct object of *remember*)
>
> It's not in the place **where** I usually put it. (adjective clause; tells *which place*)
>
> I always put it **where** I will see it when I go out the front door. (adverb clause; tells *where I put it*)

Conjunctive Adverbs

Conjunctive adverbs can appear at the beginning, in the middle, or at the end of one independent clause, but we often use them to connect two independent clauses.

Remember to put a semicolon before and a comma after the conjunctive adverb if an independent clause follows.

Conjunctive Adverb	Examples
To add a similar idea	
also	Community colleges offer preparation for many jobs; **also,** they prepare students to transfer to four-year colleges or universities.
besides furthermore in addition moreover	; **besides,** ; **furthermore,** ; **in addition,** ; **moreover,**
To add an unexpected or surprising continuation	
however	The cost of attending a community college is low; **however,** many students need financial aid.
nevertheless nonetheless still	; **nevertheless,** ; **nonetheless,** ; **still,**
To add a complete contrast	
in contrast	The cost of attending a community college is low; **in contrast,** most four-year colleges do.
on the other hand	; **on the other hand,**
To add a result	
as a result	Native and nonnative English speakers have different needs; **as a result,** most schools provide separate classes for each group.
consequently therefore thus	; **consequently,** ; **therefore,** ; **thus,**
To list ideas in order of time	
meanwhile	Police kept people away from the scene of the accident; **meanwhile,** ambulance workers tried to pull victims out of the wreck.
afterward	The workers put five injured people into an ambulance; **afterward,** they found another victim.
then subsequently	; **then,** ; **subsequently,**
To give an example	
for example	Colors can have different meanings; **for example,** white is the color of weddings in some cultures and of funerals in others.
for instance	; **for instance,**
To show similarities	
similarly	Hawaii has sunshine and friendly people; **similarly,** Mexico's weather is sunny and its people hospitable.
likewise	; **likewise,**

Conjunctive Adverb	Examples
To indicate "the first statement is not true; the second statement is true"	
instead **on the contrary** **rather**	The medicine did not make him feel better; **instead,** it made him feel worse. ; **on the contrary,** ; **rather,**
instead (meaning "as a substitute")	They had planned to go to Hawaii on their honeymoon; **instead,** they went to Mexico.
To give another possibility	
alternatively **on the other hand**	You can live in a dorm on campus; **on the other hand,** you can rent a room with a family off campus. ; **alternatively,**
otherwise (meaning "if not")	Students must take final exams; **otherwise,** they will receive a grade of Incomplete.
To add an explanation	
in other words **that is**	Some cultures are matriarchal; **in other words,** the mothers are the head of the family. ; **that is,**
To make a stronger statement	
indeed **in fact**	Mangoes are a very common fruit; **indeed,** people eat more mangoes than any other fruit in the world. ; **in fact,**

Transition Signals

Transition Signals and Conjunctive Adverbs	Coordinating Conjunctions and Paired Conjunctions	Subordinating Conjunctions	Others: Adjectives, Prepositions, Verbs
To list ideas in order of time			
first, . . . first of all, . . . second, . . . third, . . . next, . . . then . . . after that, . . . meanwhile, . . . in the meantime, . . . finally, . . . last, . . . last of all, . . . subsequently, . . .		before after until when while as soon as since	the first (reason, cause, step, etc.) the second . . . the third . . . another . . . the last . . . the final . . .

To list ideas in order of importance			

first, . . .
first of all, . . .
first and foremost, . . .
second, . . .
more important, . . .
most important, . . .
more significantly, . . .
most significantly, . . .
above all, . . .
most of all, . . .
			the first . . . (reason,
			   cause, step, etc.)
			an additional . . .
			the second . . .
			another . . .
			a more important
			   (reason, cause,
			   step, etc.)
			the most important . . .
			the most significant . . .
			the best/the worst . . .

To add a similar or equal idea			
also, . . . besides, . . . furthermore, . . . in addition, . . . moreover, . . . too as well	and both . . . and not only . . . but also		another . . . (reason, cause, step, etc.) a second . . . an additional . . . a final . . . as well as

To add an opposite idea			
however, . . . on the other hand, . . . nevertheless, . . . nonetheless, . . . still, . . .	but yet	although even though though	despite in spite of

To explain or restate an idea			
in other words, . . . in particular, . . . (more) specifically, . . . that is, . . .			

To make a stronger statement			
indeed, . . . in fact, . . .			

To give another possibility			
alternatively, . . . on the other hand, . . . otherwise, . . .	or either . . . or whether . . . or		

To give an example			
for example, . . . for instance, . . .			such as an example of to exemplify

To express an opinion			
according to . . . in my opinion, . . . in my view, . . .			to believe (that) to feel (that) to think (that)

To give a reason			
for this reason, . . .	for	because	as a result of because of due to

To give a result			
accordingly, . . . as a consequence, . . . as a result, . . . consequently, . . . for these reasons, . . . hence, . . . therefore, . . . thus, . . .	so		the cause of the reason for to cause to result (in) to have an effect on to affect

To add a conclusion			
all in all, . . . in brief, . . . in short, . . . to conclude, . . . to summarize, . . . in conclusion, . . . in summary, . . . for these reasons, . . .			

To show similarities			
likewise, . . . similarly, . . . also	and both . . . and not only . . . but also neither . . . nor		alike, like, just like as, just as as well as well as compared with or to in comparison with or to to be similar (to) too

To show differences			
however, . . . in contrast, . . . instead, . . . on the contrary, . . . on the other hand, . . . rather, . . .			instead of

Editing Symbols

Symbol	Meaning	Example of Error	Corrected Sentence
p	punctuation	I live, and go to school here Where do you work.	I live and go to school here. Where do you work?
∧	missing word	I working in a restaurant.	I am working in a restaurant.
cap	capitalization	It is located at main and baker streets in the City.	It is located at Main and Baker Streets in the city.
vt	verb tense	I never work as a cashier until I get a job there.	I had never worked as a cashier until I got a job there.
s/v agr	subject-verb agreement	The manager work hard. There is five employees.	The manager works hard. There are five employees.
pron agr	pronoun agreement	Everyone works hard at their jobs.	All the employees work hard at their jobs.
⌣	connect to make one sentence	We work together. So we have become friends.	We work together, so we have become friends.
sp	spelling	The maneger is a woman.	The manager is a woman.
sing/pl	singular or plural	She treats her employees like slave.	She treats her employees like slaves.
✕	unnecessary word	My boss she watches everyone all the time.	My boss watches everyone all the time.
wf	wrong word form	Her voice is irritated.	Her voice is irritating.

Symbol	Meaning	Example of Error	Corrected Sentence
ww	wrong word	The food is delicious. ww Besides, the restaurant is always crowded.	The food is delicious. Therefore, the restaurant is always crowded.
ref	pronoun reference error	The restaurant's ref specialty is fish. They are always fresh.	The restaurant's specialty is fish. It is always fresh.
		The food is delicious. ref Therefore, it is always crowded.	The food is delicious. Therefore, the restaurant is always crowded.
wo OR ∼	wrong word order	Friday always is our busiest night.	Friday is always our busiest night.
ro	run-on sentence	ro [Lily was fired she is upset.]	Lily was fired, so she is upset.
cs	comma splice	cs [Lily was fired, she is upset.]	Lily was fired; therefore, she is upset. Because Lily was fired, she is upset. Lily is upset because she was fired.
frag	fragment	She was fired. frag [Because she was always late.]	She was fired because she was always late.
		frag [Is open from 6:00 p.m. until the last customer leaves.]	The restaurant is open from 6:00 p.m. until the last customer leaves.
		frag [The employees on time and work hard.]	The employees are on time and work hard.
choppy	choppy writing	choppy [I like the work. I do not like my boss. I want to quit.]	Even though I like the work, I do not like my boss, so I want to quit.

Symbol	Meaning	Example of Error	Corrected Sentence
not //	not parallel	Most of our regular customers are <u>friendly and generous tippers</u>. *(not // marked above "friendly")*	Most of our regular customers are friendly and tip generously.
sub	subordinate	The tips are good, [and all the employees share them.] *(sub marked above "and")*	The tips, which all of the employees share, are good.
prep	preposition	We start serving dinner 6:00 p.m. *(prep marked above "dinner," ^ below)*	We start serving dinner at 6:00 p.m.
conj	conjunction	Garlic shrimp, fried clams, broiled lobster are the most popular dishes. *(conj marked above "clams," ^ below)*	Garlic shrimp, fried clams, and broiled lobster are the most popular dishes.
art	article	Diners in the United States expect glass of water when they first sit down.	Diners in the United States expect a glass of water when they first sit down.
Ⓣ	add a transition	The new employee was careless. She frequently spilled coffee on the table. *(Ⓣ marked after "careless.")*	The new employee was careless. For example, she frequently spilled coffee on the table.
¶	start a new paragraph		
nfs/nmp	needs further support/needs more proof. Add some specific details (example, facts, quotations) to support your point.		

E Research and Documentation of Sources

When you need to research your topic, there are two places to look for information: in a library and on the Internet.

Type of Sources

You can find the following kinds of sources in a library:

1. **Reference books, such as dictionaries, encyclopedias, atlases, and books of facts** There are general encyclopedias like the *Encyclopedia Americana* and specialized encyclopedias like the *Film Encyclopedia*. There are also general dictionaries and specialized dictionaries like *A Dictionary of Botany*. Reference books are in the reference room or reference area of the library. You cannot check them out and take them home; you must use them inside the library. Make photocopies of pages that you need.

   Note: Although encyclopedias are a good place to get basic information about your topic, many college instructors will not allow them as sources in college research papers.

2. **Books** Libraries today usually list their books in a computerized catalog. You can search for books by title, by author's last name, or by subject. Unless you know the name of an author or the title of a book, you will begin by searching by subject. You may have to look under several subjects at first. To find books on IQ tests, for example, look under the subject "IQ tests." If there are no books listed, try looking under the subjects "intelligence testing" or "testing" and "intelligence" separately. Eventually you will find what you need.

   When you find a book that you think might be useful, write down the title, the name of the author, and the book's call number. A call number is a book's address in the library. You must know this number to find the book on the library shelves.

3. **Articles in popular magazines and newspapers** Examples of popular magazines are *Psychology Today* and *Newsweek*. You can find magazine articles in two main ways. The first way is to search in an index. An index is a catalog of magazine and newspaper articles, and like a book catalog, it lists articles by title, author, and subject. Indexes are usually on CD-ROMs. There are different indexes for magazines, newspapers, and specialized subjects like psychology and business. Articles in popular magazines are indexed in the *Readers' Guide to Periodical Literature*. The *National News Index* lists articles from five major U.S. newspapers.

   A more convenient way to find magazine articles is to use an online computer search service such as InfoTrac and Ebscohost, which most libraries have. The process is the same as searching an index. However, these online services have an advantage: They allow you to print out articles directly from the computer terminal. This saves you the time and trouble of looking for the magazine on the library shelves.

Note: Be cautious about using information from popular magazines and newspapers. Some popular magazines, such as *People,* and tabloid newspapers such as the *National Enquirer* are not appropriate sources. Some Internet sources also may not be appropriate. See the next section, Evaluating Sources.

4. **Scholarly journals** For students in graduate school who do advanced research, scholarly journals are important sources of information. Scholarly journals are magazines that print academic articles, usually about a specific field of study. They are also called periodicals or periodical journals. Examples of scholarly journals are *Journal of Educational Psychology* and *New England Journal of Medicine*. Instructors in undergraduate classes do not usually require students to use scholarly journals.

Searching the Internet is a convenient way to do research, but it takes practice to do it efficiently. There are several ways to find information. One way is to type in keywords. Keywords are words that name your specific topic, such as *tattoos* or *poisonous snakes*. Search programs like Google, Alta Vista, and Yahoo will search the Internet and display Web sites containing your keywords. The more specific your keywords are, the more selective the search will be. For example, the keyword *snakes* will produce an enormous number of sites. The keywords *poisonous snakes* will give fewer, and *Central American poisonous snakes* will give the fewest.

Your instructor may allow you to gather information on your topic by performing an experiment, taking a survey, or interviewing people.

Evaluating Sources

Before you use information from an outside source, you should first determine if the information is reliable. There is a lot of outdated, biased, and false information in print and on the Internet. Your sources should be reliable, which means that the information should be current, unbiased, and true. You can judge a source's reliability by checking the following:

1. Check the date. Your sources of information should be current unless your topic is a historical one. For example, if your topic is space exploration, a source dated before 1960 would probably not have very useful information.
2. Check the reputation of the author(s). What do you know about them? You should find out their occupations, at a minimum. A reliable author is not necessarily famous; he or she just has to have special knowledge about your topic. For example, if your topic is the conditions in U.S. prisons, a letter or article written by a prisoner is reliable. However, the same prisoner would probably not be a reliable source on the topic of ballet dancing.
3. Check the reputation of the publisher. What company or organization published the information? Is it nationally or internationally known?

4. What is the purpose of the publication or Web site? Is it to sell a product, support one side of a controversy, promote a political point of view, or merely provide information?

5. Check the content. Is it mostly fact, opinion, or propaganda? Does it seem strongly biased? Are the ideas supported by reliable evidence?

6. Check the language. Does the source seem well written? Is it free from emotion-arousing words? Do you notice any spelling errors?

7. Check the quality of the presentation. Is the quality of the printing good? Is the Web site well organized? Does it offer links to other sites? Check them out.

If you aren't sure about a source, ask your instructor or a reference librarian for help in evaluating it. There are also sites on the Internet that can help. Find them by searching the keywords "evaluating Internet information."

PRACTICE 1

Evaluating Sources

Check (✓) the sources that might be useful and reliable on the topic body art (body painting, tattooing, and piercing) in ancient and modern cultures.

Print sources

_____ 1. *Tattoo History: A Source Book* by Stephen G. Gilbert. A collection of historical writings on tattooing. Includes accounts of tattooing in the Ancient World, Polynesia, Japan, the pre-Columbian Americas, nineteenth-century Europe and the United States. Published in 2001.

_____ 2. *The Rose Tattoo*. A play by Tennessee Williams, made into a movie starring Anna Magnani and Burt Lancaster. The story of a widow whose loyalty to her dead husband is tested by a handsome truck driver.

_____ 3. "Tattooing among the Maoris of New Zealand." An article by William Oldenburg in the June 1946 issue of *Journal of Cultural Anthropology*.

_____ 4. "Regulating the Body Art Industry." A doctor proposes laws to ensure the safe practice of tattooing and body piercing in the state of New York. An article written by Dr. Evan Whitman in the February 10, 2001, issue of *The New York Times.*

_____ 5. "Living Canvas." An article by Jerry Adler in the November 29, 1999, issue of *Newsweek*. Tattooing and body piercing, long fashionable with bikers and rebellious teens, is gaining popularity among the "beautiful people" of high society.

_____ 6. *Body Decoration: A World Survey of Body Art* by Karl Groning. A collection of photographs traces more than 10,000 years of body art, from the body painting of prehistoric people to the body piercing of modern punk. Published in 1998.

Internet sources

_____ 1. Tattoos.com. A Web site that provides information about tattooing and links to other sites.

_____ 2. "Tattoo." An article in the online *Encyclopedia Britannica*, found at britannica.com.

_____ 3. Body Piercing Shop. A Web site offering titanium, surgical steel, silver, and gold body jewelry. Also semiprecious gemstones and Austrian crystal. Best prices.

_____ 4. "Body-Marking." An article in the online *Columbia Encyclopedia* on body-marking, painting, tattooing, or scarification (cutting and burning) of the body for ritual, esthetic, medicinal, magic, or religious purposes.

_____ 5. Getting Pierced Safely. A Web site that explains health factors. All the facts you need if you are thinking of body piercing. Choosing a safe practitioner. Risks.

_____ 6. "The Human Canvas." A report on body art throughout history. *Discovery Online*, Expeditions series, produced in cooperation with the American Museum of Natural History.

Documentation of Sources

In academic classes, instructors may ask you to document the sources of outside information you use in a paper. There are two steps to this process.

1. Insert a short reference in the body of your paper. This is called an in-text citation.
2. Prepare a list describing all your sources completely. This list is titled Works Cited and appears as the last page of your paper.

The next few pages will show you only the basics of the MLA style[1] of formal documentation. Consult the *MLA Handbook for Writers of Research Papers* for detailed information. You can find this book and others like it in the reference area of any library.

In-Text Citations

The purpose of an in-text citation is to refer the reader to the works-cited list at the end of your paper. In-text citations are also called parenthetical references because they are enclosed in parentheses. Place in-text citations immediately after the borrowed information, usually at the end of a sentence, before the final period.

IN-TEXT CITATION

A universal language could bring countries together culturally and economically as well as increase good feelings among them (Kispert).

---

[1]The MLA (Modern Language Association) style is used in English and other language classes. Other fields of study, such as the social sciences, physical sciences, and business, use other styles.

The name *Kispert* in parentheses at the end of this sentence tells us that the ideas in the sentence came from a work written by a person whose last name is Kispert. No page number is given, which indicates that the work is only one page long.

If readers want more information about this source, they can turn to the works-cited list at the end of the essay, report, or paper and find this entry:

ENTRY IN WORKS-CITED LIST

> Kispert, Robert J. "Universal language." <u>World Book Online Reference Center</u>. 2004. World Book, Inc. 12 Sep. 2004 <http://www.aolsvc.worldbook.aol.com/wb/Article?id=ar576960>.

In-text citations are as short as possible. They contain only enough information to allow the reader to find the full reference in the list of works cited at the end of your paper. Here are some guidelines.

ONE AUTHOR

> (Clinton 17)

Use the last name of the author and a page number (or numbers, if the borrowed information appears on more than one page). Use no punctuation.

TWO OR MORE AUTHORS

> (Bamberger and Yaeger 62)
>
> (Singleton et al. 345)

If there are two or three authors, give all the names. If there are four or more, use the first author's name and the Latin abbreviation *et al.* ("and others") followed by a period.

AUTHOR ALREADY MENTIONED

> (18)

If you have already mentioned the author's name in the text, or if you are citing two consecutive pieces of borrowed information from the source, do not repeat the name in your citation. For example, if you introduced the borrowed information with a phrase such as "According to Clinton," give only the page number.

NO AUTHOR

> ("2002 Olympics," par. 12)

If there is no author, use a short title in quotation marks.

QUOTED QUOTATION

> (qtd. in Herper 1)

If you use someone's words that are quoted in a source written by a different person, begin the in-text citation with the abbreviation *qtd. in* (for *quoted in*).

ENCYCLOPEDIA ARTICLE WITH NO AUTHOR

> ("Global Warming")

For an encyclopedia article, use the author's name if you know it. If you don't know it, use the title of the article in quotation marks. You do not need a page number since encyclopedia articles are arranged alphabetically and a reader will be able to find the source easily.

ELECTRONIC SOURCE

(Kidder, par. 7)

("2000 Olympics," par. 12)

(Gardiner, screens 2–3)

For an electronic source (online or CD-ROM), follow the same system as for print sources. If there are no page numbers, use whatever numbering system the source has—section number (abbreviated as "sec."), paragraph number (abbreviated as "par." or "pars."), screen number, or no number. Put a comma after the author or short title when you use paragraph numbers or screen numbers.

Works-Cited Lists

The second step in citing sources is to list all the sources you actually used in your paper. (Do not include sources that you read but did not use.) List them alphabetically by last name of the author or, if there is no author, by the first word of the title (disregarding *A, An*, and *The*). Include information about each source as described here. Pay close attention to punctuation and capitalization, and indent the second line 5 spaces. For kinds of sources not included here, consult a more comprehensive English handbook, such as the *MLA Handbook*.

BOOK WITH ONE AUTHOR

Bryson, Bill. <u>The Mother Tongue: English and How It Got That Way</u>. New York: Avon, 1991.

This is the form of a basic book reference. Divide the information into three parts: (1) name of the author, (2) title of the book, (3) publishing information. Put a period and one space after each part.

1. Write the author's last name first and put a comma after it. Do not include a person's titles.
2. Put a colon between the title and subtitle, and underline both.
3. Write the city of publication, a colon, the name of the publishing company, a comma, the year of publication, and a period. Get this information from the title page or the back of the title page inside the book, not from the book's cover. Use the first city listed if there are several. Include an abbreviation for a state or country if the city is unfamiliar or in any way unclear. Use the most recent year. Shorten the name of the publisher by omitting words like *Press, Publishers, Books, Inc.*, and *Co.*

BOOK WITH TWO OR MORE AUTHORS

Hall, Edward T., and Mildred Reed Hall. <u>Understanding Cultural Differences</u>. Yarmouth, ME: Intercultural, 1990.

Use reverse order for the first author's name, and then write all other authors' names in normal order. Put a comma after the last name of the first author and also between authors.

BOOK WITH MORE THAN ONE EDITION

Baugh, Albert C., and Thomas Cable. <u>A History of the English Language</u>. 5th ed. Upper Saddle River, NJ: Prentice Hall, 2002.

Put the number and the abbreviation "ed." (2nd ed., 3rd ed., 4th ed., and so on) after the title, followed by a period.

ENCYCLOPEDIA ARTICLE

"Intelligence Test." <u>New Encyclopedia Britannica: Micropedia</u>. 15th ed.

Use the author's name if it is given. Sometimes the author's name appears at the end of an encyclopedia article and sometimes not. If there is no author, put the title of the article first. Enclose the title in quotation marks. Underline the title of the encyclopedia. Put the edition number if there is one; if there is none, use the year.

MAGAZINE ARTICLE

Bamberger, Michael, and Don Yaeger. "Over the Edge." <u>Sports Illustrated</u> 14 Apr. 1997: 62–70.

Put the title of the article inside quotation marks. Underline the name of the magazine. Include the day, month, and year for weekly magazines followed by a colon and the page number or numbers on which the article appears. Abbreviate the names of months except May, June, and July.

NEWSPAPER ARTICLE

Epstein, Edward A. "A Less Social Society Is Becoming Shy." <u>San Francisco Chronicle</u> 14 Sep. 1995: A-1.

This article appeared on page A-1 of the newspaper.

PERSONAL INTERVIEW

Jones, John. Personal interview. 31 Oct. 2003.

ONLINE SOURCE

Kispert, Robert J. "Universal Language." <u>World Book Online Reference Center</u>. 2004. World Book, Inc. 25 Mar. 2004 <http://www.aolsvc.worldbook.aol.com/ wb/Article?id=ar576960>.

Leroux, Kivi. "Subliminal Messages: Primetime TV Programs Educate Viewers on the Environment." <u>E Magazine</u> July–Aug. 1999. 14 Sep. 2004 <http://www.emagazine.com/july-august_1999/0799curr_subliminal.html>.

Citations for online sources need the same basic information as print sources: author, title, and date of publication. The date of publication for an online source is the date it was put online or the date it was last revised. Sometimes you cannot find an author or a publication date; in this case, just give whatever information you are able to find. In addition, you need to give these two pieces of information for an online source.

1. Your date of access. Because online sources are often revised, you need to show exactly which version you used. Put the date you accessed (visited) the site just before the source's electronic address.
2. The exact electronic address. Copy the address from the top of your computer screen and enclose it in angle brackets (< >). Copy the exact address of the Web page you used, not just the home page address. If you must divide an address because it is too long to fit on a line, divide it only at a slash mark (/).

Format of the Works-Cited Page

A works-cited list is written or typed on a separate page, which is the last page of a paper. Use the following format.

1. Capitalize the title of the Works-Cited list and center it on the page.
2. Put the list in alphabetical order by author's last name (or title of the work, if there is no author).
3. Double-space everything.
4. Indent the second line of each citation 5 spaces or 1/2 inch.

MODEL

Works Cited

Works Cited

Bamberger, Michael, and Don Yaeger. "Over the Edge." <u>Sports Illustrated</u>

14 Apr. 1997: 62–70.

Baugh, Albert C., and Thomas Cable. <u>A History of the English Language</u>.

5th ed. Upper Saddle River, NJ: Prentice Hall, 2002.

Bruce, Meredith. <u>Cybercrime</u>. New York: Wexler, 2004.

Brunish, Cory. Letter. <u>Time</u> 16 Feb. 2004: 9.

Clinton, Patrick. "Manned Mars Flight: Impossible Dream?" <u>Space Science</u>

15 Oct. 2003: 16–18.

Downie, Andrew. "Brazil Considers Linguistic Barricade." <u>Christian Science</u>

<u>Monitor</u> 6 Sep. 2000. 13 Sep. 2004 <http://csmonitor.com/cgi-bin/

durableRedirect.pl?/durable/2000/09/06/fp7s2-csm.shtml>.

Epstein, Edward. "A Less Social Society Is Becoming Shy." <u>San Francisco</u>

<u>Chronicle</u> 14 Sep. 1995: A1+.

Henderson, Lynne, and Philip Zimbardo. "Shyness." <u>Encyclopedia of Mental</u>

<u>Health</u>. San Diego: Academic Press, 19 pp. 4 May 2004

<http://www.shyness.com/encyclopedia.html>.

Herper, Matthew. "Performance Drugs Outrun the Olympics." <u>Forbes</u> 15 Feb.

2002: 30 Mar. 2004 <http://www.forbes.com/2002/02/15/0215ped.html>.

Kispert, Robert J. "Universal language." <u>World Book Online Reference Center</u>.

2004. World Book, Inc. 12 Sep. 2004

<http://www.aolsvc.worldbook.aol.com/wb/Article?id=ar576960>.

Kluger, Jeffrey. "Mission to Mars: First the Rover Lands, and Now Bush Wants

to Send People. We Can Do It Even Faster Than Planned, but Here Is

What It Will Take." <u>Time</u> 26 Jan. 2004: 42–47.

Jones, John. Personal interview. 31 Oct. 2003.

Leroux, Kivi. "Subliminal Messages: Primetime TV Programs Educate Viewers

on the Environment." E Magazine July–Aug. 1999. 14 Sep. 2004

<http://www.emagazine.com/july-august_1999/0799curr_subliminal.html>.

Pinker, Steven. "Can a Computer Be Conscious?" U.S. News & World Report

18 Aug. 1997: 63–65.

"The 2000 Olympics: Games of the Drugs?" CBSNEWS.com 9 Sep. 2000.

30 Mar. 2004 <http://www.cbsnews.com/stories/2002/01/31/health/

main326667.shtml?CMP=ILC-SearchStories>.

PRACTICE 2

*Preparing a
Works-Cited List*

On a piece of paper, write the heading "Works Cited." Then write the information about each of the following sources in a list in MLA style in alphabetical order.

1. A book entitled *Learning Disorders* by Robert W. Henderson published by Morris & Burns in Chicago in 2005.
2. A magazine article entitled "How to Live to Be 100" by Richard Corliss and Michael D. Lemonick on pages 40–48 of the August 30, 2004, issue of *Time* magazine.
3. A newspaper article entitled "Biology of Dyslexia Varies with Culture, Study Finds" on page D7 of the September 7, 2004, issue of the *New York Times* newspaper. The author's name is Anahad O'Connor.
4. An article in an online encyclopedia. The title of the article is "Dyslexia." The site's address is http://www.aolsvc.worldbook.aol.com/wb/Article? id=ar171010. The author's name is Michel W. Kibby. The Web site is *World Book Online Reference Center*. The publisher is World Book, Inc., and the copyright date is 2004. Use today's date as your date of access.
5. A Web site published by the U.S. Food and Drug Administration's Center for Food Safety and Applied Nutrition. The Web site contains an article titled "Tattoos and Permanent Makeup." The Web site's address is http://www.cfsan.fda.gov/~dms/cos-204.html. The article was updated on July 1, 2004. Use today's date as your date of access.

Self-Editing and Peer-Editing Worksheets

Self-editing and peer-editing worksheets are designed to help you become a better writer. Your instructor may choose to assign the self-editing worksheet, the peer-editing worksheet, or both.

Self-Editing

Becoming a better writer requires that you learn to edit your own work. Self-editing involves not just checking for spelling and grammar errors. It also means looking at your writing as a writing teacher does. The self-editing worksheets contain questions about specific elements that your teacher hopes to find in your paragraph or essay—a strong thesis statement, clear topic sentences, specific supporting details, coherence, an effective conclusion, and so on. By answering the worksheet questions thoughtfully, you can learn to recognize the strengths (and weaknesses) in your rhetorical skills as well as to spot recurring errors in grammar, punctuation, and sentence structure.

Peer Editing

Peer editing is an interactive process of reading and commenting on a classmate's writing. You will exchange rough drafts with a classmate, read each other's work, and make suggestions for improvement. Use the worksheet for each assignment and answer each question. Write your comments on the worksheet or on your classmate's paper as your instructor directs.

Advice for Peer Editors

1. Your job is to help your classmate write clearly. Focus only on content and organization.
2. If you notice grammar or spelling errors, ignore them. It is not your job to correct your classmate's English.
3. Don't cross out any writing. Underline, draw arrows, circle things, but don't cross out anything.
4. Make your first comment a positive one. Find something good to say.
5. If possible, use a colored ink or pencil.
6. The writer may not always agree with you. Discuss your different opinions, but don't argue, and don't cause hurt feelings.

Here are some polite ways to suggest changes:

Do you think _____ is important/necessary/relevant?
I don't quite understand your meaning here.
Could you please explain this point a little more?
I think an example would help here.
This part seems confusing.
I think this part should go at the end/at the beginning/after XYZ.
Maybe you don't need this _____ word/sentence/part.

Scoring Rubrics

When grading papers, writing teachers sometimes assign points for each writing skill. They often use rubrics such as the ones on pages 315 and 316. In each rubric, the left column shows the maximum number of points possible for each item.

Teachers may duplicate these forms to use when scoring students' work. The first rubric is for scoring paragraphs; the second one is for scoring essays.

Scoring Rubric: Paragraphs

	Maximum Score	Actual Score
Format—5 points		
There is a title.	1	—
The title is centered.	1	—
The first line is indented.	1	—
There are margins on both sides.	1	—
The paragraph is double-spaced.	1	—
Total	5	
Mechanics—5 points		
There is a period, a question mark, or an exclamation mark after every sentence.	1	—
Capital letters are used correctly.	2	—
The spelling is correct.	2	—
Total	5	
Content—20 points		
The paragraph fits the assignment.	5	—
The paragraph is interesting to read.	5	—
The paragraph shows thought and care.	10	—
Total	20	
Organization—35 points		
The paragraph begins with a topic sentence that has both a topic and a controlling idea.	10	—
The paragraph contains several specific and factual supporting sentences that explain or prove the topic sentence, including at least one example.	20	—
The paragraph ends with an appropriate concluding sentence.	5	—
Total	35	
Grammar and Sentence Structure—35 points		
Estimate a grammar and sentence structure score.	35	
Grand Total	100	

Scoring Rubric: Essays

	Maximum Score	Actual Score
Format—5 points		
Title centered (2), first line of each paragraph indented (1), margins on both sides (1), text double-spaced (1)		
Total	5	
Mechanics—5 points		
Punctuation: periods, commas, semicolons, quotation marks (3), capitalization (1), spelling (1)		
Total	5	
Content—20 points		
The essay fulfills the requirements of the assignment.	5	—
The essay is interesting to read.	5	—
The essay shows that the writer used care and thought.	10	—
Total	20	
Organization—45 points		
The essay follows the outline, and it has an introduction, a body, and a conclusion.	5	—
Introduction: The introduction ends with the thesis statement.	5	—
Body		
Each paragraph of the body discusses a new point and begins with a clear topic sentence.	5	—
Each paragraph has specific supporting material: facts, examples, quotations, paraphrased or summarized information, etc.	10	—
Each paragraph has unity.	5	—
Each paragraph has coherence.	5	—
Transitions are used to link paragraphs.	5	—
Conclusion: The conclusion summarizes the main points or paraphrases the thesis statement, begins with a conclusion signal, and leaves the reader with the writer's final thoughts on the topic.	5	—
Total	35	
Grammar and Sentence Structure—25 points		
Estimate a grammar and sentence structure score.	25	
Grand Total	100	

Self-Editing Worksheet 1
Chapter 1: Paragraph Structure

Writer: _____ Date: _____

Format

My paragraph has a title.	**yes**	**no**
The title is centered.	**yes**	**no**
The first line is indented.	**yes**	**no**
There are margins on both sides of the page.	**yes**	**no**
The paragraph is double-spaced.	**yes**	**no**

Mechanics

I put a period, a question mark, or an exclamation mark after every sentence.	**yes**	**no**
I used capital letters correctly.	**yes**	**no**
I checked my spelling.	**yes**	**no**

Content and Organization

My paragraph fits the assignment.	**yes**	**no**
My paragraph has a topic sentence.	**yes**	**no**
The topic sentence has both a topic and a controlling idea.	**yes**	**no**
My paragraph contains several specific and factual supporting sentences, including at least one example.	**yes**	**no**
How many supporting sentences did I write?	**number**	_____
My paragraph ends with an appropriate concluding sentence.	**yes**	**no**
All of my sentences are directly related to the topic.	**yes**	**no**

Grammar and Sentence Structure

Every student has his or her own personal grammar trouble spots. Some students battle with verb tenses. For others, articles are the main enemy. Some find it hard to know where to put periods.

In the space, create your own personal checklist for items that you know are problems for you. Then, throughout the term, work on eliminating these errors. Delete items you have mastered and add new ones that you become aware of.

Errors to check for include verb tenses, subject-verb agreement, articles, pronoun agreement, sentence fragments, and run-on sentences/comma splices.

Number found and corrected

I checked my paragraph for _____ errors.   _____

I checked my paragraph for _____ errors.   _____

I checked my paragraph for _____ errors.   _____

Peer Editor: _____ Date: _____

If your instructor approves, write your comments directly on the paper you are editing. If your instructor prefers that you not write on your classmate's paper, use this form, and when the directions tell you to underline or circle, copy it on the form instead.

1. Is the paragraph interesting?   ☐ **yes**   ☐ **no**

   Write a comment about a part that is especially interesting to you.

   _____

2. Do you understand everything?   ☐ **yes**   ☐ **no**

   Circle or underline any part that you do not understand, and write a comment about it.

   _____

3. Copy the topic sentence here, and circle the topic and double-underline the controlling idea.

   _____

4. How many supporting sentences are there in the paragraph? Number: _____

   a. What kind of supporting details does the writer use (facts, examples, quotations, statistics, etc.)?

   _____

   Is there at least one example?   ☐ **yes**   ☐ **no**

   b. Would you like more information about anything?   ☐ **yes**   ☐ **no**

   If your answer is yes, write down what you would like to know more about.

   _____

5. Is there anything unnecessary or that seems "off the topic?"   ☐ **yes**   ☐ **no**

   If your answer is yes, write a comment about it (them).

   _____

6. If the paragraph has a concluding sentence, copy it here and circle the end-of-paragraph signal (if there is one).

   _____

7. In your opinion, what is the best feature of this paragraph? In other words, what is this writer's best writing skill?

   _____

Writer: _____ Date: _____

Format

My paragraph is correctly formatted (title centered, first line indented, margins on both sides, double-spaced). **yes** **no**

Mechanics

I checked punctuation, capitalization, and spelling. **yes** **no**

Content and Organization

My paragraph begins with a topic sentence that has both a topic and a controlling idea. **yes** **no**

My paragraph contains specific and factual supporting sentences that explain or prove my topic sentence. **yes** **no**

How many supporting sentences does the paragraph have? **number** _____

Unity: All sentences are on the topic. **yes** **no**

My paragraph ends with an appropriate concluding sentence. **yes** **no**

Coherence: My paragraph flows smoothly from beginning to end. **yes** **no**

   I repeat key nouns where necessary. **yes** **no**

   I use pronouns consistently. **yes** **no**

   I use some transition signals. How many? _____ **yes** **no**

   My sentences are in some type of logical order. **yes** **no**

Grammar and Sentence Structure

Number found and corrected

I checked my paragraph for _____ errors. _____
               (verb tense, article, etc.)

I checked my paragraph for _____ errors. _____

I checked my paragraph for _____ errors. _____

Peer Editor: _____ Date: _____

1. Is the paragraph interesting? ☐ **yes** ☐ **no**
   Write a comment about a part that is especially interesting to you.

   _____

2. Do you understand everything? ☐ **yes** ☐ **no**
   Circle or underline any part that you do not understand, and write a comment about it.

   _____

3. Copy the topic sentence here, and circle the topic and double-underline the controlling idea.

   _____

4. How many supporting sentences are there in the paragraph? Number: _____
   a. What kind of supporting details does the writer use (facts, examples, quotations, statistics, etc.)?

   _____

   b. Would you like more information about anything? ☐ **yes** ☐ **no**
   If your answer is yes, write down what you would like to know more about.

   _____

5. **Unity:** Is there anything unnecessary or that seems "off the topic?" ☐ **yes** ☐ **no**
   If your answer is yes, write a comment about it/them.

   _____

6. Does the paragraph have coherence; that is, does it flow smoothly from beginning to end?
   a. What key noun is repeated? _____
   b. Are pronouns consistent? ☐ **yes** ☐ **no**
   c. What transition signals can you find? _____
   d. Are the ideas arranged in some kind of logical order? What kind?

   _____

7. If the paragraph has a concluding sentence, copy it here and circle the end-of-paragraph signal (if there is one).

   _____

8. In your opinion, what is the best feature of this paragraph? In other words, what is this writer's best writing skill?

   _____

Writer: _____ Date: _____

Format

My essay is correctly formatted (title centered, first line of every paragraph indented, margins on both sides, double-spaced).   yes   no

Mechanics

I checked punctuation, capitalization, and spelling.   yes   no

Content and Organization

My essay has all three parts: introduction, body, and conclusion.   yes   no

Introduction: Type of introduction (funnel, historical background, surprising statistics, dramatic story, etc.): _____

The introduction ends with my thesis statement.   yes   no

Body: The body has _____ paragraphs.

The topics of the body paragraphs are as follows:

1. _____   3. _____

2. _____   4. _____

(If there are more or fewer paragraphs, add or delete lines.)

Unity: Each paragraph discusses only one main idea, and there are no sentences that are "off the topic."   yes   no

Coherence: Each paragraph has coherence. My essay flows smoothly from beginning to end.   yes   no

   I repeat key nouns.   yes   no

   I use transition signals to show relationships among ideas.   yes   no

   I use transitions to link paragraphs.   yes   no

Conclusion: The conclusion (a) summarizes the main points or (b) paraphrases the thesis statement. (Circle one.)

Grammar and Sentence Structure

Number found and corrected

I checked my essay for _____ errors.   _____
(verb tense, article, etc.)

I checked my essay for _____ errors.   _____

I checked my essay for _____ errors.   _____

Peer Editor: _____ Date: _____

1. What kind of introduction does this essay have? (funnel, dramatic, etc.)

   _____

   How many sentences does it contain? _____
   Does it capture your interest?   ☐ **yes**   ☐ **no**
   Where is the thesis statement placed?

   _____

2. How many paragraphs are there in the body? Number: _____
   The topics of the body paragraphs are as follows:
   1. _____   3. _____
   2. _____   4. _____
   (If there are more or fewer paragraphs, add or delete lines.)

3. What kind of supporting details does the writer use in each body paragraph?
   1. _____   3. _____
   2. _____   4. _____

4. Check each paragraph for unity. Is any sentence unnecessary or
   "off the topic?"   ☐ **yes**   ☐ **no**
   If your answer is yes, write a comment about it (them).

   _____

5. Check each paragraph for coherence. Does each one flow smoothly
   from beginning to end?   ☐ **yes**   ☐ **no**
   What key nouns are repeated? _____
   What transition signals can you find? _____

   _____

6. What expressions does the writer use to link paragraphs? If there is none, write none. (If there are
   more or fewer paragraphs, add or delete lines.)
   To introduce the first body paragraph _____
   Between paragraphs 2 and 3 _____
   Between paragraphs 3 and 4 _____
   Between paragraphs 4 and 5 _____
   To introduce the conclusion: _____

7. What kind of conclusion does this essay have—a summary of the main points or a paraphrase of the
   thesis statement? _____
   Does the writer make a final comment?   ☐ **yes**   ☐ **no**
   What is it? _____

   Is this an effective ending (one that you will remember)?   ☐ **yes**   ☐ **no**

8. In your opinion, what is the best feature of this essay? In other words, what is this writer's best
   writing skill?

   _____

Self-Editing Worksheet 5
Chapter 5: Chronological Organization: Process Essays

Writer: _____ Date: _____

Format

My essay is correctly formatted (title centered, first line of every paragraph indented, margins on both sides, double-spaced).　　**yes**　　**no**

Mechanics

I checked punctuation, capitalization, and spelling.　　**yes**　　**no**

Content and Organization

My essay has all three parts: introduction, body, and conclusion.　　**yes**　　**no**

Introduction: Type of introduction I used (funnel, historical background, surprising statistics, dramatic story, etc.): _____

　　The introduction ends with my thesis statement.　　**yes**　　**no**

Body: The body has _____ paragraphs. Each paragraph explains one major step or one group of steps in the process I am writing about. The topics of the body paragraphs are as follows:

　　1. _____　　　3. _____

　　2. _____　　　4. _____

　　(If there are more or fewer paragraphs, add or delete lines.)

Unity: Each paragraph discusses only one main idea, and there are no sentences that are "off the topic."　　**yes**　　**no**

Coherence: Each paragraph has coherence. My essay flows smoothly from beginning to end.　　**yes**　　**no**

　I repeat key nouns.　　**yes**　　**no**

　I use transition signals to show relationships among ideas.　　**yes**　　**no**

　I use transitions to link paragraphs.　　**yes**　　**no**

Conclusion: The conclusion (a) summarizes the main points or (b) paraphrases the thesis statement. (Circle one.)

Grammar and Sentence Structure

Number found and corrected

I checked my essay for _____ errors. _____
　　　　　　　　　　　(verb tense, article, etc.)

I checked my essay for _____ errors. _____

I checked my essay for _____ errors. _____

Peer Editor: _____ Date: _____

1. What kind of introduction does this essay have (funnel, entertaining story, etc.)?

   _____

   How many sentences does it contain? _____

   Does it capture your interest?   ☐ yes   ☐ no

   Where is the thesis statement placed? _____

   _____

2. How many paragraphs are there in the body? Number: _____
   The topics of the body paragraphs are as follows:
   1. _____   3. _____
   2. _____   4. _____
   (If there are more or fewer paragraphs, add or delete lines.)

3. What kind of supporting details does the writer use in each body paragraph?
   1. _____   3. _____
   2. _____   4. _____

4. Check each paragraph for unity. Is any sentence unnecessary or
   "off the topic?"   ☐ yes   ☐ no
   If your answer is yes, write a comment about it (them).

   _____

5. Check each paragraph for coherence. Does each one flow smoothly
   from beginning to end?   ☐ yes   ☐ no
   What key nouns are repeated? _____
   What transition signals can you find? _____

   _____

6. What expressions does the writer use to link paragraphs? If there is none, write none. (If there are
   more or fewer paragraphs, add or delete lines.)
   To introduce the first body paragraph _____
   Between paragraphs 2 and 3 _____
   Between paragraphs 3 and 4 _____
   Between paragraphs 4 and 5 _____
   To introduce the conclusion _____

7. What kind of conclusion does this essay have—a summary of the main points or a paraphrase of the
   thesis statement?

   _____

   Does the writer make a final comment?   ☐ yes   ☐ no
   What is it? _____
   Is this an effective ending (one that you will remember)? ☐ yes   ☐ no

8. In your opinion, what is the best feature of this essay? In other words, what is this writer's best
   writing skill?

   _____

Writer: _____ Date: _____

Format

My essay is correctly formatted (title centered, first line of every paragraph indented, margins on both sides, double-spaced).   **yes**   **no**

Mechanics

I checked punctuation, capitalization, and spelling.   **yes**   **no**

Content and Organization

My essay has all three parts: introduction, body, and conclusion.   **yes**   **no**

Introduction: Type of introduction I used (funnel, historical background, surprising statistics, dramatic story, etc.): _____

   The introduction ends with my thesis statement.   **yes**   **no**

Body: The body has _____ paragraphs. The topics of the body paragraphs are as follows:

   1. _____   3. _____

   2. _____   4. _____

   (If there are more or fewer paragraphs, add or delete lines.)

Unity: Each paragraph discusses only one main idea, and there are no sentences that are "off the topic."   **yes**   **no**

Coherence: Each paragraph has coherence. My essay flows smoothly from beginning to end.   **yes**   **no**

   I repeat key nouns.   **yes**   **no**

   I use transition signals and cause/effect signal words to show relationships among ideas.   **yes**   **no**

   I use transitions to link paragraphs.   **yes**   **no**

Conclusion: The conclusion (a) summarizes the main points or (b) paraphrases the thesis statement. (Circle one.)

Grammar and Sentence Structure

Number found and corrected

I checked my essay for _____ errors.   _____
                         (verb tense, article, etc.)

I checked my essay for _____ errors.   _____

I checked my essay for _____ errors.   _____

Peer Editor: _____ Date: _____

1. What kind of introduction does this essay have (funnel, entertaining story, etc.)?

   _____

   How many sentences does it contain? _____
   Does it capture your interest? ☐ yes ☐ no
   Where is the thesis statement placed? _____

2. How many paragraphs are there in the body? Number: _____
   The topics of the body paragraphs are as follows:
   1. _____   3. _____
   2. _____   4. _____
   (If there are more or fewer paragraphs, add or delete lines.)

3. What kind of supporting details does the writer use in each body paragraph?
   1. _____   3. _____
   2. _____   4. _____

4. Check each paragraph for unity. Is any sentence unnecessary or
   "off the topic?" ☐ yes ☐ no
   If your answer is yes, write a comment about it (them).

   _____

5. Check each paragraph for coherence. Does each one flow smoothly from
   beginning to end? ☐ yes ☐ no
   What key nouns are repeated? _____
   What transition signals can you find? _____

   _____

6. What expressions does the writer use to link paragraphs? If there is none, write none. (If there are
   more or fewer paragraphs, add or delete lines.)
   To introduce the first body paragraph _____
   Between paragraphs 2 and 3 _____
   Between paragraphs 3 and 4 _____
   Between paragraphs 4 and 5 _____
   To introduce the conclusion: _____

7. What kind of conclusion does this essay have—a summary of the main points or a paraphrase of the
   thesis statement?

   _____

   Does the writer make a final comment? ☐ yes ☐ no
   What is it?

   _____

   Is this an effective ending (one that you will remember)? ☐ yes ☐ no

8. In your opinion, what is the best feature of this essay? In other words, what is this writer's best
   writing skill?

   _____

Self-Editing Worksheet 7
Chapter 7: Comparison/Contrast Essays

Writer: _____   Date: _____

Format

My essay is correctly formatted (title centered, first line of every
paragraph indented, margins on both sides, double-spaced).   **yes**   **no**

Mechanics

I checked punctuation, capitalization, and spelling.   **yes**   **no**

Content and Organization

My essay has all three parts: introduction, body, and conclusion.   **yes**   **no**

I used block or point-by-point organization. (Underline one.)

If I used block organization, I inserted a transition sentence or transition
paragraph between the two blocks.   **yes**   **no**

Introduction: Type of introduction I used (funnel, historical background, surprising statistics,
dramatic story, etc.): _____

   The introduction ends with my thesis statement.   **yes**   **no**

Body: The body has _____ paragraphs. The topics of the body paragraphs are as follows:

   1. _____   3. _____

   2. _____   4. _____

   (If there are more or fewer paragraphs, add or delete lines.)

Unity: Each paragraph discusses only one main idea, and there are no
sentences that are "off the topic."   **yes**   **no**

Coherence: Each paragraph has coherence. My essay flows smoothly
from beginning to end.   **yes**   **no**

   I repeat key nouns.   **yes**   **no**

   I use transition signals and comparison/contrast signal words to show
   relationships among ideas.   **yes**   **no**

   I use transitions to link paragraphs.   **yes**   **no**

Conclusion: The conclusion (a) summarizes the main points or
(b) paraphrases the thesis statement. (Circle one.)

Grammar and Sentence Structure

	Number found and corrected
I checked my essay for _____ errors. (verb tense, article, etc.)	_____
I checked my essay for _____ errors.	_____
I checked my essay for _____ errors.	_____

Peer Editor: _____ Date: _____

1. What kind of introduction does this essay have (funnel, entertaining story, etc.)?

   _____

   How many sentences does the introduction contain? _____

   Does it capture your interest?   ☐ yes   ☐ no

   Where is the thesis statement placed? _____

2. Does the essay use block or point-by-point organization?

   _____

3. If it uses block organization, is there a transition sentence or transition
   paragraph between the two blocks?   ☐ yes   ☐ no

4. How many paragraphs are there in the body? Number: _____

   The topics of the body paragraphs are as follows:

   1. _____   3. _____

   2. _____   4. _____

   (If there are more or fewer paragraphs, add or delete lines.)

5. What kind of supporting details does the writer use in each body paragraph?

   1. _____   3. _____

   2. _____   4. _____

6. Check each paragraph for unity. Is any sentence unnecessary or "off the topic"? ☐ yes   ☐ no

   If your answer is yes, write a comment about it (them). _____

7. Check each paragraph for coherence. Does each one flow smoothly
   from beginning to end?   ☐ yes   ☐ no

   What key nouns are repeated? _____

   What transition signals can you find? _____

   _____

8. What expressions does the writer use to link paragraphs? If there is none, write none. (If there are more
   or fewer paragraphs, add or delete lines.)

   To introduce the first body paragraph _____

   Between paragraphs 2 and 3 _____

   Between paragraphs 3 and 4 _____

   Between paragraphs 4 and 5 _____

   To introduce the conclusion _____

9. What kind of conclusion does this essay have—a summary of the main points or a paraphrase of the thesis
   statement? _____

   Does the writer make a final comment?   ☐ yes   ☐ no

   What is it? _____

   Is this an effective ending (one that you will remember)?   ☐ yes   ☐ no

10. In your opinion, what is the best feature of this essay? In other words, what is this writer's best writing skill?

    _____

Self-Editing Worksheet 9
Chapter 9: Argumentative Essays

Writer: _____ Date: _____

Format

My essay is correctly formatted (title centered, first line of every
paragraph indented, margins on both sides, double-spaced).   **yes**   **no**

Mechanics

I have checked for punctuation, capitalization, and spelling errors.   **yes**   **no**

Content and Organization

My essay has all three parts: introduction, body, and conclusion.   **yes**   **no**

I used block or point-by-point organization. (Underline one.)

Introduction: Type of introduction I used (funnel, historical background, surprising statistics,
dramatic story, etc.): _____

The introduction ends with my thesis statement.   **yes**   **no**

Body: The body has _____ paragraphs.

I give _____ arguments for my point of view and _____ arguments
for the opposing point of view.

I rebut each opposing argument.   **yes**   **no**

I support each point with a specific supporting detail such as an
example, a statistic, a quotation, a paraphrase, or a summary.   **yes**   **no**

I cite the source of all borrowed information.   **yes**   **no**

Conclusion: The conclusion (a) summarizes my arguments or (b) restates my opinion. (Circle one.)

Grammar and Sentence Structure

**Number found
and corrected**

I checked my essay for _____ errors.   _____
(verb tense, article, etc.)

I checked my essay for _____ errors.   _____

I checked my essay for _____ errors.   _____

Peer Editor: _____ Date: _____

1. Analyze how the writer organizes his or her essay.

   a. Copy the thesis sentence here. Does it state the writer's opinion clearly?

   _____

   b. Does the essay use block or point-by-point organization?

   _____

2. List the writer's arguments:

   a. _____

   b. _____

   c. _____

   (Add more lines if necessary)

3. List the opposing arguments and counterarguments:

   a. _____

   Counterargument: _____

   b. _____

   Counterargument: _____

   c. _____

   Counterargument: _____

4. What is the writer's strongest and most convincing argument or counterargument?

   _____

   How does he or she support it? _____

   Is any argument or counterargument weak and unconvincing?   ☐ **yes**   ☐ **no**

   Why is it weak? _____

   Discuss with the writer possible ways to strengthen it.

5. Do you understand everything?   ☐ **yes**   ☐ **no**

   Circle or underline any part that you do not understand, and write a comment about it.

6. What kind of supporting details does the writer use (statistics, examples, quotations, paraphrases, summaries, etc.)?

   _____

7. How does the writer name the source of each piece of borrowed supporting information; that is, what phrases or verbs does the writer use to name the sources? Write them here.

   _____

8. Is this a convincing argumentative essay? In other words, does the writer persuade you that his or her opinion is the right one?   ☐ **yes**   ☐ **no**

Index

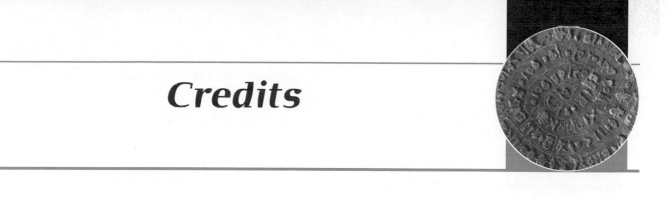

Credits

Photos

Pages 1 and 39, Antonio M. Rosario/Getty Images. **Page 2**, Nick Nicholson/Getty Images. **Page 18**, Giraudon/Art Resource, NY. **Pages 55 and 142**, Kim Zumwalt/Getty Images. **Page 56**, Erich Lessing/Art Resource, NY. **Page 81**, Neil Emmerson/Getty Images. **Page 94**, Erich Lessing/Art Resource, NY. **Page 111**, Rakoczy/Art Resource, NY. **Page 127**, Bildarchiv Preussischer Kulturbesitz/Art Resource, NY. **Pages 161 and 250**, Lee & Lee Communications/Art Resource, NY. **Page 162**, The Granger Collection, New York. **Page 179**, Erich Lessing/Art Resource, NY. **Page 194**, The Granger Collection, New York. **Page 210**, The Granger Collection, New York. **Page 230**, Giraudon/Art Resource, NY.

Text

Page 12, Q&A: Red Light Running. Highway Loss Data Institute, Insurance Institute for Highway Safety. June 2003. **Page 43**, Over the Edge. Reprinted courtesy of *Sports Illustrated* by Michael Bamberger and Don Yaeger, April 14, 1997. Copyright © 1997. Time Inc. All rights reserved. **Page 51**, World Population Growth, 1750–2150. Chart. Population Reference Bureau. 20 Oct, 2004. **Page 53**, Education, Earnings, Tax Payments. Graph. By Sandy Baum and Kathleen Payea. *Education Pays: The Benefits of Higher Education for Individuals and Society.* College Board online. **Pages 60** and **73**, Mr. Wygard's Story. Reprinted from *Management in Two Cultures* with the permission of Ryan Hadley, Intercultural Press, Inc. **Page 79**, At the Movies. You Are Where You Sit: Seating Choice Can Tell a Lot About a Person. By Harrison Shepard. Printed with the permission of Dave Butler, *Los Angeles Daily News*, July 6, 2001. **Page 82**, Understanding Chernobyl. Diagram of a nuclear reactor and excerpts from Ebbing, Darrell, *General Chemistry*, Fourth Edition. Reprinted with the permission of Sheila Harris, Houghton-Mifflin College Division. **Page 89**, Spring Cleaning, No Mops. April 8, 2002. © TIME Inc. Reprinted by permission. **Page 92**, A Japanese Betrothal. Excerpt by Daniel Inouye from *Go for Broke*, condensed from *Journey to Washington*. Reprinted with the permission of Jeniqua Moore, Simon & Schuster. **Page 96**, Shyness. Excerpt by Lynne Henderson and Philip Zimbardo, The Shyness Institute, from *Encyclopedia of Mental Health*. **Page 107**, Welcoming Back the Top Dog. Article taken from *Animal Chronicles* Vol. 15, No. 1 (Spring 2004) by Sheri Cardo. A Marin Humane Society publication. **Page 112**, We're Different but Alike. Essay by Neil Harris from *Japan Salutes America on Its Bicentennial* (1976). Reprinted with the permission of Akiko Juno, Executive Director America-Japan Society Inc. **Page 124**, Marital Exchanges. Adapted from Marriage, Family and Residence. *Humanity: An Introduction to Cultural Anthropology.* 6th Ed. By James Peoples and Bailey Garrick. Reprinted with the permission of Thomson Learning, Global Rights Group. **Page 137**, Using a New Language in Africa to Save Dying Ones. By Marc Lacey. November 12, 2004. Reprinted with the permission of *The New York Times*. **Page 139**, Share of People Who Are Native English Speakers Declining. Excerpt from article by Randolph E. Schmid. Reprinted with the permission of Judy Buelow, Valeo Intellectual Property Inc. **Page 140**, A World Empire by Other Means. © 2001 The Economist Newspaper Ltd. All rights reserved. **Page 151**, Why We Should Send a Manned Mission to Mars. Excerpt written by Melissa Joulwan. May 13, 2004. Courtesy of KQED, Inc. **Page 154**, Why We Shouldn't Go to Mars: Someday People May Walk on the Planet but Not Until It Makes Technological Sense. January 26, 2004. © 2004 TIME Inc. reprinted by permission. **Page 156**, The World Language. © December 31, 1999 The Economist Ltd. Millennium Issue. All rights reserved. **Page 158**, Brazil Considers Linguistic Barricade. Reprinted with the permission of Andrew Downie. *Christian Science Monitor.* September 6, 2000. **Page 224**, Medicine: Please Pass the Sugar. By Joel Achenbach. Reprinted with the permission of National Geographic Society. August 2004.